YOUR CHILD'S GROWING MIND

YOUR
CHILD'S
GROWING
MIND

*A Parent's Guide to Learning
From Birth to Adolescence*

Jane M. Healy, Ph.D.

Doubleday
New York London Toronto Sydney Auckland

Published by Doubleday, a division of
Bantam Doubleday Dell Publishing Group, Inc.,
666 Fifth Avenue, New York, New York 10103

Doubleday and the portrayal of an anchor with a dolphin
are trademarks of Doubleday, a division of
Bantam Doubleday Dell Publishing Group, Inc.

2 4 6 8 9 7 5 3

Library of Congress Cataloging-in-Publication Data
Healy, Jane M.
    Your child's growing mind.

    Bibliography: p. 303
    Includes index.
    1. Intellect. 2. Brain—Growth. 3. Child
psychology. 4. Parent and child. I. Title.
BF432.C48H4   1987   155.4′13   86–2058
ISBN 0-385-23149-0

This book is dedicated to all the parents who said, "That's very interesting, but what should we *do* about it?"

Contents

Foreword

During the past twenty-five years, there has been a gratifying increase in the professional and public awareness of learning differences in children. This interest has stimulated a plethora of written material directed toward a diverse readership. When Dr. Healy notified me of her intent to write this book planned primarily for use by parents, I could not help but wonder about the desirability of yet another publication related to learning. There are certainly a number of factually sound, thoughtful, and dependable works directed mostly toward the scientific community. Material specifically for parents is also contained in many books and articles, and thus, valuable information appears to be readily available.

Dr. Healy makes her important contribution not from obscure theories or fads, but on the basis of experience in the trenches—the teacher *in* the classroom working *with* the children. In particular, while she has explained current concepts of brain function in simplified terms, she has succeeded in avoiding advice to parents based upon speculation. Her approach is educational. Of special importance is her encouragement of parents to allow their children to be children; she inspires parents to provide support and love, factors that are vital to good brain development. What a refreshing difference from the strident advice of many professionals who plan to produce superkids by indoctrination rather than by education.

It is all too evident that many of the previously published works, often well-intentioned and authored by professionals—psychologists, educators, nutritionists, physicians, occupational therapists—have rendered advice that is frequently conflicting. Their recommendations are geared toward optimizing the child's development or correcting problems in learning. Their views are supposedly based upon the author's scientific knowledge and expertise; the material is often claimed to be derived from documented facts relating to brain structure and function. The parent-reader is seldom afforded the opportunity to distinguish between fact and fiction—between scientifically determined results and fictional "armchair" hypotheses of individual authors or their colleagues. Discredited research is glibly quoted as fact, if it suits the concept of the writer. The result is an amazing array of supposedly definitive therapeutic approaches—nutritional, chemical, physical, mechanical, and too often, mythical. The parent's cry for help is submerged by the "expert's" superficial, patronizing, confident (and too often expensive) claims and regimens.

The results of continued scientific research devoted to child development and learning will of necessity modify many of our currently held beliefs and concepts. However, Dr. Healy's cheerful and warm approach to parents and her constant advocacy of the child's individuality and dignity will survive future scientific advances. I am grateful this thoughtful teacher wrote this book dedicated to parents. But the children ultimately will benefit from her practical experience and wisdom.

Samuel J. Horwitz, M.D.

Chief, Division of Child Neurology
Rainbow Babies and Childrens Hospital
Cleveland

Associate Professor of Pediatrics
    and Neurology
Case Western Reserve University

Preface

This book originated in a college classroom one gloomy afternoon in 1955 when a psychology professor lost his patience with me. "Jane, for heaven's sake, stop asking questions about children's brains," he exclaimed. "We can't see them, we can't measure them, and for all we know they don't have that much to do with learning, anyway!"

I'm glad I didn't take his advice. I've kept asking questions during thirty years of studying, teaching, and being a mother to three little growing brains of my own, and I can now say with certainty that my well-intentioned professor was dead wrong. Understanding a child's brain and the way it develops is the key to understanding learning. I don't have all my answers yet, but I believe parents should be among the first to share what is known—and what it means in practical terms. It's time to bring the information from graduate courses and musty library shelves into the real world where children grow and learn.

I have tried to give you an accurate, understandable summary of current research, along with specific suggestions you can start using today. You will find stories about many real parents and children, although names and identifying details have been changed. I hope these experiences help you, as they have helped me, to unravel some of the wonderful mysteries of your own child's mind. If your time is limited, choose the chapters most helpful for you. For a full tour, however, I recommend you learn the inside story of the growth of intelligence—from the beginning.

Acknowledgments

My thanks go, first, to the many parents and children who contributed to this book by teaching me about themselves, and second, to all the real teachers who have helped me answer some of my questions —and forced me to ask many more. Many friends have helped in the preparation of this manuscript, and I am grateful to them all for reading, suggesting, and putting up with the vagaries of a writer in process. I particularly appreciate the professional wisdom and assistance of Dr. Samuel J. Horwitz, chief of the Division of Child Neurology at Rainbow Babies and Childrens Hospital in Cleveland. Finally, my fondest thanks to my family: my mother, who has always been my first and best teacher; my children, who have lifted my spirits and agreeably consented to appear in this book; and my husband, Tom, whose loving support as proofreader, business manager, and counselor is very important to me. Thank you all for giving me the freedom to explore.

Part I

BRAIN DEVELOPMENT AND LEARNING

1

Opening the "Black Box"

ONE EVENING LAST WINTER I WAS SURPRISED TO GET A CALL
from a young teacher whom I hadn't seen since she had left school
on maternity leave. We had often talked about her hopes and plans
for the baby, but tonight she sounded worried.

"Jane, I'm sorry to call you at home, but I just have to ask for
some advice about Tony. His pediatrician says he is very advanced,
and I'm doing all the things we talked about—playing with him,
talking to him, reading to him—but this neighbor of mine has just
signed up for a course which advertises ways to raise her child's IQ
by increasing his brain development. Should I be doing more? Can
parents really help build their kids' brains?"

Amy's call didn't surprise me, since I get the same question in
many forms these days. Parents often come to my office feeling pressured to do a "perfect" job despite the constraints of busy schedules,
but they are confused by conflicting theories about child development and learning. How much and what kind of enrichment does a
preschooler need? What is the best way to lay the groundwork for
reading and math? Should parents help with schoolwork? Can creativity be developed? How can parents act as a child's advocate if
school personnel aren't attuned to individual needs? What does an
IQ score really mean? What about the puzzling child who doesn't
"fit the mold"?

These questions have always been important ones, but until recently, satisfactory answers have been scarce. In this book I would like to introduce you to the new study of developmental neuropsychology, which investigates the relationship of brain development to children's behavior and learning. Combined with exciting advances in the study of human thinking, or cognition, it may be one way of finding answers about learning, individual differences in abilities, and even emotional development. Although no two human brains are alike and thus no one set of answers is right for every child, more practical information can equip parents with increased confidence and ability to make wise decisions. Still, research findings are slow to make their way into practical application, no matter how useful they may be, and surprisingly, the brain has been unpopular in professional circles. An incident several years ago made me realize how important it is to get the news around.

I met Aaron when he tripped over me as he was entering his third grade science class. As a visiting consultant, I was trying to be invisible, and apparently I had succeeded as far as Aaron was concerned. I began to suspect that this waifish-looking little fellow had a problem when he next bumped into the doorway, scattering a mass of smudged work papers whose mangled manuscript letters would have been an embarrassment to most first graders and which bore the indelible marks of teacher rejection: "Messy!" "F." Ignoring my mission to evaluate the science curriculum, I watched him struggle to organize himself around a desk, dropping his pencil and fumbling through a tattered folder for misplaced homework. A discussion of space exploration immediately attracted his attention, and his skinny arm gyrated in the air, once more knocking his pencil, unnoticed, from the desk. Recognized at last by the teacher, he delivered a stunning exposition of rocket trajectories, fuel needs, and relative astral distances.

I couldn't resist asking the principal about Aaron. "Has he ever had a neurological examination? It sure looks as if something is misfiring when he tries to translate his good ideas into action."

"Oh, no," he said. "Poor kid has an emotional problem. He's being treated by a psychiatrist. Believe it or not, he still wets his bed! His mother rejected him emotionally when he was born, and he's always had difficulty with schoolwork even though we can tell he's smart."

"Well, you might consider looking further," I ventured. I was quite sure Aaron had some problems that predated the emotional ones, but I was there to evaluate curriculum, not to do diagnosis.

Six months later I received a note in the mail from a woman who identified herself as Aaron's mother. "Thanks to your intervention," she said ("intervention," indeed!), "we took Aaron to a neurologist and found that he has had a problem since birth in one of the important lower brain centers." Since the area she described is part of a system responsible for voluntary control of motor movements such as writing, avoiding people and doorways, and yes, even bladder control, it is not surprising that Aaron was having problems despite an IQ in the superior range. "Now we understand that he isn't lazy or stupid, and he will get special help with this problem," she went on to say. "If you only knew the guilt and the anguish we have been through, you would understand why I am so grateful."

I keep that note, not only because it is the only effortless success story of my career, but also because it is a perfect example of the "black box" view of the brain. In their well-intentioned efforts to help him, the professionals in Aaron's life fell victim to an attitude which has dominated both psychology and education for many years. Lacking the technology to see, measure, or test this mysterious organ directly, they decided to ignore it. Although it now seems absurd to insist that the way a child's brain functions is irrelevant to learning, this view was tacitly adopted, with "emotional problems" becoming the handiest scapegoat whenever things weren't going well. The unfortunate result has been a "Blame Game" in which the parents, school, and even the child were accused of responsibility for problems in learning. The importance of emotions should not be understated, but this one-sided view has caused many families unwarranted anguish. Even though our knowledge of developmental neuropsychology is itself in its infancy, there is abundant evidence that the brain has an omnipresent role in all behavior and learning.

As an introduction to neuropsychology, let's take a broad look at ways in which researchers are discovering the brain and then introduce two major questions central to this book: Where does brain power come from, and what can we do about it?

Looking Inside

Research on learning is being carried out in a variety of fascinating ways; looking directly at the brain itself is probably the most exciting. With the aid of computerized scanners and techniques for measuring the intensity of electrical impulses or chemical changes, it is now possible to perform "noninvasive," or harmless, investigations of a child's brain. Television screens show detailed views of parts of the brain in minute cross section. We can even see a child's thinking "in motion"—computerized color representations of electrical or chemical changes during normal activities such as reading, or doing puzzles. Most families will never have a need for such testing, but it is producing a body of useful information about both the structure and functioning of the brain and promises to revolutionize our knowledge of how all children learn.

On a different front, work with computer "artificial intelligence" is giving scientists new respect for the brain's capabilities as they attempt to analyze and duplicate human learning abilities. They have discovered, as we will see, that the intellectual talents of even the human infant are more formidable than anyone imagined.

Other research, measuring the relationship between young children's home environments and their later school achievement, is demonstrating that certain types of early experiences produce better intellectual growth. Studies of this type consistently show that children need different types of learning at different ages, and that early experiences do make a difference in the acquisition of mental skills.

Finally, studies of adults with damage to known areas of the brain have expanded our knowledge about brain-behavior relationships and have raised some provocative questions about learning.

A Golden Screwdriver?

An adult who has suffered a stroke with damage in a small area of the left side of his brain can still write words from dictation but has completely lost the ability to read—even the words he himself has written. This puzzling case is one of many which raise the question of whether certain abilities reside in specific areas of the human brain. The search for "localization" has been a hot one, and attempts to "map" the brain have been carried out since the days when feeling bumps on the skull was a popular technique for judging intelligence. Does this mean that someday science will give us a "golden screwdriver" with which we can rewire a small part of the brain to improve a deficient ability or create unusual talent? Unfortunately, the answer is probably not so simple. Activities such as reading with comprehension, focusing attention, and the various types of memory which we employ every day require the combined efforts of millions of neural connections. Moreover, it is possible that children's brains are even more complex than those of adults.

Taking studies of adult brains and generalizing them to children is a mistake. There is a difference between studying people who have lost previously acquired skills and trying to help youngsters learn them for the first time. Nature has constituted the child's brain so that it is remarkably "plastic." The good news for parents and teachers is that there are many routes through which brain development may occur; if one part is not doing its job, other areas may take over. It is even possible that detours may form naturally if the highways to learning are blocked for any reason. Current research offers an optimistic view of our chances to help each child become a successful learner. Both personally and as a society, we may hope that parents armed with practical information will be able to kindle children's special talents and creative abilities.

Where Does It Come From?

"I'm not surprised that Sally is having trouble with math." Mrs. Strang was apologetic. "I was hopeless in math even though I was a good student otherwise." Sally, now a fifth grader who had just won the school spelling contest, was struggling mightily with her math assignments, particularly those involving "story" problems, charts and graphs, and geometric forms. We decided that Sally would work individually with the math teacher after school and practice at home with some materials designed to improve her concepts of space relationships. As Mrs. Strang left my office, I noticed that she first turned in the wrong direction before she started down the hall, and I recalled a much earlier conversation in which she confided that she didn't let Sally climb trees for fear she would hurt herself.

Did Sally inherit her math problem? Did she pick it up from poor teaching? Can we blame it on a lack of experience with physical and space relationships in her early years? How about her best friend, Megan, who started to read and calculate when she was three and gets straight A's with very little effort? Was she born smart or did her parents do something right? Should we switch the "Blame Game" to parental genes?

For years the "nature-nurture" question was debated by psychologists. Does heredity or environment play the major role in development? Now we understand that there is such a constant interaction between basic capacity and experience from the moment of a baby's conception that the question cannot be answered. Every child inherits a physical brain structure as well as certain chemical and electrical response patterns that strongly influence the ways in which the brain responds to stimuli both from outside and from within itself. Recently we have discovered that a child's personal tempo—the natural pace of responding and the speed of carrying out activities—seems to be genetically determined.

Another inherited dimension of personality may be introversion or extroversion. Some children are more outgoing and people-oriented from the beginning, and an easy or difficult disposition may also come with the package. The tendency to respond impulsively without thinking a problem through seems to be present in some families, although you will learn later how early emphasis on the use of language for problem solving may alter this style. Family patterns for the timetable of physical and intellectual development are also important. Some children pass through the stages of growth more quickly than others, although more rapid maturation does not necessarily predict a better final outcome.

Certain constellations of abilities, such as music, engineering, or literary talent seem to cluster in some families; there are also some types of learning problems, such as developmental dyslexia, which are hereditary. Studies of identical twins raised separately have also demonstrated the inherited stability of some aspects of intelligence. Since it is estimated that at least twenty to thirty separate genes are involved with intellectual ability, however, it is not easy to pin down this complex phenomenon.

Brain-Shaping Environments

Although research with infants has surprised everyone about their repertoire of innate abilities, the environment begins to exert forces immediately after conception. The growing brain is highly susceptible to structural, chemical, and hormonal influences. For example, some researchers believe that specific academic abilities, such as reading or math, may be affected by hormones secreted during pregnancy. Poor maternal nutrition or drug or alcohol abuse during pregnancy tend to produce premature babies or later physical and intellectual problems. One tragic consequence of a pregnant woman's drinking is called "fetal alcohol syndrome," in which the child suffers from poor coordination, hyperactive behavior, unusual facial features, and reduced brain size. Although this irreversible condition is associated with heavy alcohol use, the critical amount seems to vary widely among individuals.

Researchers are looking at many other environmental factors which may affect brain development before and after birth. Exposure to lead or toxins such as formaldehyde, pesticides, or certain medications may cause learning or behavior disorders. Parents whose work puts them into contact with toxic substances should be aware of the hazards of transmission to a child at home on clothing or in breast milk. Diet is important, too; a shortage of protein may retard brain growth, and a number of food substances are being investigated as possible contributors to children's learning problems. In addition to keeping informed about this fast-growing area of research, parents should carefully scrutinize a child's daily environment for potential hazards and consult a physician if they have any questions.

A Two-Way Street

Any number of influences, emotional as well as physical, impinge constantly on mental growth. The young brain's environment helps shape its development, but it is interesting to discover that this relationship is not a one-way street.

We now recognize that the child's personality and response style help determine the way he gets treated by those around him. Some children are just plain "difficult." Naturally, their behavior increases the stress, and thus affects the response, of the adults in their life. No doubt Aaron was one of these youngsters; although not at fault, he and his mother took turns sharing the blame. Understanding the problem enables us to help such children while making the parent's role an easier one.

What accounts for Sally's math problem? Undoubtedly a combination of factors. Rather than trying to pin responsibility on genes or early experiences, our job is to appreciate her particular way of learning and provide new experiences to enhance it. In short, neuropsychologists tell us that the human brain comes into the world programmed for certain aspects of learning and behavior, but many of these are susceptible to alteration. The next chapter begins our exploration of the ways in which this dynamic process takes place, and how parents can help develop each child's unique pattern of abilities.

Infancy:
Creating the Foundations
of Intelligence

IN A WELL-LOVED CHILDREN'S BOOK, DR. DOOLITTLE EN-
counters the pushmi-pullyu, a remarkable creature who is a metaphor for indecision. With a head at either end of his body, he has
trouble deciding which way to move. Many parents today feel caught
on a similar beast as they receive conflicting advice about developing
their child's intellectual skills. When should they push, and when
should they pull—or should they back off and let mental growth
proceed naturally?

Can you make your child more intelligent? Should parents try to
create "superbabies" with precocious talents? How much can we
force brain growth? Although there are no simple answers, the new
field of neuropsychology offers some useful insights into these questions. My experience suggests that specific information about brain
growth and learning is most useful for parents as support for their
own good instincts about a child's needs at different ages. During the
years when our boys were growing up, I often wished I knew more
about what was really happening inside those little heads, but the
"black box" was still a mystery. Now parents can be more informed
participants in the growth of a child's intelligence. In this chapter we
will lay the groundwork for understanding how the brain's thinking
power develops, give you a chance to evaluate your own home's
brain-building potential, and then show why collaborating with na-

ture's pattern for building brains may be a better idea than creating "superbabies."

THE DEVELOPING BRAIN

Laying the Groundwork Before Birth

Any parent can guess that a child's brain is an active, growing dynamo. A little physiology will help you understand its stages of growth. Your baby's brain cells begin to form as early as three weeks after conception, multiplying more rapidly than other body cells. Development of much of the brain's physical structure, or "hard wiring," starts now, directed by a complex genetic program. Neurons, the future "thinking cells," are produced in abundance. Many migrate to particular sections of the brain as part of subsystems that will later control reflexes, voluntary body movement, perception, and thought. Others fail to attach to any area and disappear. No one understands yet how these neurons "know" where to go, or why some don't make it, but we do know that the process occurs in spurts at specific periods of time. The quality of development during this prenatal period of cell differentiation and migration determines the future structure of the brain.

A growth spurt in the formation of brain cells lasts from the second trimester of pregnancy until six months after birth. A growth spurt of neurons occurs during the second trimester, and soon afterward glial cells, which provide the "glue" to hold the neurons together, begin to form. Since these cell systems are the raw material of a lifetime's intelligence, good care of the expectant mother is a priority. All women should be aware of the importance of good nutrition and protection from toxins or such harmful environmental forces as unnecessary X rays.

The impact of the mother's emotional state on the baby's brain is important too. Some studies suggest that pregnancies marked by excessive fear, anger, or anxiety may produce hyperactive and irritable infants. This finding is not surprising, since intense feelings release chemicals which affect the brain's functioning. Crossing through the placenta, they may find their way from the mother's bloodstream into the circulatory system of the infant.

Is this another "guilt trip" for women who have inadvertently

BRAIN DEVELOPMENT BEFORE BIRTH

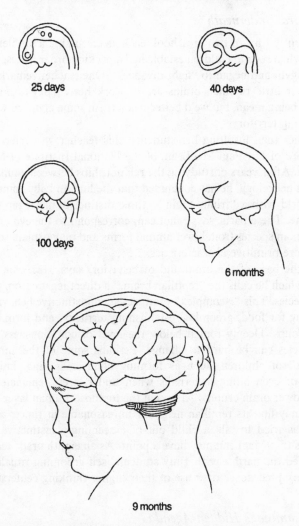

25 days

40 days

100 days

6 months

9 months

exposed their child to negative prenatal influences? While every expectant mother should be informed of the necessity for good care, much can be done after birth to ameliorate earlier problems. The newborn's brain is wonderfully malleable to experience, although its cells have already diversified into three major areas, two of which may be stuck at an earlier stage of our evolutionary history!

A Lizard Underneath

Recently I heard two preschool teachers discussing a problem that arose when several children established a pecking order for use of the jungle gym and began to "fight invaders." One teacher remarked, "I bet their little reptilian brains are at work here. They're not purposely being mean, but we'd better teach them some civilized ways of managing territory!"

Rather than insulting her students, this teacher was referring to the work of Dr. Paul MacLean, of the National Institute of Mental Health. After years of studying the relationships between animal and human neurology, he has concluded that the human baby comes into the world with a "triune brain"—three distinct brains wrapped up into one. These parts, says MacLean, correspond to the evolution of the human species from lower animal forms and may explain some of our more primitive characteristics.

At the base of the brain and of behavior, says MacLean, lies a layer which he calls the "reptilian brain," a direct legacy from primitive species. This "r-complex" produces such instinctive behaviors as foraging for food, grooming, establishing territory, and forming social groups. Deeply rooted below the level of consciousness, these tendencies can be hard to change. Perhaps some of the annoying "habits" of children, such as forming cliques, fighting, imitating peers, or even biting fingernails when under stress, emanate from these lower brain centers. Although the topmost, human layer of the brain may find its reptilian neighbor unreasonable at times, anyone who has tried to talk a child out of a seemingly instinctive habit realizes that MacLean may have a point. As an eighth grade teacher, I learned the hard way that my students' self-grooming rituals usually took precedence over use of their higher thinking centers!

The Mammal's Hidden Agenda

One tactic these teachers might try is an appeal to the second level of the "triune brain." The limbic system, which lies on top of the r-complex, is the seat of emotion. It, too, goes about its business without consulting its more rational intellectual neighbors and sometimes provides a "hidden agenda" for behavior. This brain which we share with primitive mammals confers tendencies to nurture the

THREE BRAINS IN ONE

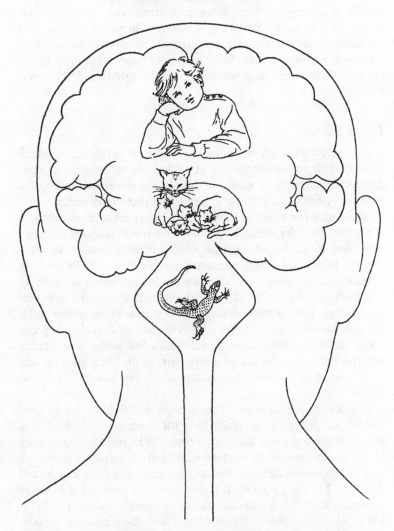

young, to flee when frightened, and to play. Many feel that the importance of this deep area has been underestimated by those who insist that our responses are determined mainly by external experiences, or that we should automatically be able to control feelings.

The limbic system is continually at work regulating hormones, drives, and some aspects of memory. Parents and teachers need to know that effective learning may depend on getting the student personally or actively involved. Movement, music, and other expressive forms are one route. Providing a positive emotional climate, and encouraging the child to express feelings and make choices, causes all learning to stick better. Some educators believe that schools' neglect of these needs may account for many problems in "motivation."

Infant Talents

Research with newborn babies has shown some tendencies which represent primitive brain systems at work. Until recently, we thought newborns were a blank slate, waiting for the environment to carve patterns of behavior. Instead, it seems that they come partially preprogrammed. For example, infants instinctively make friends with an adult who cares for them. They show preferences for their mother's voice and for gazing at patterns which resemble faces rather than objects. They enjoy things which are novel, move, or make noise. A newborn has a strong avoidance reaction when confronted with an approaching object, and will make clutching motions if he feels that he is falling. Parents may be surprised that their infant makes walking motions when held upright, but few discover that the baby can swim, too! Such reflexive talents may last a few weeks, others many months, but eventually the primitive parts of the brain yield control to the star of the show, a sophisticated newcomer called the cerebral cortex.

The cortex, our uniquely human brain, is the top layer of gray matter, which lies like a blanket over the lower areas. At birth it is like an untracked plain, but it soon begins to increase its topography of folds and fissures, its surface area, and its thinking power. A neural highway system for transmitting messages from cell to cell develops. The most important recent discovery about these message systems is that their quality depends in part on environmental stimulation. Here is a chance for parents to help their children develop strong mental equipment for learning! Let's look at the way these pathways throughout the brain develop.

Building Neural Highways

The geography of thinking does not develop automatically. At birth the brain already contains most of its billions of nerve cells, but these neurons must become organized into systems for perception, thinking, and remembering. The first two years are a period of dynamic growth for the cortex.

Amazingly, although the number of cells remains almost the same, brain weight can double during the first year of life. How? The "hard wiring" of neurons and supporting glial cells is supplemented by a growing mass of connections which link them into efficient relay systems. As stimuli seen, heard, felt, or tasted are received and then passed on, neurons fire off messages which build new physical connections to neighboring cells. Each neuron is equipped with a network of hairlike receptors called dendrites, and a single projecting axon which may vary from a few millimeters to as much as a yard in length. Scientists are excited about the finding that the growth of dendrites—and thus, the ultimate quality of an individual's thought—is responsive to environmental influences.

At birth, the dendrite spines are sparse and undeveloped, much like the branches of a young tree. During the first six months after birth they become active as sensory messages bombard the infant brain, which must learn to receive them and then pass them from one area to another. Each neuron in a message system picks up signals with its dendrites from the axons of neighboring neurons. The cells do not actually touch each other; the signals jump over a gap, called a synapse, through complex electrical and chemical processes. Synaptic connections, where learning begins, are enriched by repeated use.

Many brain cells which fail to develop synapses die, as the brain selectively "prunes" itself into an efficient information-processing system. Cells which become stimulated by picking up and relaying messages develop new dendrite spines until each sapling has become a complex, heavily branched tree. This "arborization" of dendrites is one of the main ways in which the brain grows and gains weight during childhood and adolescence.

What makes synapses and neural networks form? Conclusions about this highly complex process are still speculative, but one fact stands out. Active interest and mental effort *by the child* is the key.

THE DEVELOPING NEURON: WHERE LEARNING BEGINS

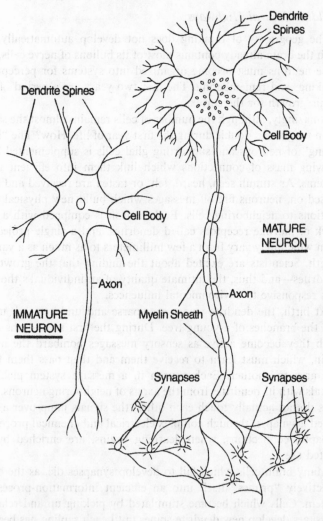

Every response to sights, sounds, feelings, smells, and tastes makes
more connections. Like a pathway through a forest, the neural traces
are at first faint, then, with successive trips, the trail becomes more
distinct and easier to traverse. The weight and the thinking power of
the brain increase in an elaborate geometric progression. The more
work the brain does, the more it becomes capable of doing.

Each child weaves his own intellectual tapestry, the quality of which may depend on active interest and involvement in a wide variety of stimuli. The home environment provides the raw material for this masterpiece.

BRAIN-BUILDING HOMES

HOME and Intelligence

A researcher sits in a family living room quietly taking notes while a mother and her toddler play together. She questions the mother on a number of factors about their daily life, trying to identify qualities of the home environment that will have long-range effects on intelligence. Studies of this type are remarkably consistent. They find that the same variables are important both for normal development and for reversing the effects of early problems.

The questions come from a commonly used questionnaire, called the HOME scale for families of children 0–3 years, which looks at six factors in a child's environment. These sample questions can help you evaluate the brain-building potential of your home. Please note that experts are divided in opinion about whether the mother or parent, who is referred to here, can effectively be replaced by other caregivers. Studies show clearly that one loving adult, who is aware of the importance of appropriate mental stimulation, should be consistently available. Use your common sense to decide how these priorities can best be met in your particular situation—and use this book to help a substitute caregiver understand your child's needs at different ages.

1. Emotional and verbal responsiveness of the parent: When the child vocalizes, does the parent respond with kind, friendly words rather than gesturing or not responding?

2. Avoidance of restriction and punishment: Does the parent refrain from acting angry, shouting at, physically punishing, or needlessly restricting the child?

3. Organization of physical environment: Is the child's world a safe place to be? Do other adults come into the home regularly? Do parent and baby get out at least three times a week?

4. Appropriate play materials: Are there toys that the child can manipulate to improve hand–eye coordination, stacking or nesting

objects, building toys, blocks, toys with movable parts, creative materials that can be used in a variety of ways? Are playthings interesting without overwhelming the child with detail? Are there toys that require the child to be an active rather than a passive participant?

5. Parental involvement with the child: Does the parent know where the child is? Does the parent look at the child often and show interest in the child's activities?

6. Opportunities for variety in daily activities: Does the parent provide outings and new things to look at and manipulate? Does someone read stories at least three times weekly? Is the other parent involved in the child's activities?

Use of this scale with families of infants who were considered either normal or "at risk" because of prematurity or adverse prenatal factors showed that a high score on the HOME index was sufficient to bring "at risk" children up to normal status on a test of intelligence by the time they were three years old. Infants from homes with lower ratings continued to show delayed development. The amount of parental interaction and the quality of the toys provided were particularly important factors. Other studies have shown that warm, loving verbal interactions between parent or caretaker and child are of particular importance in the first two years. So are praise, prompt attention, and immediate feedback. By four months, children who are talked to frequently, especially about specific objects in their environment, seem to develop better vocabularies and score better on later measures of intelligence.

Enriched Brains

There is good evidence that environments which provide appropriate and loving stimulation facilitate brain development. Studies of animals have shown that rats raised in enriched environments develop larger and heavier cortical tissue than those to whom little stimulation, either emotional or physical, is available. The "enriched" rats had more synaptic connections, and more overall cortical area in proportion to the rest of their brains. Although it is not possible to conduct such experiments on humans, we suspect that severely malnourished children may be victims of impaired brain growth, and researchers believe that other types of experience may be equally important.

Deciding what is appropriate "stimulation" for human babies is a tricky business. Other studies show that children who are heavily managed by their parents may lack certain types of thinking skills. When parents are overly restrictive in controlling and limiting activities, children show up with poorer problem-solving and mental organizational abilities. Excessive spanking or other harsh physical punishments can also limit a child's development. These findings do not mean that you should throw discipline and structure out the window. Babies and toddlers need safety and protection in order to explore new objects and situations. The security of a set of rules and reasonable limits encourages them to test their developing physical abilities against all sorts of major challenges—climbing, jumping, finding their way around new places, and extricating themselves from surprising situations.

The importance of active physical involvement for brain development was emphasized by one experiment with identical twin kittens. A revolving bar apparatus was rigged up in a patterned box designed to stimulate the kittens' developing visual systems. Each day the animals were placed in the box, but one had to work for his visual excitement; he was harnessed to pull the bar around—while his brother rode in a small basket. Although the visual input was identical for both animals, the one who did the work developed more neural connections.

How Much Is Too Much?

Beware of the pushmi-pullyu! Parents need to provide stimulation, but it is possible to become overinvolved. Don't let your eagerness to do the job deprive your child of the chance to do his own exploring and brain building. Obviously, finding the fine line between being overly directive and encouraging the youngster's problem-solving abilities is one of parenthood's major challenges. One recent survey found young mothers complaining that they were trying so hard to play with their infants that they ended up doing most of the playing while the child sat and watched. Toddlers learn many things from sitting and watching, but if Mom continually takes over, she may add more to the circuits in her busy brain than to the synapses in her child's.

The bottom line here seems to be that infants need safety, love, and conversation from their parents, or from capable, consistent caregivers. They need an environment that stimulates them to do their own exploring, manipulating, and wondering. A calm, caring home with reasonable limits but without excessive fear of punishment is a good one for brain building. As a veteran from the trenches of motherhood, however, I realize that everyone falls short of these ideals sometimes. Don't give up if the word "calm" doesn't always apply!

Guidelines for Brain-Building Play

Many parents wonder about the best way to guide a young child's play. Research again confirms common sense—get down on the floor and get involved when you have the time to be patient, and *let the child be the learner.* Here are some guidelines:

—Make sure that the child is actively interested and involved.

—If the child seems passive, start a simple activity and then try to "pass it over."

—Remember that an activity must be repeated many times to firm up neural networks for proficiency. Repetition isn't boring for young children, but if you get sick of "pat-a-cake," think ahead to the days when you will have to share the family car with this little creature. Boredom can be easy by comparison!

—Give the child positive encouragement for active exploration and investigation which builds motor and sensory pathways.

—Childproof your home for safety. Encourage attempts at new challenges.

—Carpeting and large pillows make good safe backgrounds for play.

—Keep playpen time or other restraints at a minimum.

—If possible, provide a window for the child to look out of.

—Provide low open shelves where a variety of toys, objects, and books are always accessible. Avoid boxes with jumbled toys.

—Bring in new toys or objects one or two at a time. While the brain at all ages responds to novelty, children are more likely to investigate new challenges if they are surrounded by familiar things.

—Interesting visual surroundings with bright colors—pictures, posters, calendars—can be varied to attract visual attention.

—Call attention to specific objects or aspects of the environment. Help the baby focus on one sense at a time for taking in information (look, see, touch, smell, taste, feel).

—Get in the habit of linking language to sensory input. Talk about what is happening, even with babies. Language is the means by which the brain develops its ability to act as control center for thinking, learning, and planning.

—Toys with sound or visual input improve cognitive skills, but it is important that baby be able to interact with them. Banging two pans together is far better brain food than pushing buttons to create noises produced by hidden electronic parts. The child should be able to link cause and effect—and see the parts of the toy at work.

Natural Chemicals for Learning

Appropriate stimulation does not mean keeping your child up longer and putting on the pressure. Be sensitive to nature's automatic shut-off valves, the signs of overexcitement or crankiness which show that baby has had enough. Learning seems to occur best when positive emotions facilitate chemical secretions in the brain that help messages cross synapses. These substances, called neurotransmitters, may particularly help learning when the child feels rested, in control, and secure. Exhaustion, anxiety, pressure, or fear may make it impossible for the neurons to send or receive the desired signals. One psychologist has voiced a concern that young children's hectic schedules are causing an "epidemic" of sleep disturbances. Experts are also concerned that well-intentioned parents may unwittingly short-circuit the pathways to skill development by forcing learning.

Forcing the Issue

A wave of recent enthusiasm for creating "superbabies" is putting pressure on concerned parents, who wonder if they should be teaching their child to read, play the violin, speak Japanese, or ice skate before age three. Aside from the obvious question of why children should spend time on activities which may be intrinsically meaningless to them, there is a further concern: excess pressure for learning inappropriate skills at early ages may cause problems later.

Many abilities depend on nature's maturation of particular neuron systems by coating the message-sending axons with myelin, an insulating fatty substance which helps speed messages from cell to cell. Before myelination, messages can travel along axons, but they do so erratically and inefficiently. The order of myelination formation is set by nature; overall, it starts at the top of the spine and moves up to higher, more complex, brain structures at the same time it is progressing down the spinal cord. For example, when the baby is born, structures in the lowest brain centers which are needed for reflexive sucking are well developed, but those for walking, talking, or bladder control are still not myelinated. Common sense tells us that it is useless to try and get a newborn to walk alone, but at about one year, when those connections have myelinated, it may be difficult to prevent.

Myelin formation appears to occur in cycles that precede the child's mastery of increasingly complex learning. So, although we can certainly stimulate development of cell networks when they are ready, many aspects of this growth cannot be rushed. Some research suggests that the best way to stimulate myelin growth is through helping the child understand relationships—literally making mental connections. The natural order of this learning starts with visual-spatial activities that involve touching, feeling, holding or exploring objects—water and sand play, blocks, stacking toys, puzzles, or mazes—or getting the feel of one's body in space, as in rolling, crawling, and climbing.

It is possible to force skills by intensive instruction, but this may cause the child to use immature, inappropriate neural networks and distort the natural growth process. Trying to speed learning over unfinished neuron systems might be somewhat akin to racing a limousine over a narrow path in the woods. You can do it, but neither the car nor the path end up in very good shape! Moreover, the pressure which surrounds such learning situations may leave permanent emotional debris. There is an order in which learning is programmed to take place; while it can be encouraged, it need not be forced. In the next chapter we will take a closer look at solid early foundations for higher-level skills.

Recently, I met a young mother who was feeling frustrated because her three-year-old daughter had stopped asking for the word cards which had been a part of her life since infancy. "She was reading so well," lamented Mom. "We had just done 'stamen,' 'pistil,' 'filament,' and 'petal' when suddenly she turned off." I resisted my impulse to ask why a three-year-old should read when she as yet has little to read about, and suggested she have patience. A week

SPEEDING THE MESSAGES

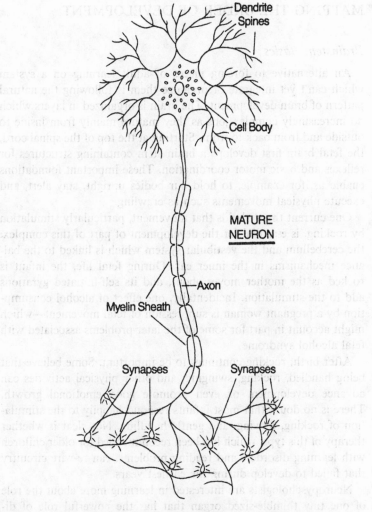

later, I saw her again and inquired if things had gotten better. "Well, sort of," Mother replied. "Yesterday she finally asked for some new words, but the only ones she wanted were 'poo-poo' and 'yuck.'" Perhaps the limbic brain has some wisdom after all!

MAPPING THE ORDER OF DEVELOPMENT

Brainstem Basics

An alternative to forcing pieces of adult learning on a system which can't yet integrate or organize them is following the natural pattern of brain development. The brain is organized in layers which do increasingly complex jobs as they mature mainly from inside to outside and from back to front. Starting at the top of the spinal cord, the fetal brain first develops a brain stem containing structures for reflexes and basic motor coordination. These important foundations enable us, for example, to hold our bodies upright, stay alert, and execute physical movements such as crawling.

One current theory holds that movement, particularly stimulation by rocking, is essential for the development of part of this complex: the cerebellum and the vestibular system which is linked to the balance mechanisms in the inner ear. During fetal life, the infant is rocked as the mother moves about, and its self-initiated gyrations add to the stimulation. Incidentally, one effect of alcohol consumption by a pregnant woman is suppression of fetal movement—which might account in part for some of the later problems associated with fetal alcohol syndrome.

After birth, rocking continues to be important. Some believe that being handled, rocking, swinging, and other physical activities can advance development or even promote good emotional growth. There is no doubt that most infants respond happily to the stimulation of rocking, moving, and gentle handling. Not clear is whether therapy of this type, which has been recommended for older children with learning disorders and reading problems, can re-wire circuitry that failed to develop during the earliest years.

Neuropyschologists are interested in learning more about the role of one tiny thimble-sized organ that has the powerful role of directing consciousness throughout life. The reticular activating system (RAS) serves as a sort of gatekeeper, allowing stimuli to enter the brain and be relayed through the limbic system to the appropriate cortical areas. Later, the child will learn to send messages back down from the cortex to focus attention, for example, on what the teacher is saying rather than on the kids playing outside the window.

Although we do not yet know how much the environment can alter these very important attention patterns, parents can help children by providing a calm environment and a regular schedule, and by encouraging them to focus on one thing at a time. Refer to Chapter 4 for specific suggestions about increasing attentional abilities as your child gets older.

Infants who come into the world "jittery" are more at risk for later attention problems. They need especially careful handling, but parents often are too exhausted to cope effectively. Enlisting the help of relatives, friends, or an outside agency may give everyone's frazzled nerves a break. Keeping the level of anxiety down is a difficult but important challenge.

Dividing Cortical Labor

Although other subcortical areas, including the limbic system, continue to develop after birth, the main action is in the cerebral cortex. The order in which its parts develop provides a map for parents interested in providing the right kind of stimulation during each period of growth.

Curving up from the back of the head over the front of the forehead, four major cortical areas, or lobes, are arranged from back to front, roughly in the order of their maturation. It is easiest to understand these complicated structures by looking at their main functions.

1. Occipital lobe—vision
2. Parietal lobe—touch and spatial understanding
3. Temporal lobe—hearing (auditory) and language
4. Frontal lobes
   a. Motor cortex—planning and regulating body movement
   b. Prefrontal cortex—last to develop fully: reasoning, memory, self-control, planning, and judgment

Each of the four lobes has a right and a left side, as the cortex is divided into two parts by a thick bridge of fibers down the middle. In Chapter 6 we will look closely at the interesting differences between these two sides of the brain. For now, I will concentrate on appropriate stimulation for motor, visual, touch, and auditory development. The major growth of the prefrontal cortex occurs later—when we get to the stage where that youngster starts to think about driving the family car.

THE GEOGRAPHY OF THINKING

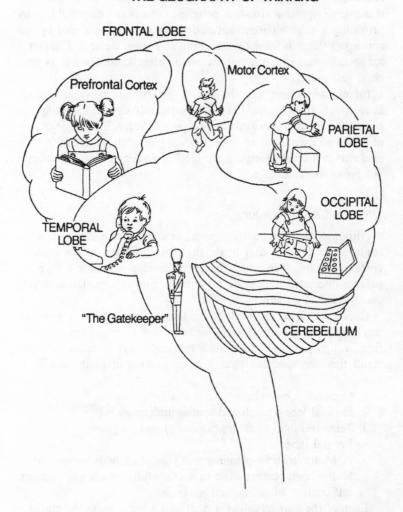

FRONTAL LOBE

Motor Cortex

Prefrontal Cortex

PARIETAL LOBE

OCCIPITAL LOBE

TEMPORAL LOBE

"The Gatekeeper"

CEREBELLUM

STIMULATING THE RIGHT CIRCUITS

Arousing a baby's interest has to be one of the easiest and most delightful jobs in the world. An active searcher and responder to every element of the environment, the infant thrives on stimulation for all five senses—but not all at once. Elaborate and expensive equipment isn't required, but a loving adult is indispensable as an interpreter, or "mediator" between the child and the confusing demands of the environment. Your overall goal should not be to "teach" your baby, but to help her discover how to organize experience for herself. The most active learners are encouraged to choose their own materials for building intelligence.

Moving and Touching

Initially, most input for the infant is through visual and motor systems. The motor cortex is developing rapidly at birth; it is responsible for planning and executing complex actions, and it must develop the ability to communicate with the cerebellum and other lower centers as well as with spinal cord connections to muscles throughout the body. Although the baby starts practicing muscle control almost immediately, integrating reflex motor movements into controlled patterns takes a long time. The baby needs many things to see and to touch with body, mouth, and hands. Initially the infant's movements seem random, but as he gets the feel of his own body in space, connections build between subcortical areas and the motor cortex to help the child organize his muscles around independent plans of action. Since the development of myelin in the spine proceeds from top to bottom, mouth, eyes, arms, and hands are used adeptly before legs and feet.

Infants love to experiment with hands and fingers, attempting to coordinate these fascinating extensions of themselves with objects they can see, getting a lesson about tactile and spatial relationships— how things relate in three dimensions. As we have noted, rhythmic movement may stimulate the cerebellum and vestibular system. Carrying a baby in a backpack provides interesting and comfortable experiences of movement, as well as visual excitement. Touching, gentle tickling, patting, and games such as pat-a-cake are natural stimulators. Most children enjoy being stroked with a variety of pleasant textures—for example, velvet, a feather, a soft-bristled brush, or cotton—or having their limbs gently manipulated.

Looking Intelligently

The infant is more skilled at looking than one might think. Newborns can imitate certain facial movements such as sticking out their tongues, and two-week-old babies recognize simple patterns and faces. Psychologists are puzzled about whether these are reflex responses or mean that the child is already starting to learn.

With practice in looking, the movements of the two eyes become coordinated around four to six months. The baby's preference for novelty suggests that visual surroundings be changed frequently—a new toy or mobile may be more stimulating than a familiar one, but familiar objects should be kept close at hand. One or two objects at a time are enough, and baby needs to practice reaching and moving toward them. One mother came home to discover that the sitter had literally imprisoned her child with good intentions—there were so many toys in the crib that he couldn't even roll over. When you are tempted to make life too easy for baby, remember the kitten who rode in the basket—and ended up with a smaller brain!

Parents can demonstrate interesting ways to play with new things. Slowly moving objects fascinate the baby, building visual connections in the occipital lobe as well as knowledge about space. If you talk softly about the toy at the same time, you begin the long, slow process of linking auditory and visual input. Learning to focus on more than one sensory modality requires neural maturation.

A variety of patterns are important: contours, horizontal and vertical lines, shapes, sizes, and colors, for example. Visual feature detectors are forming which will later enable the child to discriminate such complex patterns as alphabet letters or numerals when there is a good reason for learning them. Moreover, through such sensory experience, the child begins to form rudimentary concepts such as "like or different," "pleasant or unpleasant."

Interesting new research is questioning old assumptions about babies' preferences for color and pattern. While traditional nurseries were awash with soft pastels and cute figures, it appears likely that vivid contrasts, such as large black and white checks, herringbone patterns, and geometric shapes will turn on an infant's visual learning systems more effectively. It is important to view crib mobiles or other visual stimulators from the baby's perspective rather than from the adult's—they should be interesting, distinct, and not too complex. Combining interesting color contrasts with feelable textures, such as crocheted materials, may help integrate sensory experience—in this case, looking and touching.

Listening

Infants also need to respond to sounds, building auditory pathways that will develop the temporal lobe language areas. Although the mechanical aspects of the auditory system are in place at birth, the fiber links to the cortex are sparse and take a long time to reach adult capacity. Newborns can distinguish frequency and pitch, but finer discriminations aren't usually possible until about one year. Auditory pathways continue to develop until seven to ten years. Sounds from the environment, music, and human speech are all necessary for a well-balanced auditory diet—perhaps even before birth.

Many young babies are soothed by the rhythmic sound of a clock ticking, suggesting they remember their mother's heartbeat in the womb. This idea has been explored in a clinic at UCLA, where prenatal stimulation with earphones on the expectant mother's abdomen gives baby a taped "welcome" message from Mom and Dad at regular intervals. The intent is to increase auditory pathways for future language development. Skeptics, however, point out that most fetal auditory stimulation comes from vibrations *within* the mother's body as she speaks, and that frequency ranges from "internal" noise are more suitable for the developing brain than those of external sounds. Only near the end of pregnancy does the expanded uterus begin to conduct outside sounds with clarity.

Until we learn more about this topic, it seems sensible to give the fetus a calm, stable start without an atmosphere of pressure. By all means talk to your unborn child, but reflect carefully before you start "pushing" any type of learning. One area of proved concern is with premature babies, whose exposure to noise in incubators should be as close to the natural sound environment in the womb as possible.

After birth, appropriate auditory stimulation promotes emotional, social, and language development. Soothing, pleasant, and interesting sounds inspire curiosity and a receptive attitude toward language. A variety of sounds are important, one at a time. Music, voices, and even household noises such as refrigerators or dishwashers are good raw material, but a constant background of music or machinery noise makes sound discrimination difficult for babies. A noisy and confusing environment can be detrimental to development.

Some children may learn how to screen out human voices because they have been excessive or unpleasant. These youngsters have trouble later when they need to listen for information in school or conversation. Simple repetitive nursery rhymes, songs, and loving words help make children eager listeners. Incidentally, there is good evidence that reading books to the baby will do far more to develop a love of reading than packs of flash cards, especially if reading is associated with a loving lap and a parent's enjoyment.

Carry on a conversation with your infant. The basis of language—that it is an important way to be involved with someone—is learned from early experiences. Every time you communicate with your child, either with words or actions, you are teaching a language lesson. Baby talk to babies isn't necessarily harmful; it is an instinctive way to address infants; even young children adapt their conversation to a baby's level. It is also important to include good adult language as a model.

WARNING SIGNALS

What if a child, for some unavoidable reason, is deprived of this brain-building stimulation? The unfortunate truth is probably that certain children do not have the best foundations for brain growth. Some, too, have minor difficulties with specific aspects of learning. Although all children have their unique "quirks," I have included a list of warning signals suggested by a child neurologist. Incidentally, premature babies should always be evaluated according to their gestational age rather than actual birth date.

TIPS FROM A CHILD NEUROLOGIST

The presence of any of these warning signs should alert you to seek a professional evaluation:

1. Infant "too good"; sleeps all the time.
2. Habitual poor eye contact with parents.
3. Consistent failure to respond to voices or other sounds.
4. Asymmetry of limb movements: right and left sides of the body should be equally strong and active during the first year.
5. Noticeable delay in *many or all* of the commonly accepted milestones for motor development (sitting, creeping, walking, etc.)
6. Noticeable delay in social responsiveness: doesn't participate in pat-a-cake, peek-a-boo, bye-bye.
7. Failure to develop language within appropriate time limits.

If you have serious doubts about your child's development, don't accept "He'll grow out of it" from your pediatrician. Early detection —or reassurance—is important.

Fortunately, the developing brain is somewhat plastic. If some systems are blocked, as by blindness, for example, others develop more vigorously as they are used to compensate. One very important question is to what extent specific abilities can be changed by experience and stimulation. The answer may depend on nature's neural schedule of critical periods for skill development.

CRITICAL PERIODS

The Brain's Timing

Kittens who are blindfolded for just four days during the second month of life may be permanently blind because certain cells in the visual cortex missed their chance to be activated. Even more surprising, some animal studies show that visual feature detectors which enable us to distinguish horizontal or vertical lines may fail to develop without stimulation during a critical period. Imagine a chicken reared in a laboratory environment where vertical lines have been carefully excluded. When this poor creature is later put outside, it repeatedly bumps into fenceposts because it cannot perceive them!

Critical periods in humans are much harder to investigate, and scientists are reluctant to generalize about children on the basis of animal studies. So far it has been shown that babies born with cataracts on both eyes develop near-normal vision if the cataracts are removed prior to age two months, but are permanently impaired if they remain after six months. Such experience suggests that there are critical, or at least sensitive, periods for human brains, too. One for developing binocular vision—the ability to coordinate the images from both eyes—is thought to occur between birth and three years, and children suffering from strabismus, which results in "lazy eye," need treatment before age five for their visual cortex to be organized normally.

There may also be critical periods for auditory development. Children who suffer from *chronic or intermittent hearing loss* from early ear infections have a higher probability of future reading problems which may stem from inaccurate sound discriminations *(sh* or *ch,* for example). The human sound system is particularly sensitive to interruption between the ages of birth and four years. If sounds are blocked from entering, the child may not learn to process them accurately. Some theorists even believe that inconsistent ability to hear or hearing loss causes difficulty with more fundamental language concepts on which much higher thinking depends.

A Bizarre Story

One unique and tragic illustration of sensory deprivation during the critical period for language development is the case of Genie, a girl who was kept locked in a closet by her psychotic parents from the ages of twenty months to thirteen years. Strapped to a potty chair during the day, she was fed only baby food and "barked" at by her father, who punished her severely if she attempted to make noise. Because she had missed all language stimulation during a so-called critical period, Genie became a source of great professional interest as well as compassion when she was finally discovered and hospitalized. She developed speech after intensive teaching, but it is different from that of normal children and is directed from parts of her brain that would not ordinarily be involved. Genie's case strongly suggests that humans have a timetable indicating when certain brain cells need language stimulation.

Until we learn more, it makes sense to get all necessary systems involved for the brain's nourishment. Parents should seek expert medical advice without delay if a child has difficulty with vision, hearing, movement, or touch sensitivity. Someday we may be able to chart the timetable of neuronal maturation and plan a program for each child. In the meanwhile, it is heartening to know about another mystery of the human brain—the reason that Genie learned language at all—"plasticity."

THE PLASTIC BRAIN

Neurons Need Connections

No two brains are the same, and none of us has a "perfect" one. As raw material for the demands of thinking and learning, nature cleverly equips the infant's brain with more neurons than it needs. At birth, much cortical tissue is uncommitted, "plastic" in its ability to develop in alternate ways. Even while the brain grows rapidly during the first year of life, extra unstimulated neurons are shrinking. One intriguing theory proposes a chemical "synaptic rewarding factor," which encourages cells to make connections. When an activity is carried out, the brain stimulates itself to repeat the neural relays involved. This theory suggests that lopsided development might result if some types of sensory neurons are stimulated at the expense of others.

Fortunately, the excess number of neurons in the child's brain enables some redistribution of jobs that would have been done by damaged or poorly developed networks. Similar cortical cells or even neighboring subcortical structures may "learn" to stand in for a missing performer, particularly if the problem area is one for certain types of language or learning. Perhaps the most dramatic evidence comes from a long-term study of three children who, as infants, had had an entire half of their brain removed because they had been born with intractable epileptic seizures. To everyone's amazement, all three children developed the functions normally served by both sides, although competence in each was diminished. There are probably few functions served only by a specific group of cells in the brain, and higher thinking processes in particular require interacting systems which can be rearranged. The prognosis for bypassing damage to more specialized areas, however, such as in motor difficulties associated with cerebral palsy, is not as optimistic.

The brain's plasticity is at a height in the newborn, and no one is quite sure when it declines. We used to think that neuron flexibility diminished gradually until about age eight, when rerouting became impossible. Recently, however, there have been some suggestions that plasticity may extend even into adulthood, so there may be hope for all of us!

Coping with Problems

Although the young brain covers up to the best of its ability, small, unrecognized injuries or malformations probably are a factor in the subtle difficulties of many learning-disabled children. The problem is often not large enough to be neurologically identified by current methods, but child and parents become frustrated because certain types of learning take longer when they must be accomplished by pathways less efficient than those originally scheduled to do the job.

With new techniques of brain scanning, this whole picture may change as it becomes possible to identify even minor differences in infancy. It will take time, however, before this expensive technology is readily available for what doctors often view as "minor" problems. In the meanwhile, consider the following implications of current research:

—Make sure your child has ongoing checks of hearing and vision from early months; pediatricians are only now becoming aware of the importance of critical periods.

—If your child has recurrent ear infections, be on guard for intermittent hearing loss. Be aware that it may not show up in a one-time appointment; you may need to insist on another evaluation.

—If your child is noticeably delayed in learning certain skills, ask your pediatrician for the name of a professional who can teach you special activities to do at home. Alternate approaches through different sensory pathways are often used for rerouting, and new techniques are continually being developed.

—Don't give up if some types of learning are difficult. Remind yourself that all brains have certain strengths and weaknesses, and enjoy your child's talents rather than dwelling exclusively on difficulties.

NURTURING THE "NEED TO KNOW"

Emerging from all the data is a clear message. Each child must build individual networks for thinking; this development comes from within, using outside stimuli as material for growth. A baby will give explicit clues about what kind of input is needed and let you know when it isn't interesting anymore. Explaining things to children won't do the job; they must have a chance to experience, wonder, experiment, and act it out for themselves. It is this process, throughout life, that creates the growth of intelligence. Babies come equipped with the "need to know"; our job is to give them love, acceptance, and the raw material of appropriate stimulation at each level of development. Your own common sense, augmented by current knowledge, is the best guide.

Children's Brains at Work:
From Nursery to Schoolroom

ONE MORNING WHILE I WAS OBSERVING A PREKINDERGARTEN class in a top-ranked school, two parents were also taking a look, trying to decide whether they should enroll their little boy the following year. While he delved happily into the sand and water table, they circulated around the room. I sensed some skepticism about what they saw, and I guessed the reason. This program for three- and four-year-olds was designed to prepare children for a high-powered academic setting—but it looked like too much fun! In one corner children intently measured sand and water as they engineered a dam. Nearby, in the block area, two boys and three girls worked on a "White House" with a sliding ramp to capture "bad guys." A teacher in the art corner helped children classify wobbly clay animals for an imaginary zoo, and several youngsters in the dramatic play area discussed their shopping list for a pretend Thanksgiving dinner. One small boy spent the entire free play time fondling and talking to the class's pet rabbit.

I could see the visiting mother peering hopefully into the kindergarten room next door. When she saw five-year-olds playing, she gave up. Nudging her husband, she whispered, "This school isn't worth the money. They don't do any work here!"

As adults, we have a pretty clear idea of what constitutes "work" and "play." Most of us believe that in order to learn something, we must work hard at it, and too many have forgotten that the process of meaningful learning is both fun and exciting! Yet the human brain changes during development, and the "work," as well as the fun, that is appropriate for teenagers and adults is not right for young children. Those who believe that "valuable time" is being wasted or that their children will "get behind" if they are allowed to learn by playing are sadly mistaken.

Making sense out of experience is the key to early learning. The necessary tools are the body, the hands, and the senses, which bring new learning into the brain. Children at play are working hard at brain building. In this chapter we will investigate ways in which this assignment changes during the preschool and primary years, and how home environments can help at each age level. I hope you will also get some useful ideas about how to choose your child's first school.

SETTING THE STAGE FOR LEARNING

Enriched Environments for Toddlers

Studies show that "enriched" environments encourage the kind of play that promotes brain growth and lays good foundations for a lifetime of learning. But what does "enriched" mean at different ages?

Researchers are trying to ferret out answers to this important question. They have found that stimulating playthings are more important for cognitive development after age one than in earlier months. Availability of interesting and challenging play materials in children's homes after the first year correlates with later IQ and school achievement in reading and math. As in infancy, a child's firsthand involvement with objects and experiences is a catalyst for brain growth.

Playthings start to become important at about six months of age, but elaborate and expensive toys are not necessarily the best. A toy which the toddler passively watches or listens to is far less motivating than one which she can manipulate, interact with, or figure out. When there is only one "right way" to play, opportunities for experimentation and new discovery are limited. Common household objects, tools, cooking utensils, and gadgets are particularly fascinating because adults use them. Nesting and stacking toys or objects, containers for dumping and pouring are examples of good mental stimulators. They require active handling by the child and also teach about relationships: top, middle, bottom; small, big, bigger, biggest. Many experts believe that wooden unit blocks, in graduated sizes and shapes, are the best toy of all.

Here are some research-based ideas for creating a preschool "work" environment at home:

—Maintain reasonable rules so that the child's safety needs can be met without discouraging exploration.

—Avoid harsh physical punishment or overly restrictive discipline.

—Let the child take the lead in play. Show and guide; don't direct or boss. Be open to new ways to play or use materials.

—Don't "protect" your child from making a few mistakes—and learning from them.

—Even toddlers can make simple decisions. "What color Playdough would you like today?" "Which toy do you choose to take in the car?" Offer choices that you both can live with—and then stick to them.

—At this age it is appropriate to start suggesting that the child do some self-evaluation on occasion. "How did I do?" "Did I finish?"

—Child-sized furniture, easels, and chalkboards give a comforting feeling of control.

—Encourage children to talk about their play. Show that you are interested by listening and asking questions.

—The sensory aspects of play can be linked with language. "How does that look/sound/smell/taste/feel?" This is a good opportunity for vocabulary building (e.g., smooth, bumpy, sharp, delicious).

—As the child gets older, select a weekly topic for play exploration. For example, you might put out a magnifying glass, collecting jars, sorting boxes, and picture books for nature study. Let the child's interests guide you.

—Ideas for creative projects may be found in many magazines. Focus on the child's involvement, not on the finished product.

—Avoid workbooks or other purchased "learning" materials that "teach" rote-level academic tasks of letters and numbers.

—Easels and paints, clay, sand, Playdough, fingerpaints, water, construction paper, glue, and mud are examples of materials that help refine and organize sensory intake systems. If you tend to be fanatic about cleanliness, close your eyes and imagine little dendrites branching inside that muddy head.

I once saw a little boy who became almost panicky when he spilled some milk on the table in his day-care center. Later his teachers told me they were worried about his learning. "He's smart," they said, "but he's so afraid of making a mistake that he never tries anything that looks hard."

Help your child risk the adventure of learning.

Security to Learn

Children who feel safe because they can depend on an adult are able to reach out to new experiences. One important study looked at forty one-year-olds to determine how the security of their attachment to their mothers related to later mental development. At twenty-one months of age, the children who had felt secure at age one were more playful, more curious about a puzzle toy, more responsive to an adult playmate, and able to focus attention more effectively. They also had larger vocabularies and better scores on IQ tests. In our zest for stimulating children's minds, we shouldn't forget that a loving and safe home is always the first order of business. If you find your concerns about your child's intellect getting in the way of simple affection, stand back and ask yourself, "What's really important?"

HOW DO CHILDREN THINK?

Defining children's "work" is easier if we try to understand how thinking and learning changes at different ages. Much has been written about Jean Piaget, who tried to explain this process, but few parents are familiar with Alexander Luria, a Russian neuropsychologist who began to give us clues into the brain development which may parallel it. Although Piaget himself never wanted to tie his ideas to brain science, the connection appears to be inescapable. We have a great deal yet to learn, and these two theories provide an interesting view of how little minds look at the world—and why.

Ages and Stages

Both Piaget and Luria felt that children's thinking ability undergoes several major changes along the route to adult-level reasoning. They agreed that certain types of experience are necessary at each stage, and that a child who gets the brain food he needs has a better chance of reaching the top of the cognitive ladder. Piaget even believed that children could not move up a rung until the previous ones were firmly built. No one is sure how the speed of this climb is related to innate intelligence because life experiences are so important. To me, the most interesting and useful of Piaget's ideas is the way the child creates his own intelligence at each level: by puzzling out inconsistencies between his bits of knowledge, or "schemas," and the reality of his daily experiences.

Different Hooks

If you and your seven-year-old watch a TV program on the workings of the brain, chances are you will emerge with very different learning. An adult can "get more out of it" by hanging the new information on previous pieces of knowledge, mental hooks about biology, psychology, and years of practical experience with one's own brain. Schemas (schemata) are these mental hooks, the bits of learning that combine to form each person's scaffolding of thought. The better the framework and the bigger the hooks, the more we can remember and learn from each new experience.

Since your child's frameworks are small and immature, her learning in any situation is qualitatively different from yours. You can try to lend her your schemas by explaining them, but if she lacks the personal experience, your words will fall right off her incomplete hooks. This theory may explain why each generation seems to have to make its own mistakes instead of taking the good advice of its elders!

When you talk with your child, you can help bridge the schema gap.

1. As you solve problems together, talk through your own questions. "I wonder how I should start." "Are these two alike?" "Could I put them together?" "Is it working?" "What's going to happen?" "How did I do?"

2. Ask your child similar questions.

3. Phrase them simply and give the child plenty of time to think and answer.

4. Let the child repeat each solution several times to understand it.

5. Encourage understanding. Ask, "Why do you think that happened?" "Why did/didn't that work?"

A Small Piece of Learning

I had a conversation with a first grader the other day which taught me about one child's mental "hooks." Someone in our reading group noticed that it had started to snow. The level of excitement rose until I decided we might as well go to the window and talk about snow for a while. We ended up writing a poem called "Wet, Soggy, Snow." As the group started back to their own classroom, Marcy lingered behind, staring at the still-barren grass outside. "Why isn't the snow sticking on the ground?" she asked. Not wanting to deprive her of the chance to do some thinking (and learning) for herself, I replied, "What do you think?"

"Well," she replied, "I don't know because snow is supposed to stay there after it comes down—why isn't it?"

"It does seem to be disappearing," I acknowledged. "Do you know anything that would make snow disappear?"

Marcy thought for a moment. "Not really. Snow is cold and it stays. Well, maybe if you put water on it."

At this point I realized that Marcy's notion of snow was both inaccurate and incomplete, so there was no way she could grasp the cause and effect principle involved. Instead of trying to explain it to her, I took her outside, grabbed some snowflakes as they fell, and we watched them turn into water. Finally we felt the ground temperature and Marcy drew her own conclusions. She enlarged her "snow" schema to include her observation that warmth makes it melt, and she was forced to change her ideas to accommodate this new information. It is through countless such firsthand experiences that children develop knowledge and the ability to manipulate it mentally. *For this type of learning, parents are the first and best teachers.*

As schemas develop and enlarge, they are combined into mental *operations,* or patterns which enable the child to think about relationships in more abstract ways. For example, a two-year-old must line up blocks in order to see what they look like; an eight-year-old can think about lining them up without actually doing it, and a fifteen-year-old may be able to make combinations in his mind to test scientific relationships among them.

Levels of Processing

Does experience alone account for these changes? Luria believed that a child's ability to combine new ideas also results from maturation of three special systems in the brain which he called "functional units." I can't draw you a diagram because areas all over the brain, are involved, particularly at more advanced levels. As the child handles millions of bits of experience, the separate areas develop linking networks of cell connections. In a sense, the thinking child makes his own brain fit together!

Lower-level networks come first. At the bottom are reflex responses and learning to *pay attention,* then comes the *reception* of countless pieces of incoming information and *association* of the pieces with each other for understanding. When enough pieces have been taken in, the child finally begins to *interpret* them and *plan* responses.

How does Luria's model work in a real situation? Let's say you are trying to get your child to leave the TV set.

The *first functional unit* regulates consciousness and the ability to pay attention. This unit corresponds to the subcortical gatekeeper, the reticular formation (RAS), described earlier.

"Oops, I hear Mom's voice."

Once the message gets into conscious awareness, it is directed to a specialized reception area in the next "layer," where the *second functional unit* converts it into a meaningful signal. This message would be sent to the temporal lobe, which is the part of the cortex responsible for auditory processing. First it must be received and sorted out from other auditory stimuli:

"What did she say?"

then analyzed and organized into some sort of meaning:

"What does she mean, 'Clean up your room'?"

and finally, associated with information from other senses or from memory for complete understanding:

"Oh, I remember I left my clothes and toys all over the floor and she's having company tonight."

Only after all these steps are completed can the *third functional unit,* corresponding to the frontal lobes of the cortex, do its work of evaluating the information and planning behavior:

"Guess I'd better pick up that stuff as soon as this program is over."

For most parents, this particular example proves Luria's point that the mere presence of a neural structure does not guarantee that it can (or will) be used! Practice is the essential ingredient, and it takes all of childhood and most of adolescence to perfect and connect all the systems.

THE PRESCHOOL YEARS

Making Connections

A child's first months lay the groundwork for paying attention, taking in bits of information to each of the senses, and practicing with body movements. During this "sensorimotor" period, the brain is not ready to deal with anything beyond immediate physical experience. Around the age of eighteen months, however, most children move into a stage in which they have developed enough hooks within each sensory modality to start putting them together into bigger frameworks. They begin to understand and associate experiences. More complex patterns of movements (motor programs) are mastered, and—most exciting of all—language develops. Children with poor foundations in reception areas may fall behind when they have to start associating ideas. The higher levels at which understanding occurs are probably the most sensitive of all to environmental stimulation.

With an increasing base of neural connections, the toddler looks at the world in different ways. The development of language and symbolic play represent the beginning of abstract thought. A child pretending to talk to Grandma on a toy telephone shows that she has a mental representation of both Grandma (out of sight) and the general function of real telephones. When she asks for a cookie that you have previously put in a cupboard, she shows that she has organized and associated some ideas that take her one step beyond cookies she can only see or touch. Many believe that the roots of creativity also lie at this junction of concrete and symbolic experience.

Until sometime around age six or seven, however, channels for abstract thought are still limited. Children's "work" requires mastering their physical environments and learning to use a new symbol system, language. The preschooler remains caught on present reality with only a vague concept of past, present, and future. He has trouble with other peoples' points of view. When children in this age period are given a model of three cardboard mountains and asked what would be seen by a doll seated opposite them, they usually answer by picking the view that corresponds with their own, rather than the doll's. The ability to "decenter," or move out of one's own perspective, occurs very slowly, as any mother who expects a child to see *her* point of view can confirm! For this reason, preschool learning must arise from firsthand experience and interest. Perhaps the most important thing to remember is that the child comes at any situation with a different set of hooks than yours. Parents who respect the unique quality of early intelligence have the best chance of helping it grow.

What Should Preschoolers Learn?

After years of studying young children's learning, I am increasingly convinced that *patterns* are the key to intelligence. Patterning information really means organizing and associating new information with previously developed mental hooks. "Gifted" children have an unusual ability to pick up all kinds of patterns and relationships in everyday experience. One bright little three-year-old, who was being tested for admission into a competitive prekindergarten, had impressed everyone with her huge vocabulary and outgoing personality, but she completed the sales job when she surveyed the artwork on the wall and said, "Look! The patterns in that picture are the same as the ones in my dress."

Children who can "see" relationships and organize input at a sensory level seem to have an easier time organizing thoughts and ideas. Some youngsters come into the world with nervous systems that are better equipped for this assignment than others. Many experts believe that the withdrawal and unusual mannerisms of autistic children stem from some deficit in making meaningful connections out of experience, so that the world seems to be a terrifying jumble of sights, sounds, and feelings. The most effective treatments for this puzzling disorder seem to be those which start with trying to connect meaning to the most basic pieces of sensory input.

We are not sure how much can be done to change things at these fundamental neural levels, but while the brain is still selectively "pruning" itself before age four or five, I think it is wise to focus on helping the child make mental connections rather than on specific bits of information. Because of immaturity in parietal lobe areas that connect sight, sound, touch, and body awareness, it is still difficult to combine processes from more than one modality, such as in looking at a letter form and saying a sound to go with it, or hearing a numeral and writing it.

Even babies can be conditioned to associate two stimuli that are presented repeatedly, but this learning lacks real meaning for the child and may use inappropriate parts of the cortex instead of those best suited for the job. In fact, forced learning of any type may result in the use of lower systems since the higher ones which should do the work have not yet developed. The "habit" of using inferior brain areas for higher-level tasks (such as reading) and of *receiving* instruction rather than *creating patterns of meaning* may cause trouble later on.

Children who don't learn to search for meaning are often good "technicians" in the first and second grades because they can deal with isolated data, but when the demands for comprehension increase, they "hit the wall." They have difficulty organizing information into more abstract ideas. "I don't get it" becomes their theme song.

Helping Children Create Mental Patterns

During preschool years, the parent's job as security giver should expand to be intellectual challenger for both boys and girls. Here are some commonsense guidelines to help a child create mental patterns:

—Remind yourself often that the child's job before age six is to learn to make sense out of the world, not to memorize material that has little meaning without the necessary neural structures.

—Help your child figure out meanings and relationships in daily events; his continual "Why?" questions are a way of expressing his need to make these connections.

—Introduce skills of sequencing—arranging objects according to size, remembering words or events in order. It is beneficial to talk about abstract sequences such as cause and effect, but preschoolers must stick to objects if they are expected to put things in order themselves.

—Mental patterns are built on networks of sensory connections. Call the child's attention to patterns in the sensory world: "What does that taste like?" "Do these look alike?"

—Visual patterns are present all the time. "Look at the tree branches against the sky. Doesn't it look as if the tree has arms? Maybe we could draw a picture."

—Puzzles and commercial materials can be helpful in visual patterning. Parquetry blocks, dominoes, and kaleidoscopes are examples. "What is wrong with this picture?" links visual and cognitive skills.

—Patterning in stitchery activities is fun for both sexes, and links visual and motor development.

—Encourage auditory patterning with rhymes, tunes, familiar stories, or attention to sounds around the house. See Chapter 7 for tips on language patterning.

—For boys and girls of four and five, simple carpentry tools, wood, large nails, screws, nuts, and bolts are excellent materials for making perceptual and motor connections.

—Motor patterns need to be practiced over and over—using utensils and tools, cutting, catching and throwing a large soft ball, playing games of copying finger or body movements, for example. Self-help skills and household jobs are very important for the child to master—help your child, but encourage him to do it himself even if the job isn't done exactly *your* way! I have worked with children who are afraid to attempt even simple tasks, because Mom has always jumped in and done the job for them. They often appear inept and even disabled when they start school.

—Mothers who "hover" over children may impede the child's ability to form mental patterns of his own; one study even showed that too-frequent offering of food and drink to toddlers was negatively related to later school achievement!

—If a child truly needs help with a motor pattern, gently guide her body through the action sequence several times to lay the neural path, or divide the action into a series of smaller activity units. Don't expect a child of this age to copy complex actions (kinesthetic) which you show her (visual)—allow her to learn with one sense at a time (in this case, her body).

—Be sure to let your child make reasonable choices whenever possible. Learning to make simple decisions—and minor mistakes—is hard but necessary. Children's conception of reality needs to include close personal experience with cause and effect.

—When choosing a day-care or nursery school setting, look for one which provides varied sensory stimulation and opportunities for active movement and exploration. Look for planned and meaningful play experiences that include lots of language stimulation both from adults and other children.

What About Sports?

At a tennis court recently I was intrigued by a little girl of about five who was standing patiently outside the ladies' locker room. In one hand she clutched a limp doll and in the other a tennis racket. I couldn't help watching her for the next two hours as she first struggled through a tennis lesson and then sat and waited for her mother to finish a doubles game. I was unaccountably troubled by this docile child, who didn't seem particularly upset by her situation. Why was it bugging me so much?

Deciding to apply some of the ideas in this book, I analyzed the scene. First of all, her quiet resignation to being "good"—here defined as sitting passively and waiting on an adult's schedule—does not bode well for her future intellectual vigor. But the idea of the tennis lesson, so passively endured, also bothered me.

Research on children's athletic development is sparse, but the same principles seem to hold true. Because the motor strip in the cortex is early to mature, young children can master some large-muscle activities fairly easily. My observations suggest that many preschoolers can swim, ski, and do creative dance movements with enjoyment—if they aren't forced. Ice skating may even fall into this category, depending on how it is taught. These activities do not require intricate combinations of visual and motor skills. Sports such as tennis and baseball, however, which add fine visual-motor and visual-spatial requirements, are too much for most children until age seven or so when the brain develops the ability to combine input and output in several senses at once. As always, children will try hard if they sense their parents care a lot about an activity, but it is a shame to saddle them with expectations they can't meet or pressure for competition before they have the mental perspective to deal with it. Don't be a parental spoilsport!

A few rare youngsters are "naturals" at almost any age. If you are eager to produce an Olympic athlete and the child seems capable and eager, give it a try early on. If it doesn't take at once, however, back off and wait until that little brain and body are ready to exercise together. New research is clear on the value of spontaneous movement activities, rhythms to music, simple coordination games—all in a relaxed and noncompetitive setting.

Intellectual Building Blocks

"Play" is considered so important by child development experts that huge books of research studies have been published about it. They agree, during the preschool years, that manipulative and symbolic fantasy play are particularly important. Remember the children building the White House with wooden unit blocks? They were manipulating and pretending, but their teacher pointed out they were also "actively involved in testing two important scientific ideas: 'systems' and 'interactions,' as well as getting a solid understanding of mathematical concepts" ("We only need half as many of these." "The living room should be a rectangle, not a square."). The important notion of cause and effect was also much in evidence ("Don't make that tower too tall or it'll fall over!").

Children playing with blocks also enlarge and change their schemas of relative space ("How do I get this block to bridge these other two?"), size (each block is some multiple of the basic unit), symmetry and proportion, balance, stability, and gravity. One child, attempting to construct a roof to bridge four walls, soon discovered that the walls were too far apart, and tried out a number of hypotheses before mastering the relationships involved. Fortunately, no one interrupted her or stole her chance to learn by "showing" her how! Another youngster was busy constructing some mental schemas about number. He lined up eight blocks in a row and counted them in one direction, then backwards to see if they were the same. Then he stacked them up into a tower and counted them again—up and down. Convinced that "eight" is "eight" from all directions, he skipped off, unaware that he had just mastered an abstract mathematical idea.

The Power of Pretending

Fantasy play with others gets children to enlarge their mental frameworks, get outside their own minds, and practice using language. The children in the "pretend play" corner, planning their Thanksgiving feast, were certainly enlarging their schemas as they debated the division of labor.

"You're the mommy. You have to go to the store."

"I can't. I have to go to work."

"Whaddaya mean, work? Mommies don't work. They stay home and cook and stuff."

"Mommies do too work. My mommy works—she's a lawyer and she goes to the office and she goes to *court!* And I'll sue you if you don't play nice!"

In the process of reaching an eventual compromise, both youngsters gained information about other values and points of view, which they had to mediate through the use of language. In their "pretend" household, moreover, they were using symbols: blocks as "food," an empty can as a "telephone" and a ball as a "yucky baby." This level of learning separates human thought from that of all other species. Play, in this sense, is the gateway to metaphor, to scientific insight, and to invention. Choose a school which will encourage children to open this gate before expecting them to perform advanced mental operations.

Playtime as a Gateway to Learning

—Playtime should be relaxed and pressure-free. Constructive play usually begins only after a child feels familiar and comfortable in a setting. Activities should not be switched too often as long as the children are satisfied.

—The best play materials suggest imaginative uses rather than being too literal—materials for building a "pretend" house, for example, rather than one already fitted out with perfect furniture and accessories, lengths of fabric rather than costumes, large empty boxes, etc.

—Children use play to gain important feelings of mastery and control or deal with issues that may be troubling them. (Remember the sliding ramp to capture "bad guys"?) Adults should intervene only when necessary to preserve emotional or physical safety.

—Children can express "forbidden" feelings in play at school. For example, the "yucky baby" was frequently swatted by one little girl who, I learned later, had a new baby brother at home. She got rid of some of her feelings without doing any damage to the real baby.

—Rule-governed games are fun for adults and children and promote many kinds of learning, but they should not substitute for exploratory and pretend play.

—Children playing together often make up their own "rules" which may seem incomprehensible to an adult. As long as the children are satisfied, adults should stand aside. They don't have our schemas for rules, and we have forgotten theirs.

—Dramatic play teaches social skills more effectively than any type of instruction.

—Pretense activities are often used by a child to firm up new understandings about the world; good schools encourage and respect the quality of a child's emerging thought.

THE EARLY SCHOOL YEARS

Putting It Together: Where the Senses Meet

From ages five to seven or eight the brain is in one of its most dynamic states of change as it practices combining sensory patterns from different modalities. Maturation of a small part of the parietal lobe, at the junction where all the senses come together, makes many kinds of new learning possible, but there is enormous variability in the age when it occurs. One well-known psychologist who has applied Luria's work to American children believes it may rarely occur as early as two or three years, or as late as ten or twelve!

Only now does it make sense to ask a youngster to look at a series of written letters and "sound out" a word, to coordinate motor programs and visual skills such as in catching or kicking a ball, or later, reading music while playing an instrument. Even writing simple words from dictation links auditory, visual, and motor patterns. Children need time to practice and experiment with all these new combinations. They are adding a whole new complex of neural connections. Don't be surprised if they come up with some "weird" ideas as they fool around putting old patterns into larger new ones. What sometimes passes for "creativity" at this age may be more like experimentation. Be receptive to your child's novel ideas.

This is the age when parents first get involved in school assignments that have to be done at home. Remember that lots of repetition will be necessary before skills become automatic as they are for you (e.g., writing, spelling, using the multiplication tables, following directions—even setting the table and playing ball). It helps if you model thinking skills in everyday situations as well as with schoolwork. Here are some steps to help a child "get it together":

1. Before you try to work on anything together, make sure you have the child's attention. Your child will absorb your level of enthusiasm (or lack of it).

2. Link new information to old with illustrations, analogies, and examples; help your child make the associations. ("This is just like the problem we had with your bike—it looks as if the wheel is stuck. It reminds me of when I used to feel "stuck" in the middle of a math problem. What do you think we should do?")

3. Help the child act out the idea.

4. Show connections, common themes, or organizing principles of new material. ("These all seem to be types of flowers, even though they look different.")

5. Try to get the child to think up personal connections. (Did you ever feel the way José did in the story?)

6. Tie abstractions to concrete experience. ("Let's see if we can cut this paper in thirds. What if we cut each third in half?)

7. Pictures or diagrams help organize many types of material. Help your child make charts, maps, or lists of things in categories, or draw "cartoon" sequences to get information into manageable form.

8. Remember that the child still needs many specific instances before generalizations can be made.

Moving Toward Abstract Thought

As children start to put ideas together in new ways, they begin to get beyond the immediate physical characteristics of an object. Some of the most interesting tests of this ability are those which indicate whether a child has learned to "conserve," which basically means that the child is not fooled by physical appearances. For example, the reversible equation $4 + 5 = 9$ is the same as $9 = 5 + 4$, and even

$9 - 4 = 5$, and $9 - 5 = 4$. A younger child has a great deal of difficulty with reversibility; he believes that these things are different because they *look* different. He cannot pull out the essential relationship and thus he cannot "undo" and turn around the sequence in his mind.

Tests of conservation try to "fool" a child about the essential attributes of volume, length, area, and mass. One well-known experiment starts with two identical glasses of liquid. After the child has agreed that there is the same amount in both glasses, the experimenter pours one glassful into a taller, thinner container and asks, "Now, do these have the same amount or does one have more water?" Children below the age of seven often state assuredly that the tall one has "more," because the level of water makes it look that way. I have tried endlessly repouring and explaining, thinking a child understood because he was kind enough to say what I wanted, but the next day the tall one still had "more."

How do children get to the stage where they understand these relationships? I am willing to blame a certain amount of neural readiness, but it is clear that they must practice and experiment with hundreds of examples. The mother visiting the class at the beginning of this chapter didn't realize that her son was working on this important learning as he played at the sand table.

Remember the clay animals the children were classifying? Another major area of growth is in categorizing, classifying, and class inclusion. Ask a preschooler whether there are more dogs or more animals in the world, and he is likely to reply, "Dogs," because he is caught by the immediate notion of all the dogs he knows rather than seeing dogs as a larger class of animals. Later, the seven-year-old may successfully categorize pictures of animals into birds, mammals, and reptiles, but hesitate when asked, "If all the animals in the world disappeared, would there be any mammals left?" Many school tasks contain subtle requirements for classification; outlining is one example of a job which is difficult for students who don't get the idea of subtopics being part of one large, more abstract topic.

Turning Ideas Around

Many things which seem ridiculously obvious to adults are not clear to children. One task which is virtually impossible without conservation and good understanding of reversability is the "missing

addend" so popular in first grade math books $(3 + ? = 8)$. Teachers
and parents alike are frustrated because, at this age, most students
can learn to perform this operation only by rote—the minute they
have to remember or organize it themselves, they "forget" because
they never really understood it.

I also remember having a near argument with a six-year-old I was
tutoring one summer about whether "bigger" meant "older." She
was convinced that her daddy was older than her mommy because
he was "bigger," and I couldn't change her mind. Having tried to
make my point by every pedagogical method at my command, including waking my (large) grown son from a nap for a firsthand
demonstration, I gave up in frustration and drove to the university to
teach a class. Only as I was lecturing on Piaget did I suddenly realize
that I had been dealing with a problem of conservation—like the
water in the glass, she was convinced that "taller" was "more." This
experience reaffirmed for me the fundamental truth about learning—
you can lead the child to the problem, but you can't make the mental
leap for her. *She has to be ready, and she has to do it herself.*

Promoting Cognitive Conflict

How can we help youngsters fit those connections together? As I
learned the hard way, attempts to explain to children why their
reasoning is incorrect are doomed to fail. The trick is to get them to
see the inconsistency in their reasoning and to *want* to figure it out.
When something doesn't "fit," a state of "cognitive disequilibrium"
sets in as the child becomes aware that the immature schemas don't
work. Balanced precariously between old "comfortable" but errone-
ous ideas and the next stage, she can be pulled toward new levels by
an adult *asking the right questions.* Try these ideas for creating productive cognitive conflict:

—Remember that the child's reasoning is based on different
mental operations than yours; ask questions rather than explaining
what is "correct." (Child says, "This lemonade straw is broken."
Parent, seeing that the straw is blocked, asks, "Is there anything in
the straw that is keeping the lemonade from coming through?"
rather than, "That straw isn't broken. Here, let me clear it out for
you.")

—When the child asks you a question, respond with a question
that is just hard enough to make him wonder, but not so complicated

that it will frustrate him. Use the child's response as your guide, as in the conversation with Marcy about snow.

—At any age, hands-on experience is the first step. For example, if your child is gaining concepts of classification, you might suggest sorting the family laundry or magazine pictures into piles and then combining them with a general category label. Again, ask the question. ("Are the birds in the animal pile now? Now, let's take away all the animals. Are the birds gone? Why?")

—Help the child identify the relevant aspects of a problem. ("You seem to be looking at the height of the water in the glass. Is there any other way we could find out whether these two amounts are the same?")

—If you don't know an answer, admit it. Now you have the most exciting opportunity of all—to show your child how *you* ask yourself questions and seek information to find out answers! The best teaching I ever did was with our first school computer; the children and I learned to program it together. Believe me, we all had plenty of questions, but they learned far more from my bewilderment (which I "talked through") than they did from anything I "taught" them, and they loved the idea that a grown-up didn't know everything!

—Remember that a child in the process of enlarging or refining schemas and operations will frequently plateau and regress. Be patient with "I forget": it means the learning has not yet firmed up.

—Ask yourself, "Exactly what is it I expect this child to do, and what is her frame of reference for it?"

—Help your child see the discrepancies between his mental operations and actual reality. (Child says, "It is snowing because I put my boots on." Parent asks, "Let's think about that for a minute. Pretend we're at the lake in the summer. You have your bathing suit on. Now, let's pretend you put your boots on [Child acts out the scene]. Will that make it snow? Is it snowing *because* you put your boots on?")

—As in the above example, many of children's inconsistencies in reasoning are a result of faulty interpretation or use of language ("because," in this case.) Be alert for situations where you can use objects to work on language concepts. ("Why did you burn your mouth? Because . . .")

—Be tolerant of "wrong" answers if they are part of a process of new learning and mental exploration.

—Remember that rules can be taught, but understanding can't.

—Make sure that playing with peers is a regular part of your child's life. Children often ask each other the questions that promote cognitive conflict.

—Try to present your child with manageable problems rather than constantly providing solutions—it is her struggle with the available data that promotes cognitive growth.

—Piaget suggested that we stop worrying about how *fast* we can make intelligence grow, and concentrate on how *far!* When people asked him whether we could accelerate children's progress through each stage, he scoffed at what he termed "The American question."

A Boss for the Brain

How long does the brain's childhood last? The beginning of mature reasoning does not occur until sometime after age eleven or twelve, when the frontal lobes finally become the "boss" of the cortex. Until then, thinking has certain limits. It is natural for children to be literal thinkers, stuck in their own point of view. Preschoolers have trouble telling reality from fantasy and may appear to "lie" because of an inability to sort out the difference between what really happened and what was imagined. Children of ages five to ten tend to become very literal and rule-bound in their moral judgments, but they are also notorious for their difficulty in imagining consequences. A pleasure at hand is much more pressing than some future punishment!

Since the frontal lobes also seem to control much of what we call "motivation," a child usually has trouble planning for far-off goals or developing and executing a plan of action. Nevertheless, I frequently see parents (and teachers) who lament, "I don't understand why she is so unmotivated—she doesn't seem to be able to see why this is so important!" One family promised their son a new bike in June if he got "good grades" all year in third grade. Unfortunately, these terms were far too vague, June seemed very remote, and the plan failed.

Children of this age who need help with motivation enjoy daily tangible evidence of goals set and achieved:

—Charts, stickers or stars to keep track of small intermediate objectives

—Tangible small goals which can be measured (e.g., 90 percent on spelling tests for three weeks)

—"Contracts" made with the child for a particular objective (e.g., multiplication tables 1–5 in three minutes; no recess detention for a week) to get a desired reward

Incidentally, I believe that children should dispense their own stars, stickers, or rewards whenever possible. Instead of pasting stars on the chart, let the child do it—or better still, let him draw one in himself. It is never too early to establish the idea that we are each responsible for aiming at our goals *and* for rewarding ourselves when we reach them.

Young Brains Need Interpreters

Because that third functional unit is not completed, young children cannot objectively evaluate moral issues or even put heavily emotion-laden material into perspective. Meanwhile, parents may have to stand in to protect them and interpret input they can't handle. I once worked with a group of third grade girls who were sent to me in desperation by their teacher. Although they were all bright children, they were unable to concentrate in class and seemed to be in a perpetual state of excitement. It didn't take them long to close the door and start telling me that they were really "worried" about a lot of the sexual information that they had picked up from babysitters and the media—and which they were naturally busy exchanging with each other.

When their fears and misconceptions started to pour out, I understood why they felt so threatened by this barrage of frightening half-truths. No wonder they couldn't concentrate in class! Only one child in the group felt comfortable talking to her mother, who made a habit of limiting TV, watching it with her, and discussing what they saw. For these girls, a "learning" difficulty turned out to have far different roots.

It's a hard parental assignment, but try to be aware of potentially anxiety-producing information to which your child is exposed, and make yourself available to help put it in perspective. TV violence and even current events are hard enough for adults to comprehend, but impossible for children. They need help and lots of reassurance in dealing with the complexities of the world.

CHILDREN AT WORK

Evaluating Preschool Learning

Let's take a minute to return again to the classroom described at the beginning of this chapter to evaluate the "work" in progress. Children measuring cupfuls of sand are making mental patterns—putting together visual and motor learning with concepts of size, density, texture, volume, and fractions. Handling the materials is bringing important tactile information—and probably new dendritic connections—into their brains. Because making judgments, predictions, and plans are a part of this play, they are laying groundwork for the third functional unit. As they discuss their project, language develops, and attention is sharpened as they ignore the other play in the room.

The clay animals in the art corner integrate not only creativity and fine motor skills, but also vocabulary and descriptive language. When a parent volunteer noticed that several children were inventing imaginary animals, she encouraged them to dictate a book of original stories, make drawings, and create a plaster-of-paris relief map based on their mythical animal world.

How about the pet rabbit? It enabled one little boy to get some badly needed tactile stimulation as well as a feeling of comfort and importance as he assumed the responsibility for its feeding.

This is the type of classroom you should seek for your child, where learning that arises from personal experience helps growing brains receive, associate, organize, and comprehend at the appropriate neural levels. Far from marking time, even as late as first grade, well-planned programs like this one develop the hooks of meaning that underlie intelligence.

What's the Hurry?

The parents choosing a school for their son finally enrolled him in an "accelerated" class where children spend a lot of time sitting at desks, filling in worksheets, and being "taught." He may, of course, become an excellent student if he can overcome the monotony of this early introduction to learning. He will likely become a good "technician," unless frustration and his need to explore assert themselves. If these tasks are too inappropriate for his level of development, however, or if patterns of meaning are neglected, he could end up mistakenly labeled "learning disabled." By overlooking the cognitive potential of "play," his parents may have deprived him of the richest possible foundation for future learning.

Give your child the gift of patience for the broad-based mental experiences that will underlie joyous learning throughout life. Teaching specific academic skills before the levels of sensory reception and association are in place is like trying to build a large penthouse on an apartment building before the intermediate floors are completed. It may look good for a while, but eventually you're in for a collapse. Childhood is a process, not a product, and so is learning. In a society which often respects products more than the processes of creation and thought, it is easy to fall into the trap of anxiety over measuring achievement in isolated skills. Have faith—in childhood and yourself. Children's brains generally seek what they need, and nature has given you the instincts to help them get it.

Recently I was pleased to have as houseguests a friend from Austria and her charming five-year-old daughter, a bright little girl who has lived in two countries and is fluent in both English and German. During their visit I was particularly struck by the close relationship between mother and daughter and the little girl's sunny disposition which survived both jet lag and a hectic social schedule. In a rare quiet afternoon, we sat on my porch and talked while the child entertained herself inventing games with a few pieces of plastic packing material.

"She's so smart," I finally said to my friend, a math teacher. "Are you ever tempted to try and teach her to read or do math?"

"That's nonsense!" she replied. "I want her to be eager for it when the time comes, not spoil it for her."

Relax, parents, your children will not get behind if you allow them the time to accomplish the natural work of childhood.

4

If the Train Is Late,
Will We Miss the Boat?:
Developmental Timetables

ONE OF OUR BOYS' FAVORITE STORIES USED TO BE THE ONE ABOUT the little engine who was given the awesome responsibility of pulling all the children's Christmas presents to the other side of the mountain. I'm sure you remember that determined little fellow, puffing along earnestly with his heavy load. His refrain, "I think I can, I think I can," and finally, "I know I can!" have inspired generations of children to muster up the extra effort to go for the top—an important lesson, indeed. I wonder, though, if the shiny moral wrapping in which the gifts were delivered should carry a warning label: CAUTION! Don't expect all little engines to do the job of bigger ones, no matter how hard they try.

I firmly believe children must learn not to give up too easily, but as a learning specialist, I see many little engines who didn't make it to the top. Their gifts come in dull wrappings—unfulfilled promise, defeat—often with cards attached that say, "If only you would try harder." They droop with certainty that they are inadequate and, probably, even stupid. Yet they are often very bright children. Somehow they got derailed along the way.

Children run on different developmental timetables. By age six, teachers expect up to two years' difference in maturation among their students. Moreover, each child has a unique profile of strengths and weaknesses—physical, emotional, intellectual, and social. One of the hardest things for everyone to understand is that *bright children are not necessarily on the fastest train.* Many problems of "under-achievement" result from an incongruity between the child's neuro-logical pattern or timetable and the expectations of the family and school. In this chapter I would like to explore with you some of these emotion-laden issues so you can be a wiser judge—and advocate—of your own child's particular pattern.

THE PUZZLE OF "READINESS"

A Slow Starter

Whenever I think of developmental timetables, I remember Heather, a first grader with whom I worked because the school thought she had a learning disability. A small wistful blonde, she appeared younger than her classmates and uncomplainingly accepted the role of "baby" in group play. When playtime ended, however, her friends' tolerance decreased rapidly. One day, as usual, Heather arrived last for reading group, minus workbook and pencil. The oth-ers fidgeted while she was sent back to rummage through her desk, from which she finally produced a coverless workbook and an un-sharpened pencil. While her classmates competently located the as-signed page, she ruffled frantically through her book, unable to grasp the order of the page numbers, flipping forward, then backward, as she struggled to match her book to her neighbor's.

By the time she got there, the teacher had finished giving direc-tions, and the group was once more delayed while Heather got an-other explanation. I could see her classmates' thinly disguised impa-tience giving way to eye rolling and giggles as the lesson proceeded and Heather was called on to read aloud. Straddling her chair with determination, feet swinging with the force of mental effort, she struggled unsuccessfully to decode a simple sentence. Finally, the teacher sighed, "Mary, you try it," ending only momentarily Heath-er's daily battle in an endless war.

Would it surprise you to hear that Heather had an IQ in the supe-rior range? She did, yet her genuine confusion and inability to deal with most aspects of first grade had already convinced her that she was "stupid" and school was no fun at all. Like many bright chil-dren, she suffered acutely from the gap between her need for success and the grinding daily experiences of defeat and humiliation.

In Heather's file I found her teacher's report from the previous year. "Willing and cooperative, but immature. I recommend another year in kindergarten for Heather to gain the skills necessary for first grade." Unfortunately, her parents, convinced that she was smart enough, but a bit "lazy," had turned down this recommendation. They thought all she needed was to be "pushed." Well-intentioned, they had unknowingly put Heather on the wrong train, an express going too fast for her and dangerously aimed at an educational scrap heap. I have seen many children like Heather who never catch up. Survival is their business, and learning remains a tense and joyless process. Plunged daily into the fire of inappropriate expectations, their early promise shrivels, and nonlearning becomes a habit. They may be labeled, treated, tutored, and exhorted, but the basic issue remains unchanged. The school and the child are on different schedules.

What Causes Readiness?

For many years experts told us that school "readiness" resulted from "neural ripening," which they insisted would unfold despite environmental influences. We now know that a child's life experiences interact with the developmental schedule of the nervous system. In some cases these forces conspire to make children unready for school at the scheduled time because they are late bloomers, have a learning pattern that is different in some way, or both.

Lagging Timetables

A child who is lagging slightly in development is on the same track as the others. His train simply goes at a slower pace, although it stands every chance of reaching the same destination. This type of mild delay probably stems first from an immature nervous system. Such problems often do not show up in routine medical or school testing, however. Parents may have to act as primary diagnostician until pediatricians become more aware of the signals. Here are some of them:

1. Family patterns of slow development, "late-blooming" parents or siblings, a family history of late puberty.

2. Prematurity, which almost invariably sets back a child's developmental clock.

3. Physical or emotional problems in the early months of life.

4. Chronic diseases such as asthma, kidney disease, or ear infections. Children who spend time and energy battling such problems may not pass through stages of learning as quickly and need extra time to catch up.

5. Physical size. Developmentally immature children are often, although not always, physically small. Even large children may have a "baby-like" look compared to others of the same chronological age. (Not all small children are immature, however.)

6. Lagging social development: difficulty taking turns, sharing, or communicating with peers. A child who consistently chooses younger playmates may be expressing a need for more time to grow up. This aspect of development is one of the most important in assessing school readiness.

7. Immature, whole-body movements and lack of control over large-muscle activities, such as skipping, hopping, catching a ball, or small-muscle skills such as cutting, holding a pencil, or crayoning. Most children can go up and down stairs alternating feet by age five.

8. "Overflow movement" shows up when a child moves body parts that aren't involved in an activity—arms flap when he climbs stairs, tongue moves during coloring, feet "dance" when he sits doing a puzzle. Common in preschoolers, it is a sign of neurological immaturity in older children.

9. Difficulty distinguishing one's own left and right sides after age five or six.

10. Easy distractibility and short attention span. This child can't sit still and pay attention, particularly in a group.

11. Difficulty with eye–hand coordination. One test used to detect neurological immaturity is copying shapes, which requires cross-modal integration of fine visual and motor skills.

12. A tendency to engage in "magical" thinking, rather than confronting the realities of a situation. "If I don't notice it, it will go away" seems to be the immature child's attitude toward any demanding task (including homework, later on!).

13. Chronological age, as compared with classmates. Many "problem" learners have summer or fall birthdays and are younger than others in the same class. This situation is particularly acute for boys, who may be, on average, about six months behind girls in school readiness at age six. For this reason, girls should always be

evaluated in comparison with other girls, not with the boys in the class.

While none of these indicators alone is unusual, you would be wise to consider grade placement very carefully if your child shows several symptoms of delay.

On a Different Track

Some children don't seem so much delayed as different in development. Some of neuropsychology's most important research concerns how and why individuals vary in their approaches to learning. Children do, indeed, have "styles" for thinking and processing information, differences that are either inherited or a result of slight variations in neural development somewhere along the line. In a later chapter we will explore differences in the two sides of the brain which may account for styles of learning even in preschool years.

Children who are developmentally "different" may have trouble because their natural talents don't conform with the school's demands. For example, I know a five-year-old boy who is a whiz at block-building and can fix any mechanical device he gets his hands on (after he has it for a few minutes it needs fixing, because he takes it apart!). His room is a "disaster," but it contains a novel "kitten catcher" which he has rigged up with string and boxes, and his toy shelves hold several half-completed models of "my latest invention."

Sam sounds like a budding genius, but he will probably have trouble in school. First of all, his language development is unsophisticated. When he tries to describe something, he splashes words all over his topic without organizing them very well or getting to the point. He would much rather show than tell you about something, and he is massively disinterested in his mother's efforts to read to him. As far as Sam is concerned, pencils are only good for drawing, and he is quite unclear about the left and right sides of the page. In kindergarten he finds worksheets a drag and phonics an impossible bore, preferring to play or to build things outdoors. He has trouble following oral directions, but he can patiently figure out how to make two pieces of wood go together just right. No one can be good at everything, and the parts of his brain which control language and reading are lagging behind his other areas of advanced development.

In another culture, Sam might be considered gifted, but his school expects children to spend most of their time in first grade doing reading, writing, listening, and math papers. His pattern of learning is different, not deficient, but he may always struggle in a setting which values verbal and analytical skills more than his creative, hands-on talents.

What will happen to Sam? The things for which he is "ready" aren't in the curriculum. His father, a successful architect, remembers his own grim first grade experience and wants to give Sam another year to "get it together" in kindergarten. In this case, the teachers are reluctant because they believe Sam is smart and needs to be challenged. I hope his parents insist!

No Easy Answers

There are no easy answers to these dilemmas. Nevertheless, there is little point in forcing learning on a brain that is unequipped— either through delay or difference—to handle it. Since a parent's chances of altering the school's curriculum are limited, to say the least, it makes a lot of sense to alter the unready child's timetable by repeating one year—preferably before first grade—and working at the same time on the foundations for successful learning. While not a panacea by any means, this tactic has been extremely successful with the right youngsters. The key is whether parents see it as a positive opportunity or an admission of failure.

"Tots Flunk Kindergarten"

When a school in the Midwest decided on an extra year of kindergarten for a group of "unready" children, national newspapers flaunted the above headline. Can five-year-olds really "flunk"? Were they lazy, unmotivated, or just downright inadequate? Nonsense! From the day they are born, children are naturally motivated to learn, to master their environments, and to feel competent. Naturally, they learn best the things that are meaningful or important to them. It is our job as adults to devise tasks to harness that natural learning power, not to play the Blame Game if our demands are wrong. We can give children the desire to succeed at the things we want to teach them—by making early learning experiences interesting, successful, and fun. Forcing academic tasks on unready brains risks extinguishing the candle of intellectual excitement, particularly for children who are on different developmental timetables. Nobody wants to enter an arena where he has repeatedly suffered a knockout punch.

Answers to Parents' Questions

Why should a child repeat a year?
It can be an opportunity for neurological maturation to become more equal to academic demands.

Who should repeat?
Any child who shows clear symptoms of delay, but particularly the bright youngster, who has the best chance of catching up.

Will repeating cause emotional damage?
If parents are sold on the idea and present it positively, I have found that little emotional damage is done—certainly far less than endless years of feeling inadequate.

What grade is the best time?
The earlier the better. After third or fourth grade the chance of rebuilding attitudes and skills diminishes considerably. An exception is when a child changes schools, which is often an ideal time, even as late as high school. An older child should have a voice in the decision.

Who should not repeat?
1. If a child is socially mature, or family history indicates the probability of an early puberty, be cautious. Some parents are asking to have children held back just to give them a more competitive edge. This is a grave mistake, if the child is not immature. When their youngster enters puberty long before classmates, they usually wish they had stuck with nature's timetable.
2. If poor progress results from overall depressed ability instead of slow maturation in certain areas, repeating a grade is not a good long-term solution. Other alternatives should be discussed.

What should I say to my child?
Above all, don't threaten the child with *flunking*. The success of repeating depends on your positive attitude about it as a "new chance" to get some rewards from hard work. Try something like, "I think it would be wonderful if you could have another year to grow into first grade work. Some smart kids take a little longer to get ready for certain kinds of learning. I know it would feel good to have things seem easier for a change."

What happens during the second year at a grade level?

An extra year gives teachers and parents a chance to build capability and interest for learning, laying a foundation for success instead of failure. *We can't wait at the station and hope that repeating a grade will automatically put us on the right train.* It is important to analyze areas of strength and weakness, using the child's interests and talents to "hook" him on learning.

Sam, for example, might sit still for stories about inventors, machines, or gadgets. He might respond with interest if someone at home offered to write cards labeling his inventions, or type up his descriptions of them to read. Daddy might help him draw plans of his room to improve fine motor control and planning. He could dictate directions (in order) on how to make a "kitten catcher," and practice following other directions. At school, another year can also help him to be a leader, rather than a tagalong, and his verbal organization skills may be refined as he is delegated to explain activities to other classmates or to lead class discussions. It would be a pity to waste Sam's obvious intellect because the demands of first grade were simply not appropriate for his neurological pattern.

Stop Wiggling!

Readiness for school requires a certain degree of nervous system maturation which not all children attain by age six, or even later. Think about the expectations of an elementary school classroom—all of which may be too much for some children.

—A full school day demands concentration, physical stamina, and an ability to separate from the emotional security of home.

—Children are often expected to sit for long periods of time; for immature nervous systems this is more tiring than hard physical play.

—Students are expected to understand, remember, follow schedules and routines, keep track of supplies, and do assigned "seat work" without supervision. These are heavy demands for neural attention centers.

—A child needs to be able to handle clothing independently, and to manage personal possessions, difficult for a "clumsy" or disorganized child.

—Children entering first grade are expected to remember and follow two- and three-part verbal directions ("When I call your name, please line up and go quietly to the art room."). A lag in the skills needed for such complex auditory processing almost invariably ac-companies both delay and difference.

—For peer acceptance, children must be socially mature enough to cope with others and respond to their needs. Part of social matura-tion is directly related to limbic and frontal systems in the brain, which take a long time to come together.

—A child needs to be able to express his needs, questions, and concerns to the teacher in words without much hesitation.

—Much of the elementary curriculum involves combining modali-ties (e.g., looking at the board and writing, listening and doing, com-bining sound and written symbol in reading and math). If the child has not reached this point of neural maturation, you're in for trouble.

—Patterned fine muscle skills are required all day. Your child needs practice in cutting, drawing, holding a pencil, drawing lines with a ruler, and following a left-to-right pattern.

Experiences in early school years set a child's attitudes toward herself as a learner. These feelings are hard, sometimes impossible, to change. Unfortunately, just "trying hard" won't work if the task is too difficult. We can push, and they can try, but there is one special way in which the brain can't be rushed.

Speeding Up the Messages

Despite parents' best efforts, there are some things over which we have little control. As described in Chapter 2, there are basically two ways in which brain cells grow. First, as neurons are stimulated, message-receiving dendrites arborize, growing larger and heavier. Second, the long axons over which messages travel to other cells develop protective coatings of myelin, which make chemical trans-mission smooth and rapid. There is little myelin present at birth, and it takes about twenty years to finish the process, moving from lower structures and those responsible for motor programs (e.g., reaching, walking) to the highest centers for academic skills and abstract thought.

Since myelin formation is a necessary forerunner of efficient use, making demands on undeveloped areas may be a real mistake. We have very little information on ways to speed the growth of myelin; although it is age-related, the schedule varies widely among individu-als, and it is unclear how much—or if—the process can be acceler-ated. It seems evident that our efforts to stimulate learning must be tempered by patience until the child's mental transmission systems are equal to the task or we risk frustration, inferior skill development, and an abiding distaste and incompetence for the activity.

One little girl, who made the tough decision herself to repeat fourth grade, summed it up perfectly at the end of the following (very successful) year. "It's great to know what's going on. I used to do everything the teacher asked, but I didn't know what I was doing."

"But She'll Be Bored"

Many parents are sincerely concerned that boredom will result if their child is not pushed into more advanced learning activities. They forget that the heady experience of daily success and mastery is never boring for a child. Sometimes, too, they forget to listen. I remember one mother storming into a nursery school to complain that they weren't challenging her daughter, who had come home and announced that she was "bored at school." The teacher was surprised, since the little girl acted happy and excited about classroom activities. The impasse continued until someone decided to ask the child what "bored" meant. "Oh, it means I'm hot," she replied cheerfully. Indeed, there were some problems with the furnace, and in dance class, when she heard another child comment that he was "bored," she thought she had learned a new word! Happily, the mother apologized and the child continued to learn in a stimulating but unpressured setting. I guess the moral of that story is, listen to the child's feelings, not to your own.

Young children enjoy repetition, for it gives them feelings of control and mastery. Of course you would find a primary program too repetitive for your level of brain development, but be careful about projecting your needs. Sometimes clever children learn to use the word "boring" to avoid difficult tasks. Their parents are so panicky about slow progress that a reaction is guaranteed! If you find yourself getting caught in the trap of social pressure for choosing a school because it "pushes" academic skills before age six, ask yourself, "Whose needs are we trying to meet?"

The Fast Track

At the other end of the timetable are children who seem to advance so quickly that their parents wonder if they should skip a grade. Occasionally, in cases where the child is truly precocious in overall mental, physical, and social development, acceleration may be advised, but such children are very rare. Usually it is far preferable to keep the youngster with age mates, working with the school to develop opportunities for enrichment. In the long run, the effective use of an individual's talents—no matter how gifted he is—will hinge on his ability to communicate ideas and implement them through other people. These interpersonal skills are best gained from successful peer relationships. Intellectual stimulation is a valuable goal, but whether it warrants a compromise of social and emotional needs is a grave question for parents to consider.

Last year a friend of mine asked his son's principal for advice about the boy, small and physically immature for his age, but academically gifted. The teacher had suggested Paul might skip fourth grade, possibly because his parents were requesting extra enrichment. My friend was worried about such a major step, not only because of his son's physical immaturity, but because Paul had many good friends in his current class and seemed happy in school. After hearing the whole story, the principal casually reminded Dad that when Paul got to junior high, the boys in the locker room would not be comparing IQs. Paul stayed with his class.

What to Do?

If you suspect that your child may be a candidate either for slow or unusually rapid maturation, what should you do? First, try to be as objective as you can about the situation. Observe your child in groups of peers and strive for an objective view of all areas of development. Teachers are more objective than you, since they see your child in an age-centered context every day. Kindergarten teachers are statistically better predictors of school success than are the standard readiness tests! Listen hard if teachers use words such as "immature," "trying hard but having difficulty," "has trouble with classroom routines and with managing possessions," "needs practice in getting along with others," "seems frustrated by academic tasks."

Second, seek professional advice. If delay is the concern, you should have a heart-to-heart talk with your pediatrician to rule out unidentified physical problems. Be aware, however, that some pediatricians are notorious for saying, "He'll grow out of it." They don't see the child in school every day. It also makes sense to request an evaluation from the school psychologist, who can administer a battery of ability tests, both to get an objective opinion and to determine if either unusual giftedness or potential learning problems can be identified. Insist on the services you need from the school; this can be a turning point in your child's entire educational career, and you have a legal right to diagnostic work for suspected learning differences, including a need for an enriched or accelerated program. Sometimes, in order to get the train on the track, you need to rock the boat!

In any case, resist that urge to panic, which may cause you to start pressuring the child. Analyze ways in which you can provide pleasurable experiences at home which are directed to your child's particular needs. Above all, focus on the emotional security that underlies all mental growth and helps children with their most basic assignment—paying attention.

LET'S PAY ATTENTION

Remember the brain's "gatekeeper," that little thimble-sized gadget near the top of the spinal cord that determines what stimuli will be let into or kept out of consciousness? The reticular activating system (RAS) may be one of the most important factors in a child's timetable for learning. Some children seem to be born with better attention regulators than others, and it is important to take this into account when planning any kind of activity that requires sustained involvement.

Sometimes parents (usually fathers, by the way) tell me they insist their five- or six-year-old sit and work on phonics or math facts with them each night for up to an hour. What a way to kill the joy of learning! Although obviously well-meaning, they do not understand that, although the RAS, which Luria called the first functional unit, is fully operative by age three months, it is not under complete control until after adolescence, when a complex neural loop connects it with the limbic system and the frontal lobes of the cortex. Obviously, it is useless to expect mature attention patterns from a child, yet many adults have trouble understanding the real limitations that immaturity places on the ability to stay with one task—especially one which the child didn't choose.

Rather than making unrealistic demands, you can help your child find the best stimulus level during different activities. Each individual has instinctive drives to regulate the amounts of stimulation—auditory, visual, and tactile—that come into the brain, but young children frequently miss their own cues. Watch for signs of unusual behavior, overexcitedness, wildness, or withdrawal, which signal a need for protection from sensory bombardment. You may need to step in and decrease the level of noise, excitement, or pressure until attention systems become more sophisticated.

Helping the Attention Regulator

—Insist on a noise level in the home within reasonable limits. Some parents refer to "indoor voices" and "outdoor voices" to give children a concrete cue.

—Remember that you have a framework of experience which helps you screen out sounds, while the child does not. One little boy was terribly distracted until his mother finally realized he was frightened by the sound of airplanes overhead which she hadn't even noticed. After she explained to him what they were, he was able to concentrate better.

—Make sure the young child has a quiet space of his own to go to at any time—even if it is only a card table covered by a blanket.

—Keep adult-type stimulation at a minimum (e.g., inappropriate TV programs or adult magazines; overly exciting or alarming adult conversations). One primary school head asserts that radio and TV news is probably the worst kind of overstimulation.

—Limit TV viewing. (Be tough—it's important!)

—Support your controls with actions. (Turn off the TV; lead the child firmly to her room.)

—Let attention span develop naturally by allowing time for a child to become actively engaged in a task without interruption.

—Be sure there is someone in the home to whom the child can go to be hugged, held, and calmed down if necessary.

—Physical contact (hugging, rocking) is still necessary for children beyond infancy.

—You may need to help a young child shift focus from one activity to another; pave the way in advance. ("When you finish putting the spools in the jar, I'm going to ask you to wash your hands for dinner.")

—Prepare the child for potentially alarming or upsetting situations. ("On Halloween children will come to our door dressed in funny costumes that may look scary sometimes.")

—Establish predictable routines; insist on a regular bedtime and adequate rest.

—Some children may have trouble regulating attention because of allergic responses in the brain tissue to food or environmental substances; if you suspect allergy, check with a specialist.

—Try to identify substances or situations that create problems. Excess sugar in a child's diet may contribute to "hyper" behavior and mood swings. Again, it is worth your effort to maintain a firm hand here.

—Use words along with actions when showing something to the child; language is the ultimate mediator of attention.

The Power of Language in Regulating Attention

Luria believed that the development of the frontal lobe systems, which signal true maturity of the brain, depends on using words to guide behavior. Most adults use this brain-building "inner language" to work through problems or plans—literally talking to themselves inside their heads. Studies show that even little children perform a task better when they use "private speech" along with actions. Parents can help a toddler, for example, by describing what she is doing and encouraging her to use words herself ("You are pounding the pegs into the board. Let's say 'hit' every time you pound one."). Household tasks such as cooking present many opportunities at all ages ("Now I'm going to measure out a half cup of flour. Let's see where the half-cup mark is. Did I do it right?").

Children of all ages should be encouraged to talk through situations before plunging in and while they are working. The child with attention difficulties is a particular candidate. I frequently ask youngsters to "sit on your hands and *tell* me what you think you should do with this problem (workbook page, drawing, sentence, math equation)." They think it is funny, but it gets their brain into communication with itself, and they do a better job.

I remember one impulsive first grader who could not remember to bring both workbook and pencil to the reading table. Every day the teacher said to her, "Tell me what you will need. Now ask yourself, 'Do I have my pencil? My workbook?' " She thought this was a wonderful game, and soon we only had to say, "Have you asked yourself *the question?*" Eventually, Grace was able to do it herself. Now a sophisticated third grader, she sidled up to me in the hall not long ago with a big grin on her face. "You know," she said, "I still ask myself *the question!*"

Attention Deficits

As many as three in every hundred children have problems with attention that are severe enough to put them into the "learning disability" category. Difficulties like this are often diagnosed around age three but sometimes go unreported until the beginning of school. Extreme cases may be treated with medications which presumably "wake up" the gatekeeper, for the "hyperactive" child's main problem is directing and focusing attention appropriately. Continually at the mercy of inadequate filters for experience, they tend to be impulsive, aggressive, jittery, uncontrolled, and extremely trying to the patience of parents and teachers.

I am only skimming the surface of a major issue here. If you have a child who may fit this description, you should consult a pediatric neurologist and read one of the excellent books available for parents. Milder forms of impulsivity are quite common and should not be mistaken for true hyperactivity. They are best treated by what is called "behavioral management," with emphasis on firm guidelines and encouragement for improvement. Here are some basic principles for all children:

—Provide firm discipline. Don't accept temper tantrums or physical aggression toward others. Set a few important rules that you expect to be followed. Explain the reasons for each rule and make sure the child understands them.

—Establish a firm, predictable schedule. Don't let the child get overtired.

—Get the child's attention, with eye contact, before you give a direction.

—An overexcited child may respond to a gentle but firm touch.

Holding him by the shoulders gives the brain's control centers a chance to start over again.

—Give attention for good behavior, not bad. As soon as you catch the child "doing something right," make a fuss over it, even if it is only a little step in the right direction. If the child misbehaves, quickly send him to his room or some other quiet place for "time out."

Most attention problems probably "come with the package," but your guidance at home can help rebuild the internal structure that these little minds seem to lack. Above all, remember that the brain of a child who feels secure, loved, and happy can direct all its attention toward learning and growth rather than focusing on worries and fears.

BRAIN GROWTH STAGES

A controversial biophysicist is rattling the cages of learning theorists with new ideas about the brain's developmental schedule. Dr. Herman Epstein believes that the brain grows in a series of spurts during which it becomes more receptive to teaching and learning. According to his research, about 85 percent of children follow this schedule. While the brain—primarily the cortex—is in one of these stages of rapid growth, there is a period, perhaps as short as three months, when myelin and dendritic connections are increasing to form new channels for thought, and the brain is at its most teachable. Here are the times:

3–10 months
2–4 years
6–8 years
10–12 years (more girls)
14–16 years (more boys)

Epstein hopes that eventually there will be a way to determine exactly when these spurts begin for every child. In the meanwhile, he believes it is imperative to present interesting new material during these age periods in case of sudden readiness. Conversely, during periods when the brain is not growing rapidly, he suggests that we hold off on large quantities of new learning, concentrate on nonacademic skills, refine previous learning, and get ready for the next big push. This aspect of the theory is the one that has worried educators, who are reluctant to believe that the child may be more or less "unteachable" at some times during school life.

So far, Epstein's brain studies have not been satisfactorily duplicated, but his theory is a provocative one. Here are some of the issues it raises:

—If a major spurt in learning ability takes place between the ages of two and four years, Head Start and other preschool programs may be catching children too late for maximum effect. Certainly most language development is taking place during these years, as well as the neural growth that underlies abstract thought.

—Most experienced teachers know that some children simply are not ready to learn some things on a set schedule. When the right time arrives, however, the seed can be planted and grown in a very short time.

—It may be senseless to belabor certain academic learning tasks if the child's brain is not receptive for *any* reason. As one educational therapist put it, "If that's the day the dog died, forget learning!"

—If maximum learning potential occurs in spurts, with plateaus in between, schools should provide small-group instruction according to individual timetables. This is an enormous challenge for teachers and to the patience of parents. Even if your child isn't in the fastest group, you may need to be supportive until that next spurt.

—Three-month summer vacations could conceivably miss most of a mental growth spurt—a good rationale for summer reading!

—Periods of rapid physical development, such as early adolescence, may be a time when heavy-duty academics are not most appropriate. In the next chapter we will look more closely at the implications of these ideas for older children as we tackle the wonderful enigma of the adolescent mind.

ON THE RIGHT TRACK

Many perspectives on learning converge on one point: Children must have time to do their own mental growing. Parents are invaluable assistants, but the child is the true magician, with an instinctive need to learn, to master, and to seek out the right challenges. Adults who try to take over the show run a serious risk. By imposing demands relating to their own cognitive frameworks instead of to the child's, they can distort the natural timetable. Pushing little engines up the mountain doesn't work in the long run, because there will always be higher mountains on the other side which the child must eventually tackle on his own.

Adults who accept differences in children's developmental timetables can keep many little engines from becoming derailed along the way. Both the fast and the slow starters need an opportunity to explore the schemas of childhood on their way to the top. Since we don't have a "golden screwdriver" to alter neural growth (if we should even want to!), we must accept and work with each child's pattern. Many "late" or "different" bloomers are children with formidable potential. Lest their talents be lost to society and to themselves, let's do our best to keep them on the right track.

5

Childhood into Adolescence: Furnishing the Adult Mind

THE GROWTH OF A CHILD'S MIND TOWARD THE CAPACITY FOR adult thinking is one of the most intriguing and important puzzles of brain development. Nature builds the framework; it is up to the child, parents, and school to complete the walls and do the interior decorating. Throughout childhood, control centers move upward from the basement of reflex response toward the highest levels where the frontal lobes take over. At least twenty years are needed to finish this process, and for adults with active minds, the decorating job may never be finished!

Children need time to practice with fancier mental furnishings at each stage of development. The more they use the equipment, the more comfortable they become with it—and the better their base for the next level. The middle elementary years are an important time for consolidating early foundations, because sometime after age eleven, the mind's top floors become available for occupancy. New types of thinking are suddenly possible, but the view from the penthouse is often scary and confusing. Let's explore some of the perils—and the wonders—of the fascinating years which mark this transition.

Mental Growth in Action

One bonus of my job, working with students at all grade levels, is the opportunity to see mental growth in action. For a bird's eye view of children's thinking, consider these responses from different grade levels to the question "Why do we have laws?"

Grade One:

SUZIE: "Because some people eat bubble gum and it's *not fair* if some people have it and others don't!"

PETER: "If you're driving too fast they might give you a ticket."

RICARDO: "Because you might get hurt."

These children are all delightfully concrete thinkers, but there are some interesting differences in their answers. Suzie's answer is typical of a younger child—caught by personal, very concrete experience. Peter has moved on a bit, pushing out beyond his playground to one particular law, and Ricardo manages a rudimentary generalization. Such different levels of abstraction are common at age six and seven—an important transition point in children's ability to grasp generalizations that go beyond concrete physical experience.

Grade Five:

GEORGE: "If we didn't have laws people would go out and steal things. Car crashes would be to often because people wouldn't stop for red lights. Other people would shoot each other."

NAOMI: "We have laws because if we didn't then the world would go biserk. If we didn't have laws like 'DON'T LITTER' or 'DON'T FISH HERE' or 'NO HUNTING' then people won't know if their supposed to do this or that."

ANN: "Laws were made to protect us and to keep the world or our country safe."

These typical fifth graders wrote their answers—and their spelling is, as always, just as interesting as their ideas! Notice how this age level loves rules, law, and order—one of the hallmarks of late elementary years. Having absorbed a lot of information about the way the world works, they are still inclined to relate ideas back to concrete personal experiences. Ann is one of the few in the class who managed a more abstract statement. At this grade level there is usually less variability than at others. Let's see what happens in three years.

Grade Eight:

TOM: "We have laws to keep control of people. Laws help us to be safe. They teach us to follow directions and obey them. If you do not, you may be severely punished just as in school."

KATE: "The main reason is to keep this world under control. For example: an eleven year old boy could go into a bar and ask for a vodka, but since there are laws they prevent 11 year olds to be able to do that."

BIANCA: "Laws are very important to have in any form of group. They protect people from others. No one or group could or would survive without them. If we had no laws we would have no rights."

FRANKLIN: "We have to run by some sort of guidelines to live by and to run our society in an efficient way. If we did not have laws, we would probably be the only animals that would not have some sort of system."

Welcome to adolescence! Notice the striking contrast between two students' personal, concrete thinking (Tom, Kate), and near-adult perspectives on society's needs and universal principles (Bianca, Franklin). The rigid law-and-order emphasis of middle childhood (rules should be followed so you won't be punished) eventually gives way, for most teenagers, to larger perspectives (laws are necessary for the survival of a society), but timetables for this change vary dramatically. How would you like to be a teacher trying to plan a lesson to interest every student in this class? Something exciting is taking place, but it certainly hasn't happened to everyone! Can brain development be the key?

Everyone knows that the physical changes of adolescence are important. Neurological changes may be just as critical, but researchers are only now getting interested in the brain's transition from concrete to abstract reasoning. This chapter will summarize the most current information, give you a look inside some schools, and suggest ways parents and schools can collaborate on helping with the job.

FINISHING CHILDHOOD: THE YEARS FROM NINE TO ELEVEN

"School's OK, I'm OK."

Ages nine and ten are a relatively calm period for many children. As academic skills from the first three grades are practiced and refined, most fourth and fifth graders feel capable and in control. The brain strengthens its abilities for learning, as myelination of fibers speeds associations between senses and ideas. Late elementary grades are an ideal time to apply skills already learned. Reading to learn replaces learning to read; math becomes useful in the shopping mall or on the computer. Repeating skills and rituals lays a solid base for moving on to new challenges.

Many children at this age love to soak up information and memorize facts, but they may not reflect very deeply about them. They painstakingly copy paragraphs for reports but have difficulty paraphrasing them. Lots of practice is needed—and probably some adult help with organization and understanding. Above all, older children need plenty of time for their own brands of play. They still learn best by starting with concrete experience. The most helpful parents and the most successful teachers capture their wide-ranging curiosity in active, project-oriented learning.

Hands-On Justice

Parents can encourage teachers to exploit this delicious moment between childhood and adult learning abilities. One creative fourth grade teacher got wonderful results when she departed from the regular curriculum. Noticing that all her "sophisticated" girls were bringing their dolls to recess, she wisely figured they were expressing a need to be children for a little while longer. As she eavesdropped on the doll society, it was rocked by an argument over playground territory (remember the reptilian brain?). The girls set up a "court" to mediate the dispute, and soon the boys began to take sides, although no one was too clear on the judicial process. Sensing a golden opportunity to blend "play" with learning, the teacher scrapped her unit plans and suggested the class investigate how courts work. In the following weeks they searched out books and newspaper articles to discuss in class. Each child worked on an independent project. A lawyer father came to discuss his experiences in court and answer questions. Parent volunteers organized a visit to a real courtroom, where the judge was so impressed with these young scholars' knowledge that she let them sit in on a trial and took them on an unscheduled tour of the justice center. Finally, the dolls' own court was held, and the classroom newspaper proclaimed the result—a hung jury.

Not all teachers are this imaginative or hard-working, but all need parents' support if they try to flee now and then from the tyranny of workbooks, and from artificial standards of "competence" that put limits on intellectual curiosity. Learning prompted by personal interest works best at any age. Such "real" experiences are particularly important in late elementary years because students need help with abstract concepts such as "justice" or "law." At home, parents have an important role in seeking out opportunities to supplement the school's efforts, capitalizing on children's ready curiosity for mind-stretching conversations, family trips, and activities. The following list may give you some ideas.

Stretching the Brains of Fourth, Fifth, and Sixth Graders

—Help them begin challenging literal fact.

"Why do we go to school only on weekdays? Why five days a week?"

"Why *shouldn't* people steal?"

—Let them see that there are many points of view on issues, probably *no one right answer.*

—Play games with open-ended questions:

"What would happen if . . .

every day were Monday?

automobiles were declared illegal?

computers needed to be fed three times a day?"

"What would you do if . . .

we won the lottery?

we lost all our money?

you woke up one morning seven feet tall?"

—Help them articulate their feelings and don't be afraid to talk about yours. ("I really felt scared when I thought Grandma was seriously ill. I bet you did, too.")

—Play games of strategy which require weighing alternatives, planning moves ahead, or viewing a situation from the opponent's perspective ("Stratego," "Battleship," chess, checkers, gin rummy, hearts).

—Play "Twenty Questions." Show how to ask categorical questions. ("Is it an animal?" rather than "Is it a dog?")

—Practice allowing the child to make some reasonable choices and to experience the natural consequences. ("If you use your allowance on the record, you won't have enough to go to the movies with the gang.") Don't weaken and bail them out of minor consequences.

—If your child has trouble understanding a school assignment, look for a way to present it with pictures, time lines, maps, or objects that can be manipulated. Have fun acting out ideas or situations. Your child still learns best from concrete experience.

—Get a book of simple science experiments and try some at home. Talk about possibilities of what might happen. Make guesses together, without worrying about who's right or wrong.

—Have dinner together and talk with your child. Watch TV news together and talk about what happened. *Listen* to what your child is saying. Teachers are convinced that good family conversation times produce good students.

—Don't stop reading aloud. Encourage memorization of fine poetry or prose. Try round-robin family reading.

—Appreciate those childlike qualities even while you help him stretch. Remember, he still reasons differently from you.

STUMBLING BLOCKS TO LEARNING

Although brains work quite smoothly for most children of this age, two common and baffling quirks may show up during late elementary years.

A Problem of Output

Some children are fine until required to write something down presentably. They understand and reason as well as anyone else but can't "get it together" for homework or written assignments, which may resemble a childish-looking mess even after hours of effort. One young friend of mine, Jules, had trouble from early grades, when he couldn't organize his fingers around a pencil. He always found writing slow and frustrating—even though he was one of the brightest children in the class. Jules was clever enough to "con" every teacher out of assignments until he arrived in the middle school—unable to write a sentence. By now he had a double problem—slow development in specific motor skills plus avoidance of normal amounts of practice. At this point his parents became really worried and altered their busy schedules to help him every evening. Pitched battles ensued as they pushed and Jules dug in his heels.

Luckily, Jules attended a school where special help was available. At his parents' request, he was tested by a psychologist who confirmed a high IQ and a specific "neurological lag" that particularly affected organizing and writing down ideas. The psychologist leveled with Jules and they developed a plan together. His teachers were asked to shorten some written assignments for a while, but to insist that Jules keep up his end of the bargain. He was encouraged to shine in oral reports and class discussions. His parents were counseled in understanding his difficulty and helping him plan homework time and proofread assignments without taking over his share of the responsibility.

As the tension eased, Jules began to try harder. This year, in the eighth grade, things are going better. He is using a word processor for long assignments (more about this later), and neurological maturation seems to have closed some of the coordination gap. He still writes the bare minimum, but when I saw him in the hall recently, he confided that he had decided it was "worth it" to try for the top sections next year.

It is not too late for such early difficulties to be overcome in the middle grades if parents and teachers work together. Like Jules, many students suffer from what Dr. Melvin Levine calls "developmental output failure." Particularly with bright children, it may go unnoticed until grade three or four, when early emphasis on "decoding"—reading words—changes to a need for "encoding," which requires organizing, remembering, and restating information. Neural systems for input are working just fine, but immaturity in another part of the nervous system causes trouble at the output level. Such youngsters also have trouble organizing themselves, their possessions, and their thoughts. Pulling together information from many sources, managing time and materials, and handling heavy demands on memory may be too much for them. Calling such a child "lazy" makes the problem worse.

Having seen many boys and girls like Jules, I believe that this problem is one of the most pervasive—and difficult—of the middle childhood years and may also be a hidden cause of so-called "under-achievement" and problem behavior in junior high and high school. Not all schools are as enlightened as the one Jules attends. Many teachers, and even some psychologists, are not informed about this type of learning problem, so parents must become the first line of defense. Help from a specialist may be required—and it may be necessary to search around to find someone who understands the neuropsychological aspects of learning. Meanwhile, don't let a child like this develop habits of "lost" homework and deception ("The dog ate it." "It blew out of the school bus."). Understanding children's problems does not mean that we stop expecting anything from them! Here are some points to keep in mind:

—Some neurological differences, particularly in later-developing parts of the brain, may not show up until those areas are called upon for new kinds of school learning; when children run into trouble between third and fifth grade, do not rush to blame the teacher or the child.

—Be alert for a negative change in attitude toward school, avoidance of homework or classroom assignments.

—Make yourself available (or, if necessary, inescapable) to help with assignments that are genuinely difficult for your child.

—Keep in close contact with the school and ask for the teacher's advice about helping at home. You may need to help organize study times, assignment books, and long-range projects.

—Your hardest job will be to let the child suffer the natural consequences if he falls down on his end of the bargain. Refuse to "own" his school responsibilities.

—If problems persist, get an evaluation from the school psychologist or a learning disability specialist.

—Ask the school to provide special support services, or modify demands for written output. Keep the child's ego intact so that he can compensate for his difficulty.

—Be patient! If a task is genuinely hard, your child suffers enough from feelings of "stupidity" when he yearns to be competent. Remind him and yourself that, even in very smart people, all parts of the brain do not grow equally fast, and some need time and extra practice to do their job.

—If you cannot work with your child without damaging self-esteem (even the best parents get into "scenes"), hire someone who can. Look for a tutor who understands this type of problem.

—Remind yourself that children are not by nature lazy!

The Homework Issue

Supervising schoolwork at home puts parents on a tightrope over two fearsome chasms. On one side lies the danger of making a child overly dependent, negative, or downright defiant; on the other—school failure. What a choice! While perfect solutions are, as always, only dreams, here are some suggestions that have helped other parents.

HELPING WITH HOMEWORK

Rule No. 1: Wait to be asked.

If neither your child nor his teachers ask for your help, it probably is not needed. Trying to force a child to work with you may short-circuit his desire to come to you in the future. If you sense trouble, make an appointment with the school for advice. Remember that schoolwork is the territory of the child, who needs to feel responsible and in control.

Rule No. 2: Be available and supportive when help is requested.

Your attitude toward the importance of homework will shape your child's. If a TV program is more important to you than his need to practice multiplication tables, don't be surprised if he decides the same.

Rule No. 3: Focus on process, not product.

Often the ultimate product (the answer, the perfect paragraph, one day's assignment) is secondary to the process of learning. Think about the learning you are encouraging:

a. "If I whine enough, I can get someone else to do my work for me."

b. "Every time I ask for help, we wind up in a fight because the whole thing isn't perfect enough."

c. "It was sort of fun figuring out the answers, even though neither Dad nor I really understood the questions at first."

Rule No. 4: The final product must represent the pupil's work.

Don't deprive your child of valuable learning because you're afraid of a bad grade. You won't get invited to go along to college or a job.

Rule No. 5: Children are often hardier than they would like us to believe.

If assignments seem unreasonably long, check the following: Can she organize time effectively? Are study times at school used productively? Are telephone conversations interfering? If the child is truly overloaded, a conference at school should be scheduled with you, your child, and the teacher present to discuss the problem.

Rule No. 6: Let him fight his own battles whenever possible.

Your moral support is essential, but it is the student's job to learn to get along with people in the world—including teachers!

Rule No. 7: Provide the tools necessary for success.

Your child needs a quiet, well-lit place to study, a regular routine, and a moratorium on weeknight TV until homework is satisfactorily completed. Be tough; this is important. Older students also may need a tape recorder, typewriter or word processor, good dictionary and thesaurus, and transportation to libraries if they give you advance notice.

Rule No. 8: You don't have to know everything.

Parents feel uncomfortable when they don't know everything, but admitting your confusion and working problems through with your child may be the best teaching you can do. Even if you don't get the answer, you have both experienced "cognitive dissonance" —the basis for the most lasting learning.

The Enigma of Automaticity

Another sticky wicket for some children during these middle years is getting "automatic" on basic learning skills. Automaticity is at the heart of most daily behavior, helping us tend to routine matters so our brain's higher centers can deal with more challenging problems. For example, most people can wash dishes or pull weeds at the same time they carry on a conversation. When driving a car along an uncrowded freeway, they may think about an upcoming event, plan a dinner menu, or listen to a talk show. If a truck roars into view, however, neural control of driving instantly moves up from automatic to the "thinking brain," and everything else is pushed aside.

Most adults can listen to a lecture and take notes without using much of their brains to spell words or form letters, but if they must write an unfamiliar word with several syllables, they may temporarily lose the speaker's message. When talking, most people give their conscious effort to the ideas they want to get across. Some children have difficulty forming or using well-worn neural pathways for such "easy" tasks.

No one really understands how automaticity develops. Infant brains are busy starting a base of automatic connections as they absorb knowledge about the frequency of normal events and what can be expected in everyday situations. With practice, most learning probably becomes condensed or reallocated to lower areas, leaving the cortex free to work on more complicated problems. If you had to devote conscious awareness to how this book feels in your hands, you would miss a lot of the content!

Automaticity is essential in school. Instant recall of phonics and a basic core of "sight words" underlies rapid reading and good comprehension; if higher thinking centers are cluttered up sounding out words, fluency and understanding suffer. A youngster who stops to worry about spelling or letter formation when writing a word will have trouble writing originally or taking notes in class. In math, addition and subtraction must be automatic before multiplication and long division become easy. Middle childhood and early adolescence are the most critical times to firm up automatic skills before the child is besieged with higher-level processing demands.

Making Learning Automatic

—Children differ in the ease with which they master routine skills.

—Different types of automaticity are learned at different ages. Babies and young children must get an automatic feel for their bodies and space and for taking in and understanding sensory information. School years are the time to practice academic skills, and even adults must work hard to get new learning effortlessly embedded (e.g., your golf swing, a new foreign language).

—Remember that a child who is using cortical energy on poorly automatized "basics" will have little left for reasoning or comprehension of the task.

—Repeated practice seems to be the key to automaticity; children learn to read by reading, to write by writing.

—Drill and practice are more effective if they are varied, however, because the brain responds to novelty. Sensitivity to the child's response helps balance these competing needs.

—Synapses may get "tired" with repeated use over a long period of time. They need a short rest before becoming effective again. Changing activities for a while unblocks the pathways.

—If movement, emotional content, or personal interest are combined with practice, memory should improve. Long periods of boring repetition may cause daydreaming as higher centers seek stimulation.

—Positive feelings improve the chemical environment for efficient learning. Middle grade children love to compete with their own records on speed drills and see improvement with stars or stickers.

—There is some evidence that physical exercise increases chemical connections in the brain. One teacher published a study reporting students' improved word reading speed and accuracy after a daily jog on the playground. More research is needed to investigate this interesting idea.

—Computer drill and practice promote automaticity. This type of learning should not replace original problem solving, however, because there is a difference between automatic and conceptual responses. *All children should be encouraged to develop proficiency with original thinking and reasoning as well as with memorized skills.*

—Some people are better than others at "incidental learning." Even when concentrating on one task, they pick up and remember extraneous details. A child who is encouraged to be actively curious, investigate, and notice details may get in the habit of picking up more information than a frightened, passive child who is stifled by fears of being "wrong."

Beyond Automaticity: Parents at School

Children who achieve automaticity easily are not necessarily smarter, but it is ridiculous for them to spend time drilling on material they have already mastered. Late elementary years are a prime time for everyone to enlarge vocabulary, investigate scientific and mathematical challenges, and participate in creative activities. Because of myelination that links different cortical areas, activities connecting language with the arts may be especially appropriate in grades four to six. If your child is stuck in a classroom where drill and boredom replace intellectual stimulation, you should consider carefully whether you ought to become involved—tactfully, of course.

Children above fourth grade are mortified if their parents hang around school, and you should beware of fighting their battles for them. Nevertheless, a teacher with a large class will sometimes welcome specific offers of help. In one school, volunteer parents developed a reading club and led small book-discussion groups. Field trips and theater and museum visits can be initiated by parents, as can career talks by adults in different vocations. You might explore possibilities of creative drama, puppetry, or a videotaped production.

The issue of parent involvement in schools is a sensitive one; the child's need for autonomy is just as important as his need for intellectual stimulation. Some families prefer to concentrate on developing a home environment which encourages intellectual excitement and creativity. These years are a good time for refining artistic skills, and lessons in music, dance, or sports provide a base for future achievements. There's another trap, though—the insidious danger of overprogramming and getting hung up on "child as product."

Perfecting the Product

Several years ago, I was leaving school one afternoon when I saw a forlorn little shape hunched on the curb near my car. "What's the matter, Celia?" I asked, wondering what had reduced our most promising fourth grader to such a pile of misery.

"I missed my ride, and no one's home, and I'm going to be late for ballet," she snuffled.

Naturally, I drove her home so that she could change clothes in time for her next carpool. "You must like ballet," I ventured.

"No, I really hate it, but my mom wants me to be good."

Deciding to change the subject, I asked, "What do you like to do best?"

"I don't know. I have ballet on Monday, French on Tuesday, gymnastics on Wednesday, art on Thursday, and piano on Friday. Sometimes I wish I could just not do anything."

Celia's parents had fallen into the trap. Like many couples, they were both successful in business, accustomed to setting goals and measuring achievements. Trying to give their daughter the best chance, the most competitive edge, they arranged an "enriched" environment which ultimately convinced her that she was loved mainly for her measurable accomplishments.

These attitudes carried over into schoolwork. Celia's teachers worried about her compulsive concern over grades and her lack of time for relaxation. One of them said, "What that child needs most is to forget about her 'schedule' and go sit under a tree for a while. I don't think she has any idea what a wonderful little kid she is—she thinks her parents love her only because she's good at adult sorts of things. I keep telling her it's OK to be a child, but she doesn't know how!"

Celia is now a straight-A student in high school, but she recently wrote a theme about the price of perfection—her obsessive inner pressure to perform "not well but brilliantly." She feels "special" only because of her academic success and will "stay up all night studying if it means the difference between an A— and an A." Her worst fear is that one day she will lose "whatever I have that makes me special and capable of achieving that which others cannot." She confides, "I am not sure I will ever be satisfied, and that is, perhaps, the most terrifying thought I have ever had. The panic caused by the idea of failure is overwhelming. I only hope that one day I will be free of it."

Externally, Celia is a perfect product. What a tragedy that she has never learned to feel "special" inside herself. Her story is a good reminder that the most central—and most elusive—element of finishing childhood may be simply for parents to appreciate it while it lasts.

UNDERSTANDING THE ADOLESCENT BRAIN

Furnishing the Frontal Lobes

Somewhere around age eleven, dramatic mental events start to take place. Having mastered the world of objects, the early teenager must move on to manipulating abstract ideas—a transition from the security of concrete rules to a world of infinite possibilities and points of view. As with adolescent physical development, the timing of these changes varies widely among individuals and can be troublesome and confusing. Some believe that only about two-thirds of adults ever reach the stage of abstract thinking which Piaget labeled formal operational thought. Probably very few reach the ultimate stage, termed "problem finding," which requires generating creative solutions for abstract issues. Most agree that our society needs more people with these capabilities. How can they be developed?

Intellectual growth during adolescence seems to depend on several factors: (1) inherited potential and timetable; (2) the quality of previous brain development in reception and association areas; (3) cultural expectations; (4) the amount and type of stimulation given by school and home; (5) the child's own emotional strength and motivation to make sense out of new information and practice skills. Do these sound familiar? The principles remain the same, whether we're building the foundation or furnishing the penthouse.

The "Brain's Brain"

Although we have much to learn about neural development from age eleven to adulthood, the prefrontal cortex of the frontal lobes, often called the "brain's brain" is undoubtedly a major focus of growth during these years. While the earlier-maturing areas in the back of the brain are a vast storehouse of information, the front is a control center for selecting and acting on accumulated knowledge. Adult patients with frontal lobe disease act a lot like impulsive children. They have trouble with initiative, with analyzing the steps of a problem, thinking ahead, and planning actions; they act unrestrained and socially tactless, and have a childish sense of humor. They get some kinds of memory all mixed up and lose the ability to guide actions with words. Doctors observe frontal lobe patients who talk about what they want to do but are unable to do it.

If you look back to the diagram of the cortex on page 28, you can see the prefrontal cortex is right next door to the frontal motor strip, which gets a growth spurt right after birth and develops quickly during the early months. No wonder many believe that adult learning is based on early physical experiences!

In the normally developing brain, prefrontal areas probably become active soon after birth but aren't truly operational until sometime around ages four to seven, with a spurt of myelination near puberty which may continue into adulthood. Unlike the other cortical lobes, they do not have a direct "window onto the world" for sensory reception, so their development depends on sensory connections formed in earlier years and by the child's inner thoughts, language, and attempts to make mental connections.

Climbing into Grown-Up Thought

Early adolescent thinking reminds me of a little child parading around in grown-up clothes, stumbling a bit but acting very grandiose. Unlike the child, however, the teenager experiences unrelenting self-consciousness. Brain development enables him to glimpse all kinds of new possibilities in any situation, but it also makes him step outside and view himself for the first time. How embarrassing! One of our sons fussed for two hours about which shirt he would wear to a concert with 3000 spectators because he was sure "everyone" would notice him. Yet, even as the young teen is mortified by his own imperfection, he finds himself so special that normal rules may not apply, and a cavalier attitude toward homework or school rules sometimes follows. Parents get buffeted by sudden outbursts and inconsistencies. Remember that teenagers' confusion is greater than yours, even if they don't admit it.

Enlarged mental perspectives create a sudden awareness of "ideals," and the adolescent may ruthlessly criticize his own family. David Elkind says, "In early adolescence not only is the grass greener in the other person's yard, but the house is bigger and more comfortable and the parents are nicer." Yet difficult as they are, these youngsters are covering necessary ground, learning to build with abstract ideas just as they once manipulated their blocks.

Parents and the Adolescent Brain

—Understand that your child needs more rest than any time since infancy and that it is normal for boundless energy suddenly to give way to lassitude.

—Good nutrition, while difficult to enforce at this age, is important for optimal brain functioning. Present your adolescent with breakfast and dinner, and hope for the best. Teens left to forage for themselves are likely to subsist on "fast food."

—Have dinner, watch TV, and read newsmagazines together. Talk about what is happening. It is important to deal with abstract concepts, values, and moral issues. If your child disagrees with you, remain calm. Say, "That's interesting (original; what many believe).

Tell me about your reasons." If she shares her thoughts with you, respect them! You don't have to agree.

—New neural circuitry may slow down normal patterns of conversation and make it hard for a teenager to communicate ideas; give her time to respond in conversation.

—Girls' (and some boys') perceptions of visual patterns may go through a period of change as myelination occurs. Be patient if they suddenly seem to "lose it" when trying to organize visual input.

—Your child needs more privacy than ever before; he also needs to have you available.

—One school administrator begs parents to value their children for their "decency or personality," not for their grades or competitiveness.

—Keep up with what your child is reading in school. Read it yourself. You may be able to get a conversation going.

—Encourage deductive reasoning: "If x is true, what are the implications in situation y?"

—Expose your child to adult views of the real world: work, politics, social issues. Encourage thinking about real problems—but be ready to listen to some idealistic solutions.

—Encourage constructive involvement in the community, such as with volunteer work.

—Help your youngster express anger verbally, and encourage talking through problems.

—Expect criticism of school, of teachers, and of you. Don't undermine the school by criticizing teachers in front of your child.

—Take courage from the study that found that moderate parent-child conflict promotes mental growth and moral development.

—Remember that adolescents need to exercise their frontal lobes by playing tug-of-war with authority. Don't be afraid to set standards and stick to them. One adolescent girl admitted, "The best excuse is still, 'My mother won't let me.' "

Juggling the Abstract

With mental juggling of abstract alternatives, scientific reasoning becomes possible. Whereas younger children can form rudimentary hypotheses, they tend to get caught on the first possible solution to a problem. The classic game of "Twenty Questions" is a good example. When asked, "What am I thinking of?" the young child quickly gives a specific association ("Is it a dog?"). Older children learn to deal with categories ("Is it an animal?"), whereas an adult can evaluate and plan a strategy of broad to narrow categories ("Is it alive? Is it an animal?"). The section that follows illustrates some examples of learning situations that require adult-style reasoning, and often cause trouble for students who haven't quite gotten there yet.

Tools of Abstract Thought

Deductive reasoning: The human brain is programmed to look for rules and order in experience. Young children learn to look at many different pieces of information and put them together into a broad rule or category (all of these insects seem to have eight legs; therefore a rule for being an insect must be having eight legs); this is inductive reasoning. Only later does deductive reasoning develop—taking a general principle and applying it to unfamiliar instances, for example:

   a. "The square of a right triangle's hypotenuse is equal to the sum of the squares of the other two sides." Is this a right triangle? (If this seems confusing, you know how the student feels!)
   b. "All Latin adjectives agree with the noun in both gender and case. Add the appropriate endings to these words."

Hypothesis testing: Generating possible solutions to a problem and testing them systematically until finding one that works is the basis of scientific reasoning. For example, Piaget used a chemistry problem with five bottles of colorless liquid which could be combined in only one special way to produce a yellow color. Young children made combinations randomly and couldn't identify the important relationships. Older adolescents were able to make systematic combinations, holding different alternatives in mind until they solved the problem. Middle schoolers need help from adults who can show them how to go about considering a number of possible solutions instead of getting one idea and trying to force the facts to fit it. Open-minded approaches to everyday problems are one obvious channel toward this important growth.

Propositional logic: "If Mary is taller than Sally and Sally is taller than Marge, who is the tallest?" A child who has mastered concrete operations may be able to figure this one out. It is harder, though, to understand other kinds of propositions, such as "If it is raining, it

must be summer. It is summer. Is it raining?" or "If A or B, then C."
A good example is a direction that gives fifth graders trouble: "If it is
on your assignment sheet *or* I write it on the board, you must do it
for homework." These rules that follows the rules.

Proportion: "For every six students there are two teachers. There
are fifty-four students. How many teachers?" Problems like this require concrete materials (counters, pictures, diagrams) or a formula
until students can mentally juggle the relationships.

Second-order symbol systems: Algebra and grammar are both examples of symbol systems which stand for other symbol systems. In
algebra, numerals stand for ideas of number; algebraic terms (e.g., *x)*
are arbitrarily chosen to stand for the numerals. Grammatical terms
(e.g., a pronoun) represent classes of words which, in turn, stand for
things or ideas. This is pretty complicated stuff if you aren't too clear
on the original symbol system! Younger children can learn specific
principles of grammar (noun, verb) but should not be expected to
apply rules abstractly.

The "abstract attitude": This is the name given to the ability to
stand outside a situation and connect ideas which don't go together
in any kind of literal way. Examples are metaphor, drawing infer-
ences which are not directly stated in a text, some forms of humor,
analogies, nonliteral opposites, and a realistic appraisal of oneself. A
sensitive adult can pull children toward this type of reasoning by
asking the right questions.

These abilities don't develop overnight. Junior high students are
often poised on the brink of adult logic but need the safety of something concrete to fall back on when confronted with new ideas.
George, a seventh grader studying the novel *To Kill a Mockingbird,*
was enthralled by the plot, but couldn't understand the metaphor in
the title. When he came to his father for help, Dad suggested they
work up a literal word-by-word translation: "To Destroy Innocence." "Now I get it!" George cried.

Even adults often learn better from concrete demonstrations, but
we tend to forget that, and teenagers particularly need this kind of
support. Another type of help they need is learning to use their
frontal lobe systems to control and plan behavior.

The Importance of Inhibition

One of the most important functions of the prefrontal cortex is that of being a wet blanket—an inhibitor of excitement. Although we admire an active brain, one that is overly aroused can be a problem as it responds to too many stimuli at once and jumps from idea to idea. As the frontal lobes mature, they team up with the reticular activating system—the "gatekeeper" at the back of the brain which directs arousal and alertness. This circuit passes through part of the limbic system, forming a loop which works as a "gating system" to select and direct attention.

An important function of this loop is regulating the ability to use "feedback," which simply means an ongoing check on one's own behavior. Feedback systems help us catch our own errors and remember what we're supposed to be doing and how—and they should become more automatic during late childhood and adolescence. Students with poor feedback systems don't seem to notice when they've made a mistake; they may habitually forget to bring the right materials to class, or get distracted while doing a job at home such as setting the table. This is a frustrating situation, but there are a few positive steps that seem to help:

Helping the Brain Regulate Behavior

Verbal feedback: Studies of the developing frontal lobes stress the importance of language, particularly "inner language"—a mental dialogue with oneself. Students who are able to talk through a problem mentally before springing into impulsive action do better in school and gain higher-level thinking skills sooner. By the way, parents are the child's most important models for regulating behavior. If you act before you think, your child may adopt the same tactics. If you discipline physically instead of talking problems through, if you tend to express emotion bodily instead of with words, be aware of the pattern you are demonstrating.

Natural consequences: A parent who continually picks up the pieces becomes a feedback system which prevents a youngster from developing one of her own. Unfortunately, it is sometimes necessary to tie yourself to the sofa and let a child feel the effects of her own carelessness. If the expectations were reasonable, and she messed up,

MAKING CONNECTIONS: THE ATTENTION LOOP

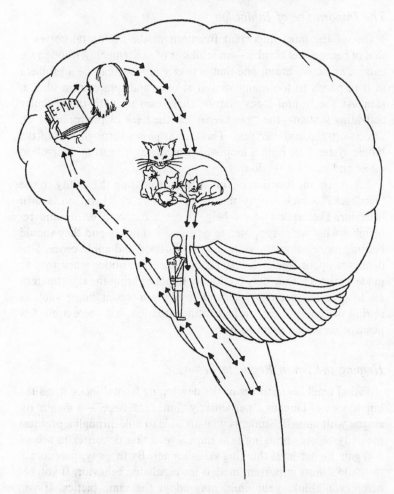

she needs at least minor consequences. This is, without a doubt, the hardest task of parenthood. Have courage. We all learn best from our errors, not from our successes. Try saying, "I'm proud of you. You made a mistake and you *learned* something from it!"

Structure: Particularly during the early years of adolescence when these control systems are being refined, the youngster may need help organizing his life, his responsibilities, and his possessions. Without taking over, you can firmly insist on certain parameters of neatness, schedule, and performance of household tasks. Reasonable expectations, consistently enforced, can help a child get a comfortable "feel" for internal control. Young teens tend to experiment with their new mental powers by pushing and testing the limits. It is your job to give them something to push against. I know it isn't easy; my psyche is still bruised from angry adolescent outbursts—but now our three young men admit that the rules were really very reassuring.

Decisions—Good and Bad

New mental perspectives give youngsters a whole new framework for personal decision making. As they practice using it, they alternate between wanting to be dependent and wanting to argue. Incidentally, because they can now see some of your point of view, they become better arguers!

One logical way to practice decision making is in making summer plans. A high school freshman came to his parents last spring for "advice." He knew that he should take a summer-school reading course recommended by his English teacher, but he really wanted a job as a lifeguard. His parents started to talk him into the reading course, but soon realized they would accomplish more by asking questions instead of giving opinions. Their son argued himself in and out of all possible situations while they tried to be interested but neutral. He finally decided to take the course, and he worked hard because he "owned" his decision. A friend whose parents "made" him take the course acted up in class and was dismissed after the first week.

Allowing kids to take responsibility is agonizing for everyone, but this is one more mountain they must learn to climb. What if this boy had made the "wrong" choice? He would still have learned a lot— including the fact that inadequate reading skills make sophomore English a drag, and that the course might be a good idea next summer. Let teenagers make choices you can live with, but be ready to take a hard line on dangerous alternatives.

POT AND THE BRAIN

Facing Facts

Teenage abuse of alcohol and drugs is a grave concern, yet many teens and parents are unaware of the brain-damaging potential of marijuana use. The active ingredient in marijuana or cannabis, THC, is a fat-soluble substance which accumulates in the lipid tissue of the nervous system. Because it does not wash out of the body like some other neural antagonists, someone smoking two joints (and perhaps only one) a week is never completely free of the drug. Its suspected effects on the brain include damage to neurons, cluttering of the synaptic clefts between them, and blocking of chemical transmitters that are needed for normal mental functioning. Moreover, marijuana may degrade in the nervous system into hundreds of organic and inorganic compounds whose effects are, as yet, only a matter of speculation.

Controversy still exists about whether THC's harm to the brain is irreversible, but specific areas seem to be particularly susceptible. One of its most pronounced effects is on the limbic system's centers for pleasure and memory. Neurologist Robert G. Heath, implanting electrodes in the brains of monkeys who were made to inhale cannabis smoke, found permanent changes in several deep areas. In the septal region, a major site for pleasurable feelings, the changes were alarmingly similar to those present in schizophrenic patients. He believes that changes in brain sites responsible for emotional behavior create marijuana smokers' apathy and "burnout"—an insidious pattern in which "the pleasure a person gains from taking a drug replaces reward for a job well done."

One major fear often expressed is that the alteration of normal pleasure pathways in the brain distorts ability to strive or achieve. Dr. Richard Hawley, who has counseled teen drug users, worries about drugs taking over the normal reward systems of the brain. Instead of pleasure in mastery of a school subject, a sport, or a creative endeavor, kids get satisfaction from nonlearning and avoidance of stress. Hawley warns, "Loss of neural function is rewarded with a surpassing pleasure." Slow brain wave patterns replace the fast frequencies of active mental effort, literally "dulling" the mind.

The user may insist that consciousness is expanded, when in reality the mind has been simplified. Like the infant, the drug user contemplates the patterns in the wallpaper.

Memory functions in the limbic system are interrupted by use of cannabis, which impairs retention, particularly of newly learned information, by blocking normal chemical transmission of messages. As long as the student can rely on "old" learning, the problem may go unnoticed, but inability to take in, synthesize, and apply new information eventually causes trouble. Both the limbic system and the reticular activating system may be involved in problems with "gating" induced by THC; capacity for focusing attention is impaired and irrelevant associations distort thought and interfere with conversation.

Burnt-Out Brains?

One of the most alarming possibilities concerns frontal lobe damage as one cause of "burnout." Although it is not feasible to implant electrodes in teenagers' frontal lobes, the "amotivational" syndrome associated with extensive marijuana use mimics many features of frontal lobe disease mentioned earlier. Dr. Robert Gilkeson attached electrodes to the scalps of teenagers who were heavily involved in marijuana use, and found distinct changes in frontal area frequencies. He, and many others, are convinced that permanent changes in frontal brain cells take place, but the definitive research about this question has not been done.

There is no doubt that adolescent brains are better off without pot. During a time of major intellectual growth, the influence of any drug distorts the process. The option of avoiding the hassles of these years is seductive for many youngsters—particularly those who lack a clear idea or ideal of themselves. Early users who later kick the habit must retrace the developmental steps which were missed, but no one knows whether full potential can be regained. Gilkeson says, "No kid who has become chronically intoxicated on marijuana for any length of time will ever be the kid he was. . . . Some losses he will never recover."

Professionals feel that increased alcohol consumption by teens presents many of the same hazards as marijuana use. Moreover, one habit often leads to another. Some long-term effects of heavy alcohol use on brain cells are recognized, but a more immediate concern for young people is its potential for addiction or distortion of intellectual and emotional growth.

How Parents Can Help

Parents and children must be on guard against the brain-damaging potential of all drugs. School counselors find that abuse commonly starts as early as age twelve. Support for drug and alcohol education and for research on the neural effects of newer drug fads, such as cocaine, are essential. Parents should also be aware that their attitudes help shape teenagers' choices regarding both drugs and alcohol. Several studies have shown that parents whose children avoid drugs tend to be:

—Described as "warm"—available for help without being overly judgmental.

—"Close to children."

—"Traditional in orientation," not afraid to set limits or discuss their own values.

—Non–drug users themselves.

—Negative about use of medications to "make you feel better" (this culturally pervasive tendency is particularly important to defy).

—Able to help keep the child's ego strength firm; teens with poor self-concepts, anxiety, or difficulty with social relationships are more likely to take drugs.

—Those who pay attention.

These ideas may sound simplistic, but we have to start somewhere. No one is a perfect parent, and none of us needs a guilt trip if a child gets into trouble. We do need better information and more attention to the influences of other adult models in our society. Parents should demand more substantive research and information on preventive strategies. In the meanwhile, if you suspect a problem, don't delay getting good professional advice.

WORKING WITH YOUR TEENAGER'S SCHOOL

The Middle School Muddle

In the light of new research, some educators are wondering whether schools are really healthy places for young adolescent brains. Middle schools and junior highs have too often been regarded as the trenches of academia where teachers complain about students' lack of motivation and await a "promotion" to high school teaching. Programs which keep early adolescents powerless as elementary school children, yet suddenly expect them to learn by teaching methods used in high school can turn off capable minds. A few innovative schools are addressing the wide range of development in grades six through nine, but they need support.

If you visit your child's school and find students acting out history lessons, drawing diagrams of reading assignments, or "playing" with math games, don't dismiss the curriculum as "frivolous." It may be based on the latest and best research about adolescent brains. Since it has been estimated that only about 12 percent of seventh and eighth graders have achieved the ability to reason abstractly, most still need to "do" in addition to sitting in lecture-style classes. This does *not* mean we need to "water down" the curriculum—rather to present it by methods which can tie abstract concepts to something in students' real experience. Believe it or not, many high school teachers find that these methods work for them, too!

The Power of Parents

It is the school's job to understand teaching methods and curriculum, but administrators listen to parents, whether they admit it or not. Parents should certainly hold schools accountable both for imparting skills and keeping intellectual curiosity alive, but some inadvertently encourage inappropriate policies. With the best of intentions they worry that a school which doesn't appear to have their child on the "fast track" may impair her future chances. One typical issue illustrates this point.

It has become fashionable to take algebra in the eighth grade, and schools feel strong parental pressure to offer this option. While a few children are conceptually ready for algebra at this level, many more are not. Experienced teachers find that, even for good math students, they must overly simplify the course in order to get middle schoolers through. Moreover, in one school district where high-achieving eighth graders were encouraged to take algebra, 70 percent of these potentially gifted mathematicians did not go on to study higher math in high school. Why? Because they were "turned off" by algebra!

Dr. Mark Tierno, who reported on this study, believes that brain development provides the explanation. Most of the students did not yet have the abstract reasoning ability for the concepts presented, so they coped by memorizing. Any subject can be memorized up to a point, but without underlying comprehension of the ideas and relationships involved, learning eventually bogs down.

Tests may be the first evidence of trouble. "I studied and studied, but when I got in there I just couldn't answer the questions," wails the student. What happened? Despite hours of work, a child who lacks the underlying cognitive development never quite gets the idea. Test taking becomes a desperate attempt to plug in isolated facts from memory, but if problems are stated differently or information must be applied, watch out! Teachers may be unaware that the basic problem is a mismatch between the levels of the pupil and the material. They blame the student for lack of effort, or decide that he "isn't really that smart after all." The student is clear on only one thing: math is not for him! Yet another year or two of development might have produced a love match instead of a divorce.

Negative Neural Networks

One of the most controversial aspects of Epstein's theory, which you read about in Chapter 4, is that brain growth often slows down between the ages of twelve and fourteen. If so, introducing heavy new academic demands for everyone in grades seven and eight could be a waste of time and enthusiasm for many students. Epstein believes that a child's learning rate—which is not necessarily related to basic intelligence—peaks somewhere around age eleven and reaches a low at thirteen or thirteen and a half. While many girls and some boys experience significant brain maturation by age twelve, many bright youngsters of both sexes await the next major growth spurt, sometime between ages fourteen and sixteen. Thus, while some middle schoolers thrive on abstract, highly verbal teaching, others are sitting in classes which might as well be in another language. Middle school teachers commonly find a range of up to six years of cognitive ability in a normal eighth grade classroom!

The scariest part of Epstein's theory concerns "negative neural networks," which may develop in a brain which is continually besieged by input it cannot process. For example, too much "teacher talk" instead of active involvement, too difficult reading material, or overly abstract math concepts have the unhappy result of reinforcing connections to *avoid* learning. We see examples in everyday life; for example, how often are you aware of the canned music in a shopping mall? You have probably learned to block many distracting or uncomfortable types of input. Similarly, a child who has learned to block classroom demands may have trouble learning even when the appropriate time comes. High school teachers agree there are capable students who seem almost negatively programmed in some subjects.

Positive Action

Some middle schools are attempting to implement recommendations from Epstein's research, but time is needed to evaluate their success. These programs center on active, involved learning and emphasize reading comprehension and writing, creative expression in the arts, manual skill development, and application of math. Epstein recommends that early teens should also memorize poetry and good literature as a base for future writing and appreciation. Parents can help implement his particular concern for teenagers' interaction with real life situations, as in volunteer work, and the challenges of nature and outdoor activities.

While the theory of "brain growth spurts" awaits further proof, some educators, ensnared in the middle school muddle, think such new approaches are long overdue. They urge parents not to let schools dismiss young adolescents as "difficult to teach," and to keep an eye out for spuriously "accelerated" courses where methods and subject matter are uninteresting, inappropriate, or even damaging. Since these years shape attitudes toward learning, the factors of mental growth should be part of the adolescent equation.

WHAT TO LOOK FOR IN A MIDDLE SCHOOL

Brain-Building Middle Schools . . .

—Have a clear sense of purpose in meeting the needs of this age group.

—Have teachers who understand the cognitive development of adolescents and enjoy working with them.

—Encourage high academic standards that are age-appropriate, not falsely accelerated classes.

—Realize that few middle schoolers are conceptually ready for algebra and other traditional high school subjects.

—Resist parental efforts to push students into inappropriate courses.

—Use sophisticated manipulative (hands-on) materials to teach math concepts (rods, geo-boards, puzzles, etc.) in addition to written exercises.

—Provide individual support for students having difficulty.

—Encourage mastery rather than a large volume of material inadequately covered.

—Take time to review material from earlier levels.

—Try to meet social, emotional, and physical development needs.

—Teach science through challenging hands-on experiences rather than relying on lectures and worksheets.

—Emphasize study skills and learning about how to learn.

—Allow students physical movement during the school day.

—Demonstrate the use of both inductive and deductive reasoning.

—Insist on original writing and speaking before a group rather than simply absorbing material.

—Capitalize on the real interests and concerns of students and allow individuals to pursue well-planned projects of their own.

—Allow for interaction with the larger community and nature outside the school.

—Challenge each child to move into more abstract levels of understanding by integrating courses in different subject areas.

—Have a well-planned program for prevention of drug and alcohol use.

—Regard music and visual and performing arts as important parts of the curriculum.

REMARKS FROM THE TRENCHES

The more I am around adolescents, the more fascinating I find them. Every day my eighth grade students amuse and delight me—and at the same time they irritate, challenge, and exhaust me. I must continually remind myself that these young adult bodies contain brains far from "finished" by adult standards. Teachers are perpetually amazed at the way kids "get it together" sometime around tenth or eleventh grade—which should be no surprise if their prefrontal lobes are still myelinating. Many late-maturing thinkers are extremely bright children, but parents and schools must hold on to their patience and good humor to refrain from pushing such youngsters into defeat or alienation. The late bloomers *can* make it to Harvard—unless adults have convinced them they are failures by age sixteen. Many psychologists believe that the alarming increase in teenage suicide is partially attributable to adults' urging teens to make choices too soon, coupled with unreasonable expectations and pressure into adults' ideas of the right decisions.

High academic standards are an important national priority, but they must be brain-appropriate for each child's level of development. As one who teaches the same students at several points during their school years, I know that for months I can beat my head (and theirs) against the wall of an inappropriate objective, only to find that, two years later, they learn it in an hour. This latter way is a lot more efficient and fun for everyone.

As at earlier ages, emotion may be the ultimate catalyst for mental growth. While you are trying to understand your teenagers' brains, don't forget to love, respect, and compliment them. Their struggle for individuality is worth admiring. Become a partner in the furnishing of a new adult mind and you are guaranteed a front-row seat for nature's most exciting developmental drama.

Part II

FOUNDATIONS OF LEARNING

"A Path to the Future":
Bridging the Hemispheres

A GUIDANCE COUNSELLOR RECENTLY RECOMMENDED THAT A ninth grade boy who was having academic difficulty be given only ten minutes of homework each night. The reason? She claimed the boy was "right-brained" and couldn't be expected to concentrate normally. His parents sensibly refused to go along with this idea, which, unfortunately, is not the only peculiar one to emerge since research about the two hemispheres has become a popular topic.

Most parents have heard about differences between the two sides of the brain, but they share professionals' confusion about their practical implications. Is there a battle going on inside children's heads as these two halves fight for control? Are some children "right-brained" learners destined to experience failure in a "left-brained" curriculum? Can a child's "learning style" be changed? What is a learning style anyway?

Despite what you may have heard, two facts are clear. Children are whole-brained learners, and the brain prefers cooperation to conflict. Moreover, anyone who claims to have answers or "cures" based on hemispheric research is undoubtedly guilty of oversimplification. In this chapter I will try to walk the tightrope between explaining what is understood scientifically and how it can sensibly be applied. I will suggest some ideas which might help children use both hemispheres effectively, linking them in an efficient and flexible system for learning.

Partners in Thinking

The first five chapters of this book view the brain sideways, in the direction of its major vertical growth from bottom back to top front. Now we switch to a horizontal perspective, which, as you might guess, also changes with age. If you looked down at the top of the forehead and could peer through the skull, you would see that the cortex is not one solid mass, as it appears from the side. Instead, it consists of two distinct halves—the cerebral hemispheres. These hard-working teammates contain two sets of cortical lobes which gradually develop specialized abilities for seeing, hearing, feeling, and thinking intelligently.

In a mature brain, a thick bridge of fibers called the *corpus callosum* carries messages in a constant flow between the hemispheres. With the exception of a few surgical cases, whom you will learn about shortly, it isn't possible to be "left-brained" or "right-brained." Even after surgery the brain fights for normalcy. Likewise, a curriculum could not be developed for only one side, since *any activity automatically engages both of a child's hemispheres.* We do not know yet how much early environment "sculpts" their balance, but there are many individual variations in the way the brain distributes the load.

Our challenge is to help children mobilize the strengths of both hemispheres to solve problems, learn, and create new ideas. Carl Sagan has optimistically termed the corpus callosum a "path to the future" because he believes that only dynamic cooperation between the hemispheres can achieve mankind's highest objectives. It takes a long time for this path to become a major highway, and each child has a special roadmap for development.

LUMPERS AND SPLITTERS

"Careless" or Too Careful?

As he stood to leave my office, Mr. Jarvis turned to his wife. "Well, we have our work cut out for us, but at least we know he isn't lazy or stupid. Now that I understand Tim a little better, I'll try to

USING BOTH HEMISPHERES

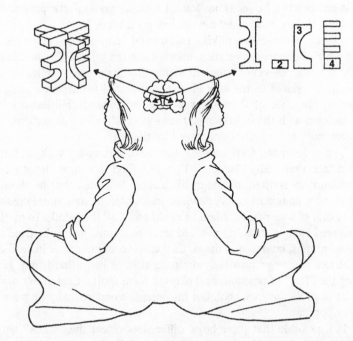

be more patient and give him positive strokes for things he's good at."

Although there is no such thing as a "typical" child, Tim Jarvis has a lot in common with many youngsters who strain the patience of parents. In fact, Tim was baffling all the adults in his life because he was so good at some things and, as he admitted, so "lousy" at others. A star soccer player and vice-president of his seventh grade class, he excelled in art and showed a real talent for design but was running into trouble with math and English. He astonished his father by his intuitive ability to figure out the relationship between wind, waves, and the speed of their sailboat, but he couldn't remember the order of the multiplication tables. He was popular with his teachers, but his report card reflected their frustration:

"Writing and spelling need attention. Tim should take more time on sentence structure."

"Tim seems to get the ideas in math, but is careless with written work. He often does not remember assignments given in class."

"Tim can understand stories very well, but he makes many careless errors when he reads out loud. I wish he would participate more in class discussions, as he always has good ideas."

I spent several hours talking to Tim and administering some tests, on which he scored, overall, somewhat above average. The profile of his abilities, however, suggested that his apparent "carelessness" might be related to the way his brain allocated hemispheric assignments. His style of thinking was weighted toward abilities usually associated with the right hemisphere—even when he was performing tasks more appropriately managed by the left.

Tim's classmate, Carl, on the other hand, was a whiz with the kind of details that really "bugged" Tim. His English compositions were meticulously written, although his teacher lamented that he should "use more imagination." A flawless oral reader, he sometimes missed the point of a story even when he could recall all the details. In math, he loved computation but avoided story problems, just as he tried to avoid graphs, charts, and maps. Carl chose computer time instead of athletics whenever possible, admitting that he had a hard time getting the "feel" of positions and plays in team sports. Carl didn't have a lot of problems in school, but his parents wondered why he wasn't very popular.

Is it possible that these boys' differences reflect the "styles" with which their hemispheres balance the load? For purposes of illustration, let's call Tim a "lumper" and Carl a "splitter." These terms are sometimes used to characterize the hemispheric modes of handling information.

Dividing Brains

Scientists first learned about hemispheric differences from adult patients who needed surgery to stop epileptic seizures. These sudden electrical storms flood the brain with uncontrolled activity; sometimes the only way to stop them is by cutting through the entire corpus callosum. Such "split-brain" patients, whose hemispheres are deprived of a chance to communicate with each other, have cooperated in research to discover how each side functions. Because cortical areas are primarily connected with sensory organs on the opposite (contralateral) side of the body, scientists are able to "feed" information into one side or the other depending on where they present it. These studies have shown that each hemisphere has its own unique style of processing information. For most people the right hemisphere learns by looking, and getting the whole intuitive "feel" of a situation, while the left tends to listen and analyze systematically. The right sees outlines and wholes, while the left arranges the details in order. The right is a *simultaneous* "lumper," the left, a *sequential* "splitter."

HOW THE HEMISPHERES SHARE THE LOAD	
LEFT: THE "SPLITTER"	RIGHT: THE "LUMPER"
Analytic-sequential	*Wholistic-simultaneous*
Provides details	Sees wholes
Listens, talks	Looks, does
Reasons logically	Reasons intuitively
Analyzes, understands time	Designs, understands three-dimensional space
Language: speech, sound, grammar	Language: single word meanings
Rapidly changing motor patterns (writing, repeated finger movements)	Manipulospatial abilities: changing environment with hands
Likes automatic routines	Likes novelty
Verbal short-term memory	Memory for sensory images
Processing rapidly changing auditory patterns (understanding speech)	Generating mental maps, conceptualizing mentally
Putting things in order	Understanding intuitively

The left hemisphere "splitter" is a natural for the analytic, sequential requirements of spoken language. It can deal with rapidly changing sound patterns such as phonics or words in sentences and fast-moving fine-motor patterns, such as writing or rapid, repeating finger movements.

While the left hemisphere thinks in words, the right relies on sensory images. Its primary jobs are important ones—maintaining control of visual space and enabling us to understand situations. It can form mental maps, organize physical exploration, and mentally "look at" or conceptualize an idea. Many believe that artistic talent, some emotions, and ability to "see" others' perspectives spring from this side of the brain.

You may have heard about all this before, but what are the implications for children's learning? First, both hemispheres are important! Thinking of the brain as a kind of mental factory helps clarify their roles in thought production.

Thought Production, Inc.

Although the adult "split-brain" cases learned to live with their mental dichotomy, the rest of us can't separate sequential and simultaneous thinking. In a simplified analogy, the right side of the mental factory is responsible for design, and the left for production. New material is received and sized up by the right "lumper," then immediately transferred to the "splitter" for analysis. As the left hemisphere decides on the order of production steps, lists the materials needed, and plans the output, the right simultaneously evaluates outside market conditions and checks production steps to see if they fit with overall objectives. For example, in copying a design, the right sees the whole configuration and keeps the parts in the proper spatial relationship while the left analyzes the elements of the drawing and orders the motor movements that guide the pencil.

One major job of childhood is to develop an efficient system. Some children, like Tim, however, seem to have an underactive production department, while Carl could use some help with design. Test profiles indicate how these differences can affect their learning abilities. Here is a summary of some major strengths and weaknesses at age twelve:

TIM: A "Lumper"

Strengths	Weaknesses
Large-muscle (global) sports (soccer, swimming)	Small, patterned motor sequences (writing)
Spatial relationships (sailboat, mechanical drawing): tests at high school level	Auditory short-term memory for words: tests like an eight-year-old

Visual creativity (excels at art and design)	Following sequential directions
Learning by doing (carpentry, mechanical gadgets)	Language expression, grammar, accurate oral reading
Doing puzzles without small internal details (seeing "whole")	Getting math equations in order (analyzing and sequencing)
Getting along with peers	Hearing and remembering homework assignments, taking notes in class

CARL: A "Splitter"

Strengths	*Weaknesses*
Linear-sequential computer programming	Large-muscle sports, sense of field positions
Phonics, grammar, story details	Comprehension of "big picture" (reading comprehension, relationships)
Math equations	Math concepts; unfamiliar story problems
Algebra (formulae)	Geometry
Handwriting	Maps, charts, graphs
Organizing time, outlining	Imagination, creativity
Auditory memory for words or digits	Social awareness

I will give suggestions for balancing these learning abilities, but first let's address the question of how the boys' differences came about. Were they born this way? How much does early experience influence hemispheric balance? What role do parents have? Actually, each child comes into the world with a special pattern, but early environmental influences have much to do with its realization.

WERE THEY BORN THIS WAY?

Infant Specialists

When a baby is born, the brain's top layer, or cortex, is waiting for experience to turn on the switches. The right and left hemispheres, although clearly defined, are not yet functionally connected, since the bridge between them is one of the last membranes to be "finished" with coatings of myelin. Most experts now believe that the two hemispheres start out primed for different types of work because they already prefer certain types of experience. Sequential noises, such as a series of clicks, provoke greater brain wave activity in newborns' left hemispheres, whereas visual flashes of light arouse the right side, which also responds to nonverbal musical notes or the sound of the washing machine. From the beginning, the left hemisphere has a tendency to act as "boss." You might notice, when you talk to your baby, that she turns her head more often to the right than to the left. This common tendency toward right-turning (remember, the left hemisphere controls the right side of the body) is viewed as evidence that the left hemisphere is responding to your words.

With the development of language comprehension and speech, the left hemisphere in most people increasingly dominates over the right. It gradually gains in ability to deal with sequential, automatic movement. One study evaluated whether three, four, and five-year-olds were better at using their right or left hands for different kinds of activities. The right hand (left hemisphere) was better at sequential motor actions, such as finger tapping or peg moving, whereas the left hand (right hemisphere) preferred visual-spatial tasks such as copying another person's hand postures.

EXERCISING BOTH HEMISPHERES
Sample Activities

SPLITTING	LUMPING
Sequential: Analytic	*Simultaneous: Visual-Spatial*
Fine-motor activities	Large-muscle play
cutting out small items	team sports

coloring inside lines	gymnastics
detailed needlework	climbing
finger games with sequenced movements	free play (tag, etc.)
Listening to language	Free-form drawing, painting
Talking about events	Looking at pictures
Putting things in order, making lists	Making and using maps
Understanding time sequences	Following mazes
Music: the words	Music: the melody
Writing sentences	Manipulating mechanical devices
Describing objects systematically	Dramatizing
Using phonetically rearranged languages (Pig Latin)	Finding hidden pictures
Repeating directions in order	Seeing or creating patterns
Listing steps in an activity	Easels, paints, fingerpaints, clay, craft activities

HELPING THEM WORK TOGETHER

Games which combine visual and verbal cues (e.g., "Simon Says")

Visualizing pictures from listening or reading (make a "mental movie")

Large block play with a story attached

Describing actions with words

Talking about manipulating toys or mechanical gadgets

Verbalizing intuitive discoveries ("How did you know that? What clues did you use? What came into your mind first?")

Describing problem-solving experiences ("Can you tell me how you did that puzzle?")

Memorizing math facts to music

Spelling words backwards, remembering number sequences backwards

Keeping the score of the game in your head

Doing proofs in geometry (proving an intuitive process with sequential logic)

Writing up science experiments

Cooking by following recipes

Watching TV and then retelling the story in order ("First they found the treasure, and then . . .")

Doing electrical wiring from a sequential plan

Building models from directions

Reading music

Telling time from a nondigital clock

One Side Instead of Two

Several dramatic cases prove that hemispheric organization can be altered to some degree. Imagine yourself as a parent with a terrible decision to make: Your child has been afflicted since birth by a rare convulsive disorder which does not respond to medication. Neurologists find that one side is seriously injured, causing continual, violent reactions throughout the brain. The remedy is even more drastic than the "split-brain" operations: removing the entire hemisphere which is the source of the trouble.

A few families have made this agonizing choice for surgery. The operation, termed "hemidecortication," rarely performed, has offered an opportunity to observe plasticity in action. As these children grew up, doctors were astonished by their apparent normalcy. It soon became evident that either remaining hemisphere could assume many of the duties of its missing neighbor. Children without a left hemisphere developed language and learned to read, while right hemidecorticates could perform visual-spatial tasks such as mazes and map reading.

Long-term studies, however, show that overall ability is lower than might be expected if the child's brain had been able to develop normally. The younger the brain at the time of surgery, the greater its potential for redistributing assignments, but any such compensation has its cost. The best-functioning brains have two lively hemispheric partners.

Thinking Styles

As we consider the implications of all this information for parents, it becomes clear that, while no normal environment will make a child "left-" or "right-brained," children differ in the way they deploy thinking skills. Here's a summary of some major points:

1. *Hemispheric specialization* probably is present from birth, but development is shaped by the demands and input to the brain. Heavy auditory-verbal stimulation may increase left-hemisphere capabilities and vice-versa. Deaf children, for example, show a pattern of hemispheric organization different from that of hearing children.

2. *Lateralization* means the pattern in which abilities such as language are distributed between the two sides.

3. *Hemispheric dominance* is one side's tendency to determine the style of processing to be used for a job. In our highly verbal society, the side with language in it, usually the left, is more often dominant, but for visual, wholistic thinking, the right may need to be the leader.

4. Individuals vary in their ability to activate the appropriate hemisphere for different demands. Such flexibility may be a major factor in intellectual ability.

5. *Hemispheric style* is a term used to suggest an individual's preferred way of processing information when there is a choice of strategy to be used. For example, in putting a puzzle together, you can use a predominantly analytic strategy by naming each piece and assembling them in a logical order, or you can work from the whole outline, using mainly visual clues. Although both hemispheres are working, one may set the tone.

6. Younger children may tend to use a right-hemisphere style, acting on situations globally without analyzing them; as verbal demands increase, the left side takes over more often. An activity such as reading may be handled in different ways at different ages.

7. Plasticity of the hemispheres probably declines by the beginning of adolescence.

Integrating Design and Production

The hemispheres communicate by way of the corpus callosum, the thickest network of connections in the entire body. It is one of the last pathways in the brain to be completed and it may hold the key to mental efficiency by activating and suppressing hemispheric control. For example, in reading, both visual and verbal abilities are used, but if the language hemisphere doesn't take charge, accuracy, fluency, and comprehension may suffer.

Parents who want to help their children build this pathway to the future can follow three major guidelines:

1. Encourage a wide variety of activities to engage all parts of the brain.

2. Let the child's interest direct learning. Connections develop in response to demands from the child's brain, not from an adult's.

3. Don't expect full hemispheric integration until after puberty.

Here are general guidelines for each age level:

Birth to three years: The baby and toddler may still be using primitive brain areas for many tasks that the cortex has not yet taken over. During this period the child essentially has a "split brain," because the corpus callosum has not myelinated. You may have noticed a young child transfer a crayon from one hand to the other when crossing the center of the paper. This inability to cross the body's midline may be one sign that the hemispheres are still working independently. We can't expect a child of this age to put things together—either physically or mentally. She can't effortlessly coordinate two sides of the body, or link words and images for reasoning. She can't picture the characters in a story in her mind, remember complicated directions, or solve problems that she must "see" in her head. ("Sally walks behind Suzie. Who walks first?") These years are important foundations for expanded use of both hemispheres. Refer to "Exercising Both Hemispheres" for suggestions.

Four to six years: New connections start to form as the corpus callosum undergoes its first major development around age four. Simple, interesting activities combining right and left hemisphere skills become important challenges. Many children instinctively begin to use words to help them manipulate puzzles or plan the use of art materials. Real-life challenges build connections—especially when the child has a *real* reason to solve them. Tying shoes, for example, combines small, sequential motor movements with a visual-spatial task.

Wise parents use these years to link language with creativity and visual-spatial skills which build bridges to abstract reasoning. They pass up rote-level memorization tasks designed to make the child (or the parent) look impressive.

A nursery school teacher told me one story about a mother who was anxious to make her little girl appear intelligent by teaching her some important facts. When the teacher reported that Susie had succeeded in tying her shoes for the first time, Mother brushed off the news. "Tell us whose picture is on the one-dollar bill, Susie," she demanded.

Agreeably, the child replied, "Washington Redskins!"

To build hemispheric bridges, stick with things that have meaning for the child.

Six to ten years: Hemispheric division of labor may be affected by school demands for reading, writing, spelling, and computation. Children who tend to be "lumpers" often experience difficulty and begin to think they are "stupid" because their individual style seems out of place. They require extra practice with language, seasoned with recognition for their visual or creative talents, and special help with the skills of reading and solving math equations. Conversely, "splitters" adept with production tasks (sounding out words, computation) may risk becoming one-dimensional if their school fails to emphasize comprehension and original thinking. Parents have a major responsibility during these years to understand their child's preferred style and provide supplementary experiences for balance. Encouragement of creativity may increasingly fall to the family. Go together to museums, children's concerts, plays; try sculpture, creative movement, or drama. If this is not your "bag," give it a try anyhow. You are a wonderful example of "parent as learner," and you may even build a few bridges of your own!

Eleven years and up: This is the age for the final maturation of the "path to the future," but remember that the pattern is less plastic than in earlier years. By now your child has a distinct learning style, which adult expectations should take into account. Children who still "march to a different drummer" probably have strong creative talents. Help each child respect his own style, but don't give up on making connections. For many children, this is a time when new myelin growth or changing hormone balances help things suddenly fit together, if the emotional climate permits. Let the youngster know that his brain is gaining wonderful new powers—it's worth the effort to try again on some old problem areas. Because of the increased abilities of the corpus callosum, visualizing stories or "seeing" and turning ideas around mentally should become easier, but some young teens, especially girls, may experience perceptual confusion and need verbal strategies for talking through maps, geometric problems, or complex visual displays.

During this period of rapid change, parents take on more of a spectator role. Don't forget to applaud! In addition, keep providing supplementary cultural experiences and lots of conversation about thoughts and ideas.

Waiting for the Bridge

In a recent parent conference, the father, a neurologist, was sympathizing with his second grade son's spelling difficulties.

"I realize now," he explained, "that I am still hopelessly confused about all the words I learned before I was in sixth grade. Then, suddenly, spelling just came together."

Fortunately, he hadn't already been pressured into believing he was a failure. If your child has trouble making connections of any kind, I would suggest that you focus hard on keeping the road open until the bridge has a chance to develop.

Building Bridges Between the Hemispheres

—Using two parts of the brain at the same time is a talent that develops with age and practice. The farther apart two areas are, the easier it is to use them together. (It is easier to carry on a conversation while drawing a picture than while writing a letter.)

—Emotional state may alter the chemical balance which helps messages cross between hemispheres. Excess pressure or anxiety may block mental bridges.

—Food allergies may slow down transfer time across the corpus callosum. Since traditional skin tests are not a reliable detector of food sensitivities, you should keep track of any substances that seem to make your child tired, grouchy, listless, less mentally alert, or "hyper." Food additives, dyes, sugar, and chocolate are particularly suspect.

—When transfer time is impaired, the most complicated thinking goes first.

—Some parents inadvertently give different signals to each hemisphere. If your words say, "That's OK" but your body signals are negative, your child's brain will be understandably confused.

—Your own hemispheric style influences the activities you choose for your child. Be aware of it and don't limit varieties of adventure. If you hate puzzles or word games, for example, let your child know that you are approaching a challenge together.

—Help your child learn to estimate in math. Seeing the big picture before starting gives a framework for understanding. Young children find this very hard.

—Visualization—also hard for young children—is one of the most important ways to link the right hemisphere with left-hemisphere language use. At first, read stories out loud while you show pictures; then have children draw pictures of their own. Eventually, suggest that they close their eyes and make a "mental movie" while you read a short passage. Ask, "What color was the queen's dress in your imagination? What did the house look like?" Don't be surprised if it takes a lot of practice. You can start gently around age four.

Not Enough Bridges?

Recently, I received a cry for help from a kindergarten teacher. Charles, she reported, "has a high verbal IQ and wonderful language comprehension but is miserable in school. He is exceptionally awkward with crayons and scissors, frustrated because he can't write his name, and he resists clay and fingerpaints because they are 'messy.' He is socially inept, can't seem to imagine or pretend, and always waits for a teacher to tell him how to use new materials. He is so clumsy in gym class that the other children are starting to make fun of him. I found him crying in the hall yesterday."

After observing Charles in the classroom, I understood the teacher's concern. The only joy this handsome little boy showed was when his turn came at the computer. He kept to himself despite the teachers' tactful efforts to get him involved.

When we voiced our concerns to his mother, she was surprised. She recognized that Charles was verbally advanced and was proud of the fact that he spent most of his time at home playing with video games and the computer. No, they didn't have an easel, paints, crayons, clay, or fingerpaints in the house, but Charles loved books and stories. Since they lived in an apartment, he got outside only for supervised walks to the park. His parents thought they had provided their son with the latest and best tools for learning. What happened?

As with most cases, this one does not divide neatly down right-left hemisphere lines. I wonder if only parts of each hemisphere had gotten their exercise. A fully developed callosal bridge spans all parts of the cortex—feeling, touching, manipulating, seeing, hearing, expressing, and reasoning. Perhaps Charles's environment, enriched in one sense, but deprived in others, had limited his potential to make connections at several of these levels. My guess is, when the time had come to start connecting two mental continents, parts of each were still unexplored.

It is hard to write a prescription for mud pie making and tree climbing, but I might have told this mother about the studies showing that animals raised in the wild have thicker, heavier cortical tissue than do those who have been domesticated. The wild animals are forced to solve a wider variety of problems, interacting physically with environmental challenges. For Charles, we settled for suggesting activities to balance his skill development: finger games, painting, sewing cards, bead stringing, large motor games, movement activities—and some free play "in the wild." Above all, Charles needs help in making connections with other children.

THE QUESTION OF HANDEDNESS

Whose Responsibility?

Experts disagree about how much genetic responsibility you have for the way your child's hemispheres become lateralized. Many believe that there are distinctive trends in families, showing up in similar learning styles or in choices of related professions over several generations. One avenue into this puzzle has been the fascinating question of right- and left-handedness.

Handedness is in part genetically determined. Approximately 90 percent of all people are right-handed, but up to 30 percent may carry genes for left-handedness. Most newborns show right-sided preference by lying on their backs facing right with their right arm outstretched. Firm hand use preference is usually established before age six. To determine handedness, several tests should be used: for example, eating with a spoon, writing, throwing, hammering, and threading a needle. If a child does any of these with the left hand, he is classified as "not right handed."

Each hand is connected to the opposite cerebral hemisphere; it was once assumed that a dominant right hand reflects inherited left-hemisphere language lateralization, and vice-versa, but the situation is not that simple. While it is true that almost all right-handers have speech housed in the opposite left hemisphere, so do 60 to 70 percent of non-right-handers. A few non-right-handers have speech in the opposite right hemisphere, and some in both sides.

Just because speech is in one side, this hemisphere is not necessarily the one which is "dominant" when there is a choice of response style. There are both right- and left-handers who prefer to be lumpers rather than splitters, who feel more comfortable with visual, nonverbal thinking. At this time, other than some questionnaire-type tests whose accuracy is unproven, there is no nonmedical way to categorize people as to a dominant hemisphere. Probably most adults, both right- and non-right-handed, use different strategies depending on the requirements of the situation.

Nevertheless, there is evidence that non-right-handers are different. They may have language more evenly distributed between the two hemispheres, giving them a "reserve" in case of damage to either side. Lefties with left-handed relatives may have different patterns of brain organization than those without. Some believe that nonfamilial left-handers were meant to be right-handed but suffered some subtle early damage which changed things around. An unusually high percentage of non-right-handers is found among children with developmental disabilities, including reading problems. Needless to say, this area of research is being carefully pursued.

Hands, Brains, and Families

Interesting new findings come from the Harvard Medical School, where two researchers proposed that left-handedness may result, not from injury, but from different brain cell development caused by an excess of testosterone, a male hormone, before birth. They think this condition tends to occur in certain families, altering normal hemispheric balance and predisposing a child for language and reading problems. They also suspect a connection with the immune system, since these families are particularly susceptible to allergies, migraine, and autoimmune diseases (e.g., rheumatoid arthritis, celiac disease, lupus). This theory could explain the tendency for non-right-handed-ness and learning problems to occur in certain families. Other cur-rent studies confirm the family connection but implicate the allergic mother's autoimmune system as a causal factor in altered hemi-spheric patterns.

Interestingly, individuals and families with reading problems often excel in visual-spatial or creative fields (engineers, artists, architects). If this sounds like your family, have courage. In addition to their formidable talents, they may also prove to be *less* susceptible to cer-tain other kinds of disease. Everyone will be awaiting more clues into this mystery.

Have you ever noticed a child writing with his hand hooked up around the top of the line of print instead of holding the pencil underneath the writing as most people do? Biopsychologist Jerre Levy proposed that the hooked, or inverted writing posture indicates same-side brain and hand specialization, rather than the usual oppo-site connection. A left-handed "hooker" would have language in the left hemisphere, and vice versa. Not enough is known as yet to make responsible suggestions about what you should do if your child is a "hooker," but it may be a sign that other learning tasks are being approached in a divergent way—and it probably isn't something that the child can easily change.

Sometimes neither side seems to be able to take control. Ambidex-terity which persists after age six may indicate that the child has not yet settled on one dominant hemisphere for language processing. This lack of an effective boss has been blamed for reading problems and language disabilities. An extreme example of the latter is stutter-ing, which some believe can result if the hemispheres competed to produce each word.

Should We Change Handedness?

Some parents feel they should insist a child use the right hand, but forcing the issue may create a new set of problems. Such pressure has even been suspected of causing stuttering by confusing innate brain organization or, more likely, by creating emotional conflict. Given current information, the best advice seems to be to let your child be the guide about which will be the preferred hand.

I once knew a four-year-old girl whose father, a physician, insisted she use her right hand instead of her preferred left because he thought he could force her left hemisphere to become dominant. He was convinced that this switch would counteract a family tendency toward reading problems. When he asked my opinion, I reminded him that even top neuropsychologists are hesitant about tampering with the developing brain. More important, the child was clearly a nervous wreck. Undeterred, he persisted, and I lost track of the case until two years later when a tutor called me. She had been hired to work with the little girl, who had just been diagnosed as having a learning disability—accompanied by emotional problems. Would she have had it anyway? I don't know.

We need better information on this whole subject. In the meanwhile, what should parents keep in mind?

—Specialists who study growing brains assert vehemently that we do not yet know enough to fool around with children's development in any way that violates common sense.

—If members of your family are non-right-handed, you may transmit the tendency even if you are right-handed.

—If your child is not right-handed, it does not mean that he will automatically be either reading disabled or a visual-spatial genius, but he may have a better statistical chance for both.

—Ambidexterity may suggest incomplete language lateralization, putting a child more at risk for delay in language or reading. If your child does not have a hand preference by age five, shows signs of language delay described in Chapter 7, and has difficulty with school readiness, you might consider a professional evaluation. Please try to shield the child from your anxiety, however. You don't want to *create* a "problem"!

—Likewise, if your family includes people who suffer from allergies, migraine, or autoimmune disorders and reading, spelling, writing, or speech problems, keep an eye on the early learning patterns of your children.

—Boys are more at risk for all developmental language disorders than are girls. Prenatal testosterone might play a role in this scenario.

—At this time, there is no solid evidence that "mixed dominance" of hand, foot, or eye are of any diagnostic importance.

"THE OTHER DIFFERENCE" BETWEEN BOYS AND GIRLS

Alike but Different

After a recent parents' meeting, one mother came up to me with a question which was obviously troubling her.

"I don't know what to do about my five-year-old twins," she confessed. "I'm doing my best to raise them in a 'nonsexist' environment, but Shauna spends a lot of time playing 'house' with her friends, and Buddy only wants to build things and run around the neighborhood. No matter how much I encourage them toward other activities, they seem to be stereotyping themselves!"

I didn't have a quick answer to this one, either, because the topic of sex differences is hotly debated in professional circles. First of all, there are many more differences between children of the same sex than between the sexes. If we lined up all the boys and then all the girls in the United States on the basis of almost any characteristic, there would be lots more in the overlapping group of boys and girls together than out at the different ends.

Nevertheless, two important strands of research are confirming what parents have known all along: Overall, boys and girls prefer different activities and excel at different skills. They may even think differently. Much of this variation is clearly due to environmental factors, but some of it may reflect biological variation in brain organization.

Females score better on tests of verbal skills. Female infants are more sensitive to voices, particularly their mother's, and are more easily startled by loud noises. The majority of girls talk earlier than boys. They score better on tests of verbal abilities throughout elementary years, tending to master reading and writing sooner and to excel in grammar and spelling. They are more verbally fluent and do better on tests of naming objects quickly. Females, overall, rely more on talking, and have fewer language disorders and better hearing throughout life. Generally, they are superior to males in fine motor movements. Socially, they are more sensitive to others' facial expressions; girls, but not boys, recognize photographs of their mother as early as four months. They pick up "clues" from the environment more subtly; this ability for incidental learning may account for the phenomenon of "woman's intuition."

Males, on the other hand, excel overall in tests of visual-spatial skills. They are better at moving three-dimensional objects around in their minds and understanding relationships in the physical world. Studies in different cultures have shown they are better at solving mazes—a task which many women find irritating. Here in the United States, boys consistently do better in mathematical reasoning (not necessarily computation); in one study they outpaced girls at age thirteen in the "highly gifted" math category by thirteen to one. By tenth grade, the majority of boys of normal IQ have passed most girls up in math. This differential could be related to their tendency to solve problems by touching and looking instead of "talking" them through, since higher math requires a type of abstract reasoning based on relationships in the physical world.

Many boys shine at activities requiring large body movement, and they show more aggressive behavior. They are less dependent on others' reactions for their own judgments, being more influenced by the objective characteristics of a situation.

Before we conclude that these differences are all rooted in biology, however, it is important to remember two facts: There are many children of both sexes who don't fit the pattern, and it has often been shown that adults tend to treat boys and girls differently—even when they think they do not. No one can measure how these subtle pressures have contributed to the differences between the sexes.

Sex and the Hemispheres

New techniques have been developed to test differences in the activity of the two hemispheres. Special earphones direct competing messages into left and right ears to see which (opposite) hemisphere responds to various kinds of stimuli. Likewise, pictures or printed words are flashed into the left or right visual fields to test each side's capabilities. Combined with studies of electrical brain wave patterns, this research indicates that many girls have earlier left hemisphere language lateralization, but overall abilities more widely distributed. Consequently, they are better able to use both hemispheres interchangeably, which may account for their skill at picking up nuances of a situation or doing several things at once. How many women's husbands wonder how they can talk on the phone, cook dinner, and discipline the children all at the same time?

Boys (and some girls) seem to have more assertive right hemispheres, particularly when they are young. Their interest in large-motor and visual-spatial play activities (climbing, building, manipulating) accompanies later maturation of left-hemisphere language centers—and puts many little boys at a disadvantage in school, although this right-hemisphere exercise may make them better at math later on. By the time language is fully lateralized, it is shoved firmly into the male left hemisphere; consequently, when information comes in, more of an either-or choice of strategies must be made. Boys may miss information because they are concentrating on another kind of input. Yet they score higher in tests of abstract thinking because they are not as dependent on outside cues.

What accounts for these differences? Perhaps it is true that male hormones in the womb "masculinize" brain organization, creating greater right-hemisphere development and slowed language lateralization. So far, no one has pinpointed all the reasons for prenatal hormone balances, but look for continuing research on this topic. In light of the findings about reading problems, left-handedness, and allergies, I was intrigued to see a study of one group of children, mainly boys, who were exceptionally gifted in mathematics and thus were presumed to have superior right-hemisphere functioning. They proved twice as likely to be left-handed and six times more likely to have allergies than the general population.

What Can Parents Do?

We are only beginning to understand the influence of sex differences in our society. Perhaps you wonder, "What's wrong with differences, anyway?" and they may, indeed, be inevitable. Nevertheless, if a child is going to be penalized at any stage in the learning process because of lagging development, parents will want to take some action.

—There are certain individual differences that you can't do anything about. Each child's basic pattern of brain organization is valuable. Parents are often the main cheering section for one whose pattern is slightly divergent from school expectations. I think the term "nontraditional learner" is a helpful one for describing such youngsters, whether male or female.

—It is impossible to sort out the effects of environmental influence, but you and the school may be orchestrating gender differences by subtle attitudes of which you are not aware.

—Male and female brains have slightly different organization at the level where right and left hemispheres take over separate jobs. From what we know about plasticity, however, this pattern might be modifiable by early experience.

—Young boys (and some girls) suffer needlessly in early school years if they lack verbal and fine motor skills. Likewise, your daughter (or son) may bog down in mathematical and some types of abstract reasoning if she lacks visual-spatial ability. We don't know if—or how much—you can shape these abilities, but it makes sense to plan activities with an eye to balance. Consult the suggestions listed under "Expanding Learning for Boys and Girls."

—Encourage your school to appreciate each child's talents. When I go into a second grade classroom and see that all the spelling papers with smiley faces have girls' names on them, I understand why boys sometimes grow up resenting the female of the species.

—Boys' later-blooming verbal abilities put them more at risk for early learning problems; they may be better candidates for grade retention in the early years. If your son has a late birthday, consider his learning pattern carefully before you enter him in kindergarten. A professional evaluation may be helpful.

—Early-maturing brains seem to develop superior language skills, whereas later maturers of *both sexes* tend to be better at visual-spatial reasoning and other right-hemisphere skills. Since some girls have this latter pattern, they should be encouraged to excel at activities which suit them. We could use more good female engineers and architects! Boys who are early mental maturers may show superior verbal skills.

EXPANDING LEARNING FOR BOYS AND GIRLS

Attitudes

—Be aware of subtle pressures you exert. Parental models may be one of the most important factors in creating sex differences.

—Fathers seem more likely to perpetuate sex stereotypes with children than do mothers.

—Boys may be placed "at risk" for educational problems by a lack of responsiveness in their mothers; girls are more "at risk" if they lack exposure to challenges.

—Praise high-potential girls for achievements just as you would praise boys. Don't lower your expectations for either sex on the basis of anticipated differences.

—Don't assume that girls can't do math or boys won't be interested in reading. Your assumptions may become self-fulfilling prophecies.

—Be alert to your child's "style" of responding and its influence on your interactions. For example, a child who is very context-sensitive will sense your moods and say things to make you feel positive toward him, and vice-versa. You may need to help some boys be more sensitive in their personal relationships. Tell them what you want them to say. ("It really made me feel uncomfortable when you didn't respond after I told you about my new job. If you made a comment, I would know you were interested.")

—Be sympathetic to some inevitable pressures in school that are unfair. Whereas expectations in primary schools are sometimes more appropriate for little girls, some college entrance exams may favor male performance.

—Help all children learn to rely on their own judgment. Girls in science class tend to look to adults or peers, while boys are better at judging their own work.

—Don't provide too much assistance as children confront unfamiliar equipment or activities. They will gain skill and confidence if they "tough it out" themselves. New challenges call out talents from both hemispheres and force them to work together.

Activities

—Provide all children with toys and experiences that appeal to both hemispheres. Our best guess is that the brain becomes organized according to the stimuli that come into it.

—Show your child how to play in a variety of ways, avoiding sex stereotypes. Mother may be surprised how much fun she can have with an electric train or a set of blocks; Dad can read to his son in addition to playing baseball with him. Boys can enjoy needlework and girls love carpentry.

—Since children have strong toy preferences even before age three, just providing variety isn't enough. You may have to sit down and *play* together. Your interest is the best motivator of all, and having fun is sure to help the hemispheric partnership.

—Encourage children to use mechanical and scientific equipment: telescopes, microscopes, cameras, radio kits, and science kits. Let them take things apart. Girls may need to *talk* their way through, and boys should also be encouraged to use words describing what they are doing and seeing.

—You may need to help some children broaden their contexts and help others focus theirs. Broadening means calling attention to elements in a situation that they have missed. ("While you were watching TV, did you notice that Dad was having a phone conversation with your school bus driver?") Focusing calls for specific suggestions. ("While you're watching that TV program for social studies, why not save your talk with Sue until later?")

—Some children may need help relating ideas to their own experiences ("When the characters in the story couldn't achieve their ambition, did it remind you of the time you didn't make the first team?"), whereas others may profit from a push toward more abstract, less personal thinking ("You noticed that it is harder to squeeze the icing out of the narrower tube; can you figure out a rule about how force and the size of a tube are related?").

—Remember that many children—even into teen years—must manipulate the environment to learn; they don't get information well by only listening.

—More verbal children may need to talk through problems in math, chemistry, and physics.

—The LOGO computer language, in which children learn programming by moving a "turtle" on the screen, may help the development of visual-spatial concepts and reasoning. I would avoid the overly simplified versions of LOGO on the market and use this program as it was originally intended—after children are about five years old.

—You can help both sexes develop lagging spatial skills by play that involves manipulating and exploring three-dimensional space and objects.

BACK TO THE LUMPERS AND SPLITTERS

Strategies for Learning

Let's return to specific recommendations for Tim and Carl. Although there are as many styles of learning as there are individuals, flexibility in presenting material can help most children understand and remember more easily. The idea is to capitalize on the child's natural "style," while boosting weak areas with extra help. I like to make suggestions on the basis of practical observation of a child's strengths and weaknesses.

Carl, our splitter, is big on facts, details, and "right" answers. More interested in information than in people, he is an industrious, well-organized student. Depending on the school he attends, his lack of creativity and insight may be a problem, but youngsters like Carl generally do well in traditional classrooms. They thrive with a lecture method of instruction and objective, short-answer tests. Their weaknesses show up when they must stand back and view the whole forest, instead of concentrating on the individual trees. Often a child like this becomes lost unless someone tells him where he is supposed to be going.

Carl had a habit of getting caught up with details and missing the main point of class discussions. I gave him this drawing of the forest and the trees and suggested his teacher take him aside when he started to get enmeshed in splitting and ask, "Carl, can you stand back and look for the forest, or are you bumping into trees?" One day, he looked up in pure frustration and said, "I haven't even gotten to the trees. I'm stuck in the bushes!"

Carl benefited from being encouraged to look for the big picture before he started anything. We tried to help him see connections and understand how details fit together to make wholes. One tactic that helped him pull ideas together was summarizing a paragraph or a story in only ten words. He learned to think about his main idea before he tried to make a point in a discussion. His teachers tried to provide Carl with a framework before he started to plug in isolated facts. They discovered that many students liked a verbal outline and a blackboard diagram of the general ideas to be covered at the beginning of a lesson. ("Today we're going to talk about the causes of the

SEEING THE FOREST OR THE TREES

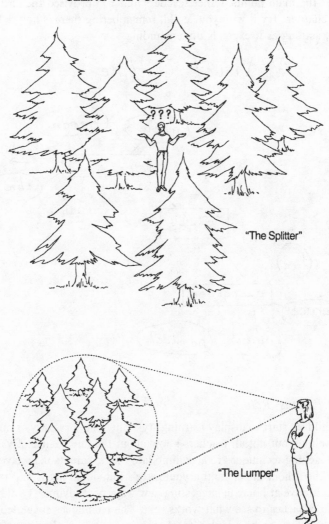

"The Splitter"

"The Lumper"

American revolution. You will need to think about what we have learned about life in the colonies before you can understand them.") They used time lines and other devices to put facts into perspective.

Drawing diagrams of ideas is hard for many people. Since I have been using this technique with students, however, I am a convert. They don't care how inept I am; they love the way it helps them "see" the main points. Other teachers and I improvised the ones in this chapter. Try it with your child, remembering there is no "right" way, as long as it expands understanding.

A Visual Outline

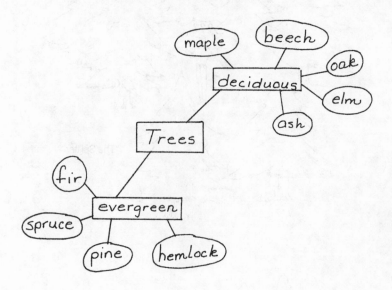

The Parents' Role

Children start to display learning style differences as early as nursery school, but not all teachers know about the importance of varying teaching techniques to accommodate them. Parents may have to help the school understand a youngster's individual needs and take the initiative at home in suggesting new ways of studying. Try different approaches to see what works best. The techniques suggested in this chapter can be adapted to almost any age level. Parents often remark that their learning patterns are similar to those of their children, so they have strategies of their own to share. Unfortunately, some also limit the child's early experiences because of their own preferences.

We will never know how different Carl might have been if he had received more encouragement for creative, visual, and wholistic

Mapping Ideas:

Some Causes of the Civil War

thinking during early years. He never enjoyed three-dimensional puzzles, mazes, or "hidden pictures"—and since Mother hated them, too, they were never in the house. He really liked lining up his collection of toy cars, practicing writing numerals, and building with plastic blocks that snapped together in set patterns. Instead of free-form art activities, he was encouraged to color inside lines. This child probably had a predisposition toward sequential, analytic processing, and his early environment did little to alter it. Should we try to expand children like Carl into more versatile thinkers? As scientists probe hemispheric development, this question will take on increased significance.

Weird but Wonderful

Then there's Tim. A nontraditional learner who needs to see and do rather than listen, who reasons with images rather than words, Tim is on the other end of the splitter-lumper scale. He can see whole forests easily, but usually lacks the patience to go in and analyze the trees. He jumps into the middle of situations and may intuitively come up with the right solution—or one which is way off base. He can't organize himself—or his strategies for school work.

"How can he read so carelessly and still get the idea?" his English teacher asks. "Tim gets the answer but can't write out the equation," complains his math teacher. Sometimes, if people are willing to listen as he struggles to describe it, his idea is "weird but wonderful." The Tims of this world usually have a harder time in school than the Carls, but not because they lack ability. If your child is like Tim, your work is cut out for you, but the first step must be to get rid of the words "lazy" or "stupid."

Understanding Tim's strengths and weaknesses helps explain some of his inconsistencies. For example, he liked math until seventh grade, but now found himself unable to "get it." He didn't realize that, in elementary school, math class had involved a lot of *doing,* writing on the board, and manipulating objects and shapes. Now, he was in a class where the teacher taught by talking. Considering Tim's difficulty with remembering even one sentence at a time, it is no surprise he was in trouble. I explained to Tim that he needed to ask the teacher to *show* in addition to telling him and that he needed to write problems in his notebook as well as sit and listen (or fail to!). Fortunately, his teachers were all willing to cooperate because they recognized that he really wanted to improve.

Tim was missing homework assignments which, teachers being only human, were often given quickly at the end of class: "Oh, by the way, tomorrow's homework is to do all the odd-numbered examples on pages 17 and 20 and write a short paragraph about the effects of climatic conditions on fossil formation." Forget it! (That's what Tim usually did.) Tim's parents went in to school to explain that he needed to have directions *written down* or given more slowly. He may eventually need to use a tape recorder, as some students do, in high school lecture classes. Simultaneously, he can practice trying to remember longer and longer chunks by repeating them back and working on better note-taking skills. Understanding his style does not mean lowering our ultimate expectations for him.

At home, in addition to reassuring him that all this work is worth the effort, Tim's parents can help him organize longer reading assignments in a visual form. Tim loves mapping ideas to help him remember what he has studied. It is also never too late to work on language development and expression of ideas at the dinner table; these habits may carry over into increased classroom participation.

Parents can help with auditory memory by practicing a limited number of directions at a time ("Please go upstairs, close your bedroom window, and bring down a bar of soap."). They will undoubtedly have to help him organize his homework time and be available to proofread reports. A typewriter or word processor will help him with fluency in his writing. Students like Tim often like to study to music; if it works, let him.

Tim may need special help from a tutor or teacher who understands his learning style. The bad news is that he will have to work harder in school than some of his friends. The good news is that he can succeed—both in school and, more importantly, when real life exerts a different set of demands. The ultimate success of many "lumpers" confirms this pattern as *different, not inferior.*

Does accepting divergent learning styles mean lowering academic standards? *No!* Helping children achieve and enjoy learning can only improve the intellectual climate. Parents and teachers must take the time and effort to meet individual needs without caving in on expectations. Truly, we all have our work cut out for us!

Different Drummers

This chapter has been about making connections and balancing differences—between the hemispheres, between the sexes, between individuals. We are just beginning to explore neural variations underlying the colorful mosaic of human talent. Differences make us interesting and provide society with a broad pool of abilities. Underlying the history of human accomplishment are myriad combinations of left and right, male and female, lumpers and splitters. The most effective thinkers are those who can link their mental talents in varying combinations—who can see ideas and plan their implementation, grasp a total problem and analyze its elements, create and communicate.

We're not sure where people get their unique styles of taking on the world, or how much we can—or should—change them. It may be true that atypical hemispheric organization produces the best thinkers of all! The suggestions in this book are for expanding, not altering. I hope you will apply them with the love and common sense which are your parental gifts. By broadening bridges, you can ease your child's intellectual passage, for differences often cause children pain. Adults are privileged, because they are respected and even acclaimed for uniqueness. They choose the arenas in which they wish to appear and avoid those where they are inept. Children are not so lucky. If their skills are unbalanced, if they aren't good at some school tasks, there is little respite from inadequacy. Parents, frustrated by their child's defeats, can easily lose sight of talents which reach beyond the classroom walls.

One little girl, a fourth grader whose main strengths are creative and intuitive, came up with an important thought one day as we were discussing a story about prejudice. Face clenched in concentration, she struggled mightily to find words for her idea. Here they are:

Feelings About Others
Some people are nicer
Because their brains
Are differently attached to their hearts
Than other people's.

No matter how your child's brains are attached, I hope you can respect that singular pattern even as you work to integrate its design. Society needs pathways to the future built by effective, flexible, and interesting minds.

"Do Pigs Have Wishbones?":
Unfolding Language

ONE EVENING A NUMBER OF YEARS AGO, WHEN OUR YOUNGEST son was about four, I was preparing dinner and studying for an exam on children's language development while he pursued his favorite hobby of rearranging the kitchen cupboards. Suddenly he gazed up, regarded the pork chops in my hand, and asked, "Do pigs have wishbones?" I remember laughing at this "cute" comment and jotting it down on a scrap of paper, but I don't recall how I responded; quick explanations were the rule in those days of return to graduate study and part-time work. No doubt Doug was left to contemplate the mysteries of wishbones on his own.

Not long ago, with student days and exams far behind me, I came upon that scrap of paper stuck in a dusty cookbook. After years of studying other children's language development, I was struck by the irony of having overlooked the importance of my own son's words. With those simple four words, Doug, like most children of his age, showed that he had mastered the most complex rule system of the human intellect in a few short years—with no formal instruction. I didn't pay much attention at the time, but that funny question, with all the learning that lay behind it, presaged well for his future with reading, writing, organizing solutions to problems, reasoning about abstract ideas, and even leadership ability. Moreover, by using language, Doug was building his own brain!

I have learned a great deal since that day in the kitchen, and I would like to help you appreciate, better than I, your own children's language development. To understand how you can take the most constructive role in helping it unfold, we should first consider the four things that a child must learn: its purposes, its mechanics, its meanings, and its rules.

THE PURPOSES OF LANGUAGE

Nature's Mysterious Device

Where does language come from? Experts have waged intellectual fisticuffs about whether it is all preprogrammed or determined by input into specialized areas of the brain. As usual, the answer lies somewhere in between. Both "language," a general term for the use of verbal symbols, and "speech," its means of expression, are an instinctive reflection of humans' need to communicate. Did you know that a two-month-old reaching out with one finger pointed is practicing a form of language? Have you noticed how, by the age of six to nine months, *without knowing a single word,* a child can participate in a "conversation" and even control it? (If you doubt this, watch baby and Grandma sometime.) Nature has built the basics of language into most infants' brains.

A deaf child starts to babble at the same age as do hearing children, so we know that auditory stimulation is not necessary for prelanguage development. One of the most intriguing theories has proposed a "language acquisition device" somewhere in the brain which makes it inevitable. No one has yet located this mysterious machine (which I whimsically picture as a small square box with lots of wires sticking out), but scientists have yet to come up with a better explanation. Infants around the world who are exposed to different languages and dialects all babble remarkably similar sounds. They produce vowels before consonants and are instinctively sensitive to sound differences. Infants' left hemispheres can already sort out human speech from noises in the environment. You might say that children are biologically programmed to talk.

One young mother takes great delight in reporting her infant daughter's progress to me. "Only two months old, and I swear she's imitating me. I say 'hi,' and she says 'i-i-i-i.' My husband says it isn't possible." Her husband has underestimated the power of the language acquisition device—and also the verbal inclinations of many females of the species, who usually operate on a slightly faster speech timetable than their male peers. Yet despite the brain's predilection, it takes coaching from the environment to build the staggering number of neural connections required for further development.

The deaf children who start to babble do not develop speech without special intervention, although they show their predisposition to communicate when taught sign language. Hearing language is a must, and the better the language environment, the better the outcome. Parents have a bigger role in this critical area of learning than in almost any other. Fortunately, nature has also programmed parents instinctively to become their child's best teachers. The first lesson they present is about loving communication.

Primitive Purposes

An infant's first communication usually takes the form of a piercing wail, which sounds as if it arises from a primitive part of the brain. It does. Early vocalizations emerge from the limbic system, which is the early "mammal brain" responsible, among other things, for emotion. As the child begins to coo, babble, and receive verbal messages, new networks in the upper-level cerebral cortex begin to form. By six to nine months the higher centers can assert some control over their primitive neighbor. Yet language throughout life is closely linked with emotion, and it is important to remember that children who get enough cuddling and unconditional love have a better chance at learning language—and everything else.

Full language capabilities take decades to develop, for the necessary cell networks are slow maturing ones. Specialized centers need to be stimulated so they can take over the jobs of listening, speaking, and understanding. Most children invite your assistance. Even two-month-olds seek out face-to-face interaction. The adult's positive response is instinctive—and important. If Mother, for example, acts "different," seeming aloof or upset, the infant responds with body language signaling distress. During the first six months a strong bond with a parent or caretaker is important for many reasons: to set good patterns of personal interaction, keep the limbic system purring, and teach the rules of the game of conversation.

Learning the Game of Conversation

Did you know that playing peek-a-boo is a language game? It teaches turn taking, the first lesson. Between four and nine months this concept is practiced over and over, and most children skillfully pick up the idea. They begin to learn that "talk" involves waiting for your turn as they imitate adult words and sounds. There are other rules to be learned: gestures go along with sounds and help everyone understand what is meant; you can get people to do things for you by making noises of various kinds; people respond when you "talk" to them. Sometimes they even know what you mean: "Well, how did that taste, Jimmy?" Jimmy wiggles eloquently and emits a loud burp. "Oh, you liked it, didn't you!"

All of these reasons and conventions for using language come under one heading—*pragmatics.* Children who lack them are at a serious disadvantage because they have trouble using language as a tool. Much "social maladjustment" stems from such poor understanding —not of the words themselves, but of the game of conversation. Such children can't size up where the other person is "coming from" or understand how to incorporate others' points of view into their behavior. They may verbally barge into situations or withdraw wondering why no one seems to like them.

Helping Children with Purposes for Language

Look at this listing of seven reasons for using language, and notice how many are based on interaction with others.

1. **Instrumental:** To satisfy needs and wants.

"Lou, if you would like a cookie, please use words to ask me instead of whining and pounding on the shopping cart."

2. **Regulatory:** To control the behavior of others and of self.

"Let's talk about a fair way to decide who plays with the truck now. Then we'll talk about how you'd like to take turns."

3. **Interactional:** To establish and maintain contact with others.

"While I'm getting dinner, I love it when you stay near and tell me about your day."

4. **Personal:** To express choices, assert the self, and take responsibility.

"Don't be afraid to tell me which one you want; I'll let you know if I don't have enough money."

"If you feel sad, it might help to talk about it."

"Why don't you talk to Ms. Smith before school tomorrow. I would be proud if you could try to solve this problem without asking me to call the teacher."

5. **Learning:** To ask questions and get information.

"I don't know if pigs have wishbones, but that surely is an interesting question. I'll help you ask the butcher when we go to the store tomorrow."

"I like to have you ask questions about things you're interested in —it lets me know you're building your brain for thinking."

6. **Imaginative:** To pretend, to create images and patterns.

"Let's take turns making up stories about a pretend trip we would like to take."

"Let's think of all the things that would happen if our street turned to chocolate pudding. Can you make a picture in your mind of what it would look like?"

7. **Representational:** To inform others, to tell about ideas.

"Please tell me your ideas about whether we should go to the library this morning or wait until after dinner."

"Your report for science sounds so interesting; can you explain to me how a battery works?"

"Would you like me to help you and Mark organize a debate about that?"

These lessons don't end when school starts. Maturation of language pathways is not completed until at least adolescence, and possibly later. Parents can demonstrate all these purposes and patiently help a child experiment with them. Endless "why?" questions are wearing, but they are the foundation of language as a tool for thinking, a major implement for intellectual growth.

CHARACTERISTICS OF LANGUAGE-BUILDING HOMES

—Children find adults' voices pleasant to listen to (at least usually!).

—Children see parents using language to communicate and solve problems. Adults encourage "talking through" situations before taking action.

—Parents or caretakers share activities and talk about them with each child, and give frequent praise.

—Adults respond positively to childrens' attempts to communicate. They listen when the child talks, refrain from interrupting, and show pleasure in the child's use of language.

—The family does not emphasize silence or submission as signs of being "good." Children are encouraged to "play" with words and express feelings verbally.

—Adults create "slots" for childrens' participation in family conversations.

—The child is encouraged to talk about what is happening during play with puzzles, blocks, etc., and to describe what they are doing or thinking. ("Tell me what your block house looks like." "How is that shape different from this one?")

—Children must use language to have needs met. Whining, crying, or gesturing do not get children what they want.

—Adults modify their own talk to the child according to his ability to understand. They also rephrase and expand the child's speech to teach more advanced forms. (Child: "I dooed it." Adult: "Yes, you did the whole puzzle, didn't you? Now would you like to do this one?")

—Records, "talking" picture books, tapes, and other toys which encourage listening skills are used.

—Television does not substitute for conversation. Children learn to formulate and not just to soak up input.

Mother or "Mother Figure"?

Studies of early language strongly emphasize the mother's role. What if she is not the primary caretaker? This question is a hard one to answer, for it is clear that there is a biological base for mother-child interactions that lay the foundations for communication. Yet warm and loving physical care is not enough. A normal child who had been well cared for and loved by deaf and mute parents had abnormal language when he began to receive regular therapy after he was three years old. Fortunately, he was young enough to make up the lost ground, but the message is clear: Exposure to language is necessary. If you must choose a mother substitute for your child, or even a frequent babysitter, insist on consistent, affectionate care and a real concern for good language development. Check out grammar, vocabulary, and voice quality as carefully as you check on health and reliability. Don't have your child encouraged to "be quiet" for convenience, given poor models of speech, or cheated out of a rich vocabulary. Find someone who enjoys conversation and reading, who will discipline with words rather than physical action. Likewise, when choosing day-care settings, put good language near the top of your list of "musts."

Here are a few suggestions for you—or your child's caretaker—to build the pragmatic base for language learning:

—Associate talking with warm, personal interactions. Young children understand loving physical contact better than long strings of words.

—Initiate games of sharing and turn taking. Take turns banging a spoon on a tray. Build a tower and let the child knock it down. Take turns "talking," even if half of the conversation sounds like gibberish.

—"Where's your tummy? Where's your toe?" is a good example of an instinctive parent-child game that teaches both communication and vocabulary. "What does the kitty say?" is another favorite.

—Show your child from earliest months how to look into someone's eyes when talking to them. This comes naturally to most children. If your child habitually avoids eye contact, stop, gently turn his chin, say, "Look at my eyes," and wait for eye contact before you go on talking. Repeated problems may signal an underlying difficulty.

—Use attention-getting phrases such as "Look here" or "See?" to make sure the child is "with" you.

—When a child is old enough to start conveying meaning, let her know when she has not made herself clear, and why. ("When you said you didn't want to go and then got your coat, I wondered what you meant.")

—Help your child get you to do things tactfully. ("I liked it when you said, 'Daddy, please help me when you're ready.' It made me feel as if you cared about what I was doing, too.")

—Don't confuse a child with "body talk" different from your words. If you are irritated or upset, express it in a reasonable and honest way.

—Adults and older children instinctively "pare down" their language to the child's level. Trust your instincts when you find yourself simplifying.

—If the child has older siblings, encourage them to talk to the baby. You will be astonished at what good teachers they are, and they will bask in the praise and warm feeling that their help elicits.

—Children learn better at first if there are only two speakers, but family conversation is important too. The child should not always be the center of the conversation, as observing "grown-up" talk teaches the rules.

—Dramatic play, dolls, and puppets help children put themselves in another person's place. Practice exchanging roles ("You be the mommy now and I'll be the little boy.").

—Let young children be important message-bearers. ("Please tell Daddy we will be ready to go in ten minutes.") Good practice for remembering things they hear.

—Encourage contacts with peers. Children learn about language from social play. You may need to bite your tongue as they work out minor differences.

—Let your child teach you how to do something or give directions for an everyday action. Follow the directions exactly to show the effect of her words. A classic example is describing how to make a peanut butter sandwich. You may get some mutual laughs trying to spread the peanut butter before picking up the knife or opening the jar! Such direction-giving skills are rarely perfected before middle school years.

—Young children gradually learn to handle indirect messages. If you say, "Would you like to help me clean the dog's pen?" don't be offended if your child responds, "No," and goes on playing. One mother was looking at pictures with her little girl and asked, "Do you see what the animals are doing?" "Uh huh," agreed the child. Until "indirection" is mastered, you may need to be more specific if you expect a response.

—Your sensitivity also provides a lesson in inferring information. If your son comes in and announces, "The swing is broken," and there is no swing in your yard, you might answer, "Oh, you must have been playing at Jimmy's house." Inference takes a long time to develop because it goes beyond the concrete facts presented.

—Above all, make language input pleasant for your child. Children who have learned to "tune out" adult voices because they were loud, bossy, or hurtful may start school with poor listening habits.

Missed Lessons

I once tested a little boy who was labeled a "misfit" in second grade. His teacher thought he might have a learning disability because he was unable to remember the simplest directions. He had difficulty answering questions and often "said the wrong thing" to other children. After testing Paul, I knew exactly what she meant. He looked terrified when asked a question; tears actually appeared in his eyes several times when he had to express an idea. He needed to have most questions repeated, and he couldn't say back more than three numbers in a row, but he was good at block puzzles and making sense out of pictures. This profile is, indeed, typical of children with language disabilities, and I was quite confident of my diagnosis until Paul's father came to pick him up and asked to see me privately.

"I don't want to blame my wife for Paul's problem," he confided, "but she doesn't have much patience. Actually, she yells at the kids all the time—sometimes she even swears and puts them down in a real nasty way. Our other ones fight back, but Paul just acts like he doesn't hear it at all. I feel terrible telling you this, but I thought you should know."

So much for my clear-cut diagnosis! How much did Paul's negative experiences with listening and conversation have to do with his language disability? The "problem" was a real one at the time I saw him, but its source remains open to speculation. Learning to "tune out" had enabled him to survive at home, but it wasn't helping at school! We tried to help his mother understand Paul's needs, and a specialist worked with him on skills of listening and expressing himself. Now a teenager, he is still a "loner" who has trouble relating socially to his classmates. I often wonder what would have happened if his first language teacher had taken the time to give him all the lessons.

MILESTONES IN COMMUNICATION

Ages for each stage are approximate:

By 2 months: responds to Mother's speech

Birth–9 months: cries, smiles, vocalizes, laughs, reaches out, makes gestures of giving, pointing, showing

By 2 years: can cooperate in communication; understands how to ask and answer, take turns in talking

can use language for different purposes (to get something, to tell about something, to relate to others)

By 3 years: gives related response to question

changes topics rapidly when talking

By 4 years: pretends conversation on toy telephone, waits for "answer"

By age 10: can stick to a topic

varies conversation according to listener

can use language to give "hints"

understands social "rules" for language use

There is no question that some children pick up the forms and uses of language more easily than others, and Paul might have had difficulty despite the most loving attention. Most language problems are not the parents' fault! Variations in language development sometimes reflect differences in intelligence. On the high end of the scale, one of the hallmarks of giftedness is precocious vocabulary knowledge and use of words for expressing and playing with ideas. Yet some children with delayed language development are bright. Research on hemispheric dominance suggests that language problems may run in certain families who make up for this relative weakness by extreme capability in fields requiring visual and spatial expertise. How do you know if your child is learning language on schedule? Some of the earliest signs are in the mechanics of language—how accurately it is received and pronounced.

MASTERING THE MECHANICS

Taking in Language

Like any production system, language has two main parts: input and output. Without good raw material going in, the quality of the output inevitably suffers—in auto factories and in the language production system. The name given to the ability to use sounds is *phonology.* Phonological development starts when sounds of speech activate waiting neural networks.

First of all, the child must be able to pay attention. Ability to focus on important sounds and differentiate them from background noise originates far down in the brain. It comes naturally to most infants, but you can help by providing an environment where noise is reasonably controlled. "Talking" with just one person at a time also helps.

Second, the child must be able to discriminate one sound from another. Is Mom referring to a "block" or a "clock"? It's easier if the object is available for reference. The "critical period" for mastering sound discrimination is probably between birth and five years; if the brain doesn't get its practice during these years, the child may have later difficulty with reading, spelling, and speaking clearly.

Getting Out the Words

One of our neighbor's children said "pasketti" for spaghetti so often that the whole family renamed this staple. Such confusion of sounds shows that the left hemisphere hasn't perfected its management job. First, sounds in the word must be received clearly, in the right order, and held in "short-term memory" long enough for the brain to register them. Then the order must be recaptured and forwarded to the speech apparatus for production. A diagram of this part of the input-output system might look like the illustration on page 154.

During the first year the brain gets lots of practice hearing and imitating sounds, but most children are not ready to produce real words until after their first birthday. Like many other skills, this development cannot be forced, for it depends on maturation of connections from the brain to the speech apparatus. Other brain areas, maturing simultaneously, take care of the short-term memory that is required. Simplified consonant-vowel combinations and mispronunciations are typical of first words: "poo" or "poon" for "spoon," "ga-ga" or "goggy" for "doggy." Articulation and memory improve with increased practice and longer words. Here are some suggestions for encouraging development of the mechanics of speech:

—Adults tend to speak more clearly and pause longer between sounds than in adult speech because fast, rapidly changing sound patterns are confusing for children. Being sensitive to the child's response prevents your shutting down the system by overloading it!

—It's OK to exaggerate the contours of your voice to help the child get the message. Scaling down words is good for babies

BUILDING LANGUAGE: REPETITION WITHOUT MEANING

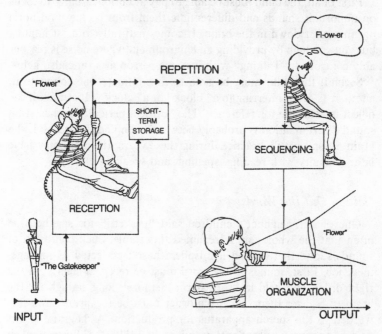

("mama," "nana"), but baby talk which models incorrect pronunciation is not necessary.

—Early games of imitating tongue movements help build the speech apparatus. Practice imitating different pitches and volume.

—Get a book of childhood games to find possibilities for language building. Games of syllable repetition are excellent practice. When the child can repeat one syllable ("ba"), try two ("ba-da") and three ("ba-da-ba"; "ba-ga-da"). Later, try words. Keep it easy enough to be fun. Preschoolers and even older children benefit from games remembering and repeating words in order like "Grandmother's Trunk," "Telephone," etc.

—Games with rhyming words help later listening and reading.

—"Pig Latin" and similar games help older children remember and sequence sounds. Children with reading problems often have trouble here.

—Children differ widely in their tendency to imitate adult speech. If the child seems unresponsive, make food or other treats contingent on some kind of verbal effort.

—Children need time to think of the right words and pronounce them; don't steal their chance to learn by doing it for them.

—If your child mispronounces a word, gently repeat it correctly. Do not expect accurate articulation of all sounds until after age seven.

—You can help with attention by touching or holding the child gently (on the chin or shoulder) while you are talking. Ask, "Can you say it back?" You may need to rephrase and simplify. Don't ignore a habit of "tuning out."

—Some children have unusual difficulty sorting out important talk from background noise. They need a limited noise environment.

—Listen with interest whenever your child wants to tell you something, and try to refrain from interrupting.

—Excess emphasis on perfection spoils the game. If you find your anxiety level building, pull back. Language which is tangled up with unpleasant feelings is hard to unravel.

—Your enthusiastic response is the trigger for your child's continued language development. Don't fall into the trap of trying to "drill" language skills; good speech develops in a context of everyday events and play.

MECHANICAL MILESTONES

Because of individual differences among children, these ages are only approximate.

First 4 months: Can distinguish between different sounds (one to two months), cooing.

6 months: Babbling (may use sounds not in English language).

9–18 months: First syllables (consonant-vowel: "ma," "ma-ma").
First consonants, usually *p, m, t,* and *k.*
First vowels, usually *a, i, u.*
Babbling may continue even after child acquires words.

By 3 years: Speech can be understood.

4–5 years: Can pronounce consonant clusters (e.g., *sm, sp, tr, cl*).

6 years: Can pronounce and distinguish between all vowel sounds.

8 years: Can pronounce and distinguish between all consonant sounds.

> *7 years:* Can remember and repeat five numbers in a row.
> *10 years:* Can remember and repeat six numbers in a row.

Mechanical Problems

Sometimes this finely tuned phonological system misfires some-where along the line. The most commonly diagnosed language prob-lem is with clear articulation. If your child is very slow in developing commonly acquired sounds or does not have intelligible speech by age three, you should first have a doctor rule out any primary physi-cal problem. Then you should seek an evaluation from a well-in-formed speech and language clinic or private therapist. Although often self-correcting, articulation disorders can be a harbinger of other language and school problems. Early help is important, while the system is still as plastic as possible.

All children repeat TV commercials and other familiar messages; it is normal when accompanying other efforts to communicate spon-taneously. A few children with a peculiar language disorder called "echolalia" don't learn to express themselves in their own words. They repeat slogans inappropriately *in place of original speech,* sounding strangely "flat," without the normal contours of the human voice. Such children usually have several signs of developmental dif-ference and are easily identified as language delayed.

Approximately one tenth of all children—mainly boys—stutter at some time during their early years. Most cases clear up spontane-ously within one year, and only 1 percent of adults are stutterers. If your child starts to stutter, ignore it for a while and keep the atmo-sphere as unpressured as possible, since perfectionism and anxiety worsen the condition. If it persists, get a professional evaluation. Stuttering may occur because language control is temporarily com-ing from both right and left hemispheres instead of just from one side.

Until the age of five years, language may not have found its perma-nent home in either side, particularly for boys. As the left hemi-sphere takes over its role as language boss, speech becomes easier and faster. Some experimenters are trying to help the brain gain language abilities by directing special tapes of music or voices into left or right hemispheres. This notion is still very controversial. Keep your own ears open to these developments, but be skeptical of anyone who promises dramatic "cures" or claims that one type of treatment can cure many different problems. Above all, steer away from any system in which language training is made unpleasant for children.

The Multilingual Dilemma

Babies of all cultures babble similar sounds at first. Soon, however, they drop the ones to which they are not exposed, and it becomes increasingly difficult to get them back. If you have ever tried to learn another language, you will probably agree. Is this a good reason to teach children foreign languages during the most sensitive period for mastering sounds? The answer to this question hinges on both the reason and the method for the "teaching." Most children who grow up in bilingual homes master both languages. For a while their overall development is a little slower, but they eventually catch up and become fluent in both. Their learning is based on the best reason—communication—and the "method" is everyday interaction with family members. This is true for *most* children. A brain with inefficient circuits for language, however, has real trouble grappling with even one set of sounds, meanings, and grammar.

Adolescents and adults can usually learn a second language as well as children who receive early instruction in a language not spoken regularly in their home. Pronunciation and inflection may never be quite as good, but older students have better strategies for mastering the rules of a new grammar. There is nothing wrong with exposing young children to foreign languages, *if* (1) the child does not have an incipient language problem (see warning signals later in this chapter); (2) the child is interested and learning is nonstressful; (3) the language is presented orally in the same way children master their natural language; (4) understanding of rules of grammar is not demanded.

There has been some discussion about whether the right hemisphere bosses the job in the learning of a second language after puberty. Research in this area may stimulate new ideas and clarify the rather muddy issue of when to introduce foreign languages in schools.

LEARNING THE RULES

The Wug That Flimmed

Four-year-old Molly listens intently. "Show me," her teacher says, "the horse kicked the cow."

Molly happily seizes the toy horse in front of her and delivers the cow a satisfying clout.

"Now listen and do this," says the teacher, "the horse is kicked by the cow."

Molly hesitates. "He just did that," she protests.

By the age of four, most children have mastered an astonishing number of rules for word order, which make up the grammar, or *syntax* of a language. Like Molly, they show sophisticated comprehension until they hit the toughest grammatical structures. How do they learn these rules? By listening, listening, listening and practicing, practicing, practicing. Growing brains sop up language and magically wring out grammatical principles without even being aware that they're doing it.

"Alright, Molly, here's another toy. Pretend this is a strange animal called a 'wug.' You try to finish what I say about the wug, OK?"

"OK!" Molly is thoroughly enjoying this game.

"This is one wug. Now there are two of them. There are two . . . ?"

"Wugs!"

"Good girl. Now listen. This wug likes to flim. Now he is . . . ?"

"Flimming!" Molly chortles and makes the toy do a little dance on the table."

"Good. Yesterday he . . . ?"

"Flimmed."

What is the purpose of this nonsense talk? It certainly isn't a vocabulary lesson. The teacher has just demonstrated that Molly can apply rules by adding appropriate endings to words she has never heard before. No one can explain why young children generalize all of these rules in a standard order; even children who are delayed in their language development follow the same pattern, only more slowly. When a new rule is first learned, it is usually overapplied, explaining why Molly says "I runned" instead of "I ran," and why a three-year-old asked for "a chee" when she wanted one piece of cheese. Most children have mastered almost all language rules by the time they begin school. Later-developing structures are the passive voice ("The horse was kicked by the cow."), time sequences which have the words reversed ("Before you mix in the flour, please beat the eggs."), comparative forms (big, bigger, biggest; some, more, most), and irregular plurals (mice, women).

Rule Problems

Some children have trouble latching on to these rules. Problems may result from poor models of grammar at home, from hearing difficulties during early years, or possibly from some delay in the brain's circuits. A child who has trouble remembering word sequences will have difficulty producing them. For some, repeated exposure just doesn't seem to "take." Here are examples from the speech of children who need some help:

Patsy, age 6: "Once upon a time there was a boy, and he said, "At this store is too big." "I want the one with not the hat."
Ben, age 9: "On a big field there is two boys in the early morning because they didn't sleep all night."
Carol, age 10: "A index is a thing and in the back of the book and it's all arranged." "Here are some characteristics I am going to tell."

These children all have an adequate command of vocabulary and a clear idea of what they mean. The problem lies with stringing words together to express the idea. Subtle variations from standard form ("on" instead of "in" a field; "tell" instead of "tell about") show problems with the nuances of oral language. When they hear their phrases repeated, they may not be aware that anything is wrong. Could an enriched language environment have helped? We really don't know, since syntactic problems are among the most difficult even for professionals to treat. The confusion may lie at a more basic neural level where the brain picks up, recognizes, and remembers patterns of all kinds. Thus, play experiences which help the brain learn to organize incoming information and learn about rules and relationships may even be important in developing grammar! There are also many ways for parents to involve children in the patterns and rules of language:

—Children demand and need lots of pattern repetition. Repetitive patterns, such as nursery rhymes, are one of the best ways to organize young brains around language.

—Expose your child to good language from the beginning. In addition to talking, start reading aloud. Avoid books with "pop" language and slang-like expressions. I remember how tired I used to be at the end of the day, but now I wish I'd taken even more time for story reading.

—Don't stop reading out loud when the child learns to read. Families traveling by car have a special opportunity for round-robin reading; we found it settled irritations and postponed the inevitable "How much longer, Daddy?"

—Children love to go to plays and puppet shows. Be wary of taxing little brains with too much excitement, and keep them infrequent and special.

—Don't trust TV to give your child good language input. One provision in the parental bill of rights is control of the on-off switch!

—Children learn syntactic rules from helpful adults. Parents tend to correct meaning more often than grammar, but you can tactfully *reshape and expand* a child's talk. If Molly says, "I runned," Dad might say, "Yes, you ran," (reshaping) then add, "You ran to get the smallest box you could find, didn't you?" (expanding).

—Linking all language learning to everyday happenings helps understanding and memory. Use concrete objects to show what you mean whenever possible. ("Look, the bat hit the ball. The ball was hit by the bat.")

—When looking at pictures together, show your child different ways to talk about one event. "See, the man is going shopping. He wants to shop for food because his children are hungry. What a big bag he has! It is bigger than the other one, but this one is the biggest of all."

—Children need to hear many questions in order to pick up the interrogative form. Practice asking Why? What? When? Where? Who? and How? questions and show your child how to answer them.

—Follow your natural tendency to increase the complexity of your sentences as your child gets older. Check understanding by asking her to restate what she thinks you said. Some children act as if they understand when they really don't.

—You can devise games using prepositions. Hiding objects and giving clues is one example. ("It is *under* something." "Look *inside* something green.") Demonstrate how you use prepositions in everyday talk. "See, I'm putting the tomatoes *beside* the pears.")

—Be patient. These rules are incredibly complicated. Often, too, the child's idea and desire to tell you about it is more important than the exact wording.

MILESTONES IN LANGUAGE RULE LEARNING

These are only a few of the many grammatical structures children master. There is wide individual variation in this aspect of language development.

18–24 months: Combines two or more words in sentences.

By age 3: Constructs sentences of three or four words.
Uses noun and verb phrases ("dat big doggie," "him want cookie").

2–4 years: Uses verb tense markers (walked, walking, runned).

3–4 years: Uses auxiliary verbs, negatives ("I won't can do").

8 years: Uses irregular plurals (women, mice).

MOVING INTO MEANING

A Question of Semantics

The patterns of a child's personal experience are the template for language understanding and expression. Attempts to teach children language by drill don't work very well because meaning is missing. When children learn language in their natural setting, meaning comes with the package because there are all kinds of props in the situation. While Mother talks about a toy, she holds it out for the child to touch. When Dad says, "Let's go for a walk," he gets his jacket out of the closet. Parents have an instinctive tendency to label objects and to provide an ongoing commentary about daily activities. Language linked to everyday events ultimately expands to descriptions, story plots, and abstract ideas. It is a long but direct route from "See baby" to the implications of "Strike while the iron is hot."

The term "semantics" is used for language meaning, from single words to long texts. While specific areas of the left hemisphere prob-

ably control sounds, grammar, and some aspects of meaning, overall
semantic abilities are hard to pin down because they go hand in hand
with mental development. A typical child repeated the above proverb
perfectly, but wondered, "Didn't they get burned when they hit the
hot irons?" Although he understood each word, his thinking was
simply not sophisticated enough to get beyond the literal meaning. It
is impossible to build language (or reading) comprehension unless
basic thinking skills are part of the program.

Learning words and their meanings is all tied up with concept
development because words are symbols. Exactly how do you know
what a "dog" is? There are some pretty odd-looking dogs walking
around, yet an adult can almost always say with certainty, "That's a
dog." How do you know that something is a chair—and not a bench,
or a stool? Somewhere inside your brain you have mental pictures of
your typical dog and chair, which you compare with each new animal or "object to sit on." If the new one is close enough to your
prototype, you feel confident about using that label. Knowledge of
word meanings is stored in the brain in "semantic networks" which
connect millions of prototypes for things, events, and even abstract
ideas such as "freedom" or "mercy."

How do children develop semantic networks? From firsthand experiences with objects in the real world, and from hearing words
associated with those objects and then with other words. "Go car-
car," shouts a toddler as a bus passes by. "That's a bus," explains her
mother. "You ride in a car, and you ride in a bus, but a bus is bigger.
A car is smaller than a bus." A semantic network for "vehicles" has
just been born. Patiently, slowly, adults help children braid the
strands of experience, language, and thought.

Patterns of Relationship

Comprehending language is basically a question of understanding
relationships. One early relationship problem is learning about pronouns. "You give it to me," means different things depending on who
says it. Most children, however, master "I-you" and "my-your" con-
fusions by about age three—a remarkable feat of abstraction. Continued trouble with pronouns may signal some underlying difficulty
that should be investigated.

Prepositions are another way to express relationships. What is
"above" anyway? It might mean where an airplane is flying, or on

top of a printed line on a page. "In" and "out" mean different things if you're talking about the cereal's relationship to the cupboard or Bill's membership in the club. Other parts of speech can also be confusing. What is "little"? Molly is little compared to Dad, but she is not little compared to a goldfish. "Here" and "there" change depending on where you are. Fortunately, the human brain seems well adapted for this kind of work—if the child has good foundations for understanding physical relationships.

At this point we need to add a whole new layer to our input-output system. In the diagram on page 154, input was simply repeated without any understanding, as when you read aloud in front of a crowd of people and then have no idea what you read about. You can also repeat mathematical formulae or words in a foreign language, but unless you have some associations to plug them into, they fall right out of your brain at the same time they fall out of your mouth! The illustration on page 164 shows what happens when we move up to a level where incoming words get associated with familiar information from semantic networks.

Expressing Meaning

Did you notice there's still a gap in the system? What happens to all the good ideas churning around in the topmost layer? Take a pencil and draw in a line to connect comprehension and sequencing words. Label it "formulation"—expressing an original message. Children these days may not get enough practice formulating sentences and conversations as they watch TV, play video games, or "talk" to a computer. Good language output takes lots of practice, and schools which encourage predominantly the "input" side—reading and listening without having to express or write down ideas—deprive students of the most critical tools for using their knowledge.

For your child's future success in conveying ideas, writing, and thinking, please don't accept spaghetti talk that winds around without going anywhere. "Oh, like, well, you know, well like he could, you know, but . . ." Formulating ideas into sentences refines knowledge circuits, sharpens logical thinking, and avoids "fuzzy" understandings. A society which cannot communicate its ideas verbally may be in for trouble.

BUILDING LANGUAGE: CONNECTING WITH THOUGHT

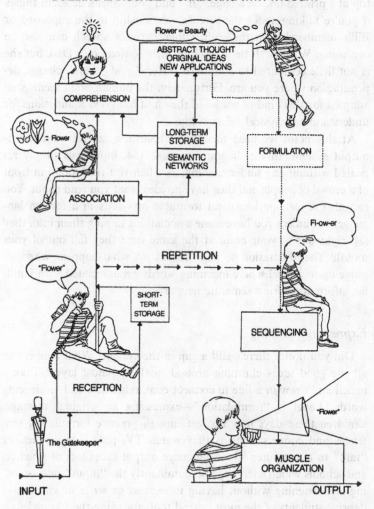

MILESTONES IN MEANING

All ages are approximate.

Before 1 year: Understands words spoken by others.

9–18 months: First words; usually names or action words.

18–24 months: Two-word combinations.
                 Possessives, negatives, questions.

> Uses objects symbolically in pretend play (stick = horse).
>
> Beginning use of "and."
>
> *3–4 years:* Can get an entire idea into one sentence.
>
> Comparative terms: big, little.
>
> Pronouns I-you, my-your.
>
> Past tense.
>
> "Why" questions; use of "because."
>
> *4–5 years:* Can follow three simple commands.
>
> "If . . . , then . . ." concepts.
>
> *By age 6:* Some use of passive voice ("He was bumped.").
>
> Simple opposites (big-little, tall-short, hot-cold).
>
> Terms: because, so, then, but, well, just, again, still, already, not yet, too, over, under, on top of, into, up, down.

Unfolding Meaning

Learning to understand language goes along with learning to use it. When you discuss happenings in your child's life, make plans or read together, describe an event or a person, you demonstrate the connection. Here are some suggestions.

—Always use language in a real context if you want to promote the best semantic growth. Talk about what the child is experiencing.

—Work on attaching meaning to words by "showing" what you are talking about. ("See, now I'm putting the button into the buttonhole—like this." "Look, this is the way I peel the orange.")

—Help your child build a good base of understanding by putting "talk" with age-appropriate play experiences. Get down on the floor and show how to talk about what's happening (be sure the child "gets the floor" to talk too).

—Imitating words and phrases is a first step, but the ability to repeat something does not signify understanding. If you wonder whether your child has understood, ask him to *show* you what he thinks it means.

—A mother's style of conversation influences her child's. Some mothers tend to use talk as a practical tool for interaction ("I can tell you're enjoying that applesauce; would you like some more?"), and others tend to convey information ("Applesauce is made from apples. They are fruits, like bananas.") It is probably a good idea to mix these two styles.

—Repetition is the key to children's understanding. Children looking at books repeat to themselves what their mothers have said about the pictures. Even if you think you will start to scream if you read "The Gingerbread Boy" one more time, hang in there!

—As the child gets older, encourage her to retell stories in her own words. Retell the plots of TV shows in the order of events.

—Vocabulary building goes on all the time. Here are a few possibilities:

> Use the names of household objects.
>
> Point out and name things while you are walking or driving.
>
> Name things in pictures as you look at magazines together.
>
> Think of as many kinds of houses as you can (igloo, hut, mansion); ways of doing something (fast, slowly, deliberately, joyously).
>
> Act out words whenever possible to show meaning ("See, my face is joyous now.").
>
> Teach verbs by examples: "See, that boy is running. That one is climbing a tree. The girl is jumping rope."
>
> Demonstrate prepositions ("I'm putting the egg into the cup." "I'll hide the pencil behind the bookcase.").
>
> Expand modifiers ("How many words can we think of to tell about how the princess looks? About how the monster is walking?").
>
> Play games with opposites ("I say dark, you say . . ." "The knife is sharp, the eraser is . . .").

—Help your child generalize meanings. "The knife is sharp. (Can you say a word sharply? Can you find anything sharp about someone's face?)"

—It is all right to use some words that the child doesn't yet know or understand provided the situation is familiar. Children make the best progress after infancy with adults who gently stretch their understanding. Studies show that fathers may tend instinctively to challenge the child, while mothers are more sensitive to their current level.

—When using an unfamiliar term, you might call attention to it. ("Here's a special word for that kind of dog—it's called a 'collie.' ")

—Children remember a thing better if they are asked to tell about it themselves. ("Now that I've explained where to go after school today, why don't you tell me again so I know you understand?").

—When choosing a day-care setting, look for an emphasis on language understanding. Children must have verbal interactions with adults, not just with other children.

—Teach relative terms with demonstrations. ("This orange is bigger than the lemon. Which is bigger, the orange or the grapefruit?").

—If the child asks an illogical question, try to rephrase what you think she wants to know.

> CHILD: Why is the airplane?
>
> PARENT: Do you mean, "Where is the airplane?" It just went too high for us to see behind the clouds.

—If a young child hasn't responded to a question in about five seconds, you might repeat or rephrase it.

—Family meals are a wonderful chance for children to develop both understanding and expression. Try some conversation starters to get everyone involved: ("I'd love to hear what each of us was doing at eleven o'clock this morning." "The nicest thing that happened to me today was. . . . What about everyone else?") Help younger children be a part of the conversation.

Being head language coach can be tiring, but some parents take their responsibilities so seriously that they wear out the child instead. Unfortunately, incessant stimulation can cause circuits to overload and shut down. The brain also needs quiet times in which to put together the new connections.

Faltering Formulation

"I don't know how Bea can have a language problem. She talks all the time!" This mother is right about her daughter in one respect. Bea, age seven, does indeed chatter like a magpie, but when you stop to listen, it is hard to figure out what she is talking about. Here is the way she retold a story about a boy who went on an imaginary space mission and discovered a new planet.

"Well, there were all these . . . ah . . . things and they came at him and he was, he was, well, real scared and then he got back in the —you know—in the space thingey, and he pushed the . . . pushed the button and they went fast and he was scared when the things came but at the end they got back and he went in his . . . um . . . bed and that's the end."

While this child isn't exactly at a loss for words, the words she uses don't do a very good job. I call this "peanut butter" talk: if the child spreads enough of it around she may succeed in covering the subject. This particular example illustrates a rather severe problem of "cluttering" with extra words and repetitions. Other children with milder problems are just off center when they try to answer questions or impart information. If you find your child tossing too much talk that misses the topic, try to encourage more thought and fewer words. "See if you can pick just three important ideas from the story [perhaps boy, space trip, new planet]. Now let's start with telling who the main character is. When did the story happen? Where? What did he do? How did it end?"

Another problem this child shows is in "word finding." Instead of being able to think of a word—usually a noun—she uses fillers or roundabout talk. Common examples are: "The ah-ah-ah—you know . . ." "Thingey." "Stuff." One eight-year-old couldn't think of "doorknob" and said "doorpuller." Another called the coatrack the "hanging-up thing." A six-year-old defined a nail like this: "You put it down with a hammer in wood." Fuzzy talk like this is common (and cute) among younger children, but if it is chronic or persists into school years, you should give it some attention. Reading and writing skills are based on the ability to call up familiar words, and such word retrieval difficulties ("dysnomia") may signal future problems.

There are a few things you can do at home. First, give the child time to think of what to say. Pressure makes things worse. Second, don't accept "You know," "stuff," or other substitutions. Gently probe for a meaningful word or help by supplying one. One helpful game is trying to name a series of common objects or pictures as fast as possible. Fast color naming is also good practice. Remember, though, keep it fun. If language causes tension in your home, get professional help.

The boxed material lists other symptoms which may indicate a problem with language. The presence of *several* of these signs warrants a visit to a speech and language clinic or specialist. You probably can't change your child's basic pattern, but parents and professionals working together can make a big difference.

WARNING SIGNALS

All children show some problems with language as they grow. If you notice several of these signs, however, you should obtain a professional evaluation of your child's language development. (Premature infants may be expected to show some delay because of immaturity.)

Absence of cooing or babbling during first six months

Repeated failure to make eye contact with caretakers

Persistent difficulty with turn-taking games

Trouble with sucking, chewing, or swallowing

Excess drooling

Persistent difficulty imitating tongue movements

"Strange-sounding" voice (may result from physical causes)

Acquiring single words and phrases and then stopping all speech

No communicative use of expressive speech by age three

"Echolalia": repeating set phrases, such as TV commercials, instead of spontaneous speech; inappropriate repetition without intentional communication

Extreme problems "understanding" or relating to peers in play situations

Stuttering that is severe or that persists more than one year

Age-inappropriate syntactic errors

Persistent pronoun confusion after age three

Delayed or absent asking of questions

Use of language only to label or request things rather than to comment on activities or events in the environment

Frequent articulation errors persisting after school age

—Substitution of one sound for another

—Omission of sounds

—Sound distortion

—Addition of inappropriate sounds

Frequent word substitutions; difficulty retrieving familiar words

Frequent irrelevant responses ("What do you like to do at school?" "Sally goes to my school but we have different teachers.")

Persistent inability to come to the point

Difficulty with abstract meanings of words

Purposeful withholding of speech

Unblocking the System

I once had a student whose mother was ready to give up on her. "I can't understand how Marie can be *so* slow. Every time anyone says anything to her, she gets this vague look on her face and says, 'Huh?' She's been doing that ever since she was little, and now she's about to flunk eighth grade. I can't believe she's really that dumb!"

Marie turned out to have an IQ that astonished everyone—including Marie. While she was indeed a slow language processor, she had superior abilities to reason and possessed an extensive vocabulary if anyone gave her time to use it. Yet she had learned to play the "dumb" game very effectively. It took a combination of language therapy, help in school, and much encouragement to convince both mother and daughter that she was really OK. Everyone's hard work evidently gave Marie the steam she needed, for her mother later called me to report that she is now on the honor roll in her high school. She still has to concentrate hard when people talk quickly to her, and it takes her a long time to read assignments, but she is a hard worker. I credit her mother's support for giving her the self-confidence to bypass some blocks in the system.

THE MAGIC OF INNER SPEECH

Language Builds Brains

Can the use of language increase the brain's ability to think? Neuropsychologists now believe that "inner speech"—the silent conversation that most of us carry on with ourselves—creates physical connections in several important parts of the brain. If you want your child to be a success in school, this ability may be the most important one of all. The best way to teach it is by example.

Let's say your toddler is trying to sort different-colored plastic chips into piles. If you demonstrate saying, "Blue, green, yellow" as the chips are sorted, your child should be able to sort them faster and learn a valuable lesson about the power of words in guiding actions. From the age of about four, you can show a child the magic words: "First I will . . . and then I will . . ." Ask a school-aged child who has difficulty with a math problem, "What is the question that you're supposed to answer? What steps could you take to get it?" Very often, this simple process results in, "Oh, I get it now!"

The ability to use words to guide actions is age-related. The more practice children get, the better the connections. First graders think it's lots of fun to "teach" parents by giving directions. Older elementary children can play such games as two players sitting on either side of a "wall" where they can't see each other. The child arranges colored blocks or other objects in some sort of pattern and then tries to get the other player (you, perhaps) to duplicate the design by describing what to do ("Pick up the purple triangle and put it at the top. Then take a red square and make it touch the triangle right underneath.") You can also help older children plan ahead with words—writing out time schedules for major assignments, listing parts of an assignment in order, etc. Any activity that mediates actions with words can be regarded as brain-building material.

One language technique that is effective with impulsive children involves five steps that put higher brain centers in charge of actions:

1. What do you have to do? (Identify the problem.)
2. How do you think you should go about doing it? (Evaluate the method for attacking the problem.)
3. What will you need to do first? (Plan the attack.)
4. Are you following your plan? (Check the progress.)
5. Did you finish what you had to do? (Check the outcome.)

Working on these five steps takes a particular brand of patience, but all children will benefit from the time you spend teaching them to build their own brains with inner speech.

THE PIG'S WISHBONE

I hope you can now share my excitement as I look back at a four-year-old's seemingly simple question. It is one of the marvels of the human mind that children master the purposes, mechanics, rules, and meanings of language without explicit teaching. Adults' participation in the process of developing language is an instinctive gift to the intellects of the next generation. Be gentle and trust yourself to help unfold each layer. If I really had a pig's wishbone, I would wish you and your child a joyous journey together.

8

What Is Intelligence?

"GUESS WHAT!" MY NEIGHBOR CONNIE BOUNCED THROUGH THE kitchen door, waving an official-looking envelope. "We got a letter from Meg's school saying they want to give her an intelligence test to find out if she should be put into a 'gifted' class. I know you're familiar with this kind of testing. Is it really valid? Should I prepare Meg for it? Will we get the results? I hope they won't make her feel like some sort of guinea pig!"

I was delighted to learn that my little friend's talents had been recognized, but I was sympathetic with her mother's questions. Parents are naturally concerned about what test scores mean and how they will be used. Many wonder about their validity and their relevance to success in school and in life. Well, the same questions are being asked by professionals. No one has even agreed what "intelligence" is! The use of IQ tests is continually challenged, and some psychologists believe we should adopt entirely new approaches to the whole question of mental ability.

This chapter will summarize current views on intelligence and show you some benefits—and pitfalls—of IQ testing. We will consider the important issue of parental influences, genetic and environmental, on IQ and glance at two particular aspects of human mental ability, memory and motivation. Finally, some new ideas may encourage you to be a more informed participant in the growth—and measurement—of your child's "intelligence."

INTELLIGENCE: TRADITIONAL VIEWS

The Mystery of "g"

What makes some people smarter than others? In any society we find a range of abilities for dealing with life's demands. Individuals who are "superior" may be more clever at solving everyday problems, more adaptable when confronted with new challenges, or quicker in learning the skills of the prevailing culture. "Intelligence" might be quite different in a society of hunters or farmers than in ones dominated by computer programmers or dancers. Yet some psychologists continue to search for one general factor underlying all intelligent behavior; according to this theory, some people have more of it, and some have less.

Psychologists in Europe and America began trying to test people for an innate general learning ability, often referred to as "g," about a century ago. Observing differences in individuals' speed and efficiency for learning, they searched for differences in the brain's processing of incoming information such as sounds and visual stimuli, or memory for lists of numbers or nonsense words. Some measured brain size, but no one ever found proof of a "bigger is better" theory. More recently, scientists have pursued it in specific parts of the brain —particularly at the synapses, where messages are transmitted from neuron to neuron. So far, we lack the technology to ascertain whether mental ability resides at this basic level, but some researchers are investigating the speed of children's electrical brain wave patterns. Also, as we shall see later, some new infant studies are coming up with a factor that looks suspiciously like g.

Single-factor theories of intelligence have always been controversial. Most experts deny that human mental ability can be explained so easily—or that it is all innate, because so many aspects of a child's environment contribute to intellectual achievement. The g in tests of school children has turned out to be closely associated with verbal ability—which parents can influence! Perhaps new technology for studying the brain will settle this argument. In the meanwhile, the scene has been dominated by completely different views of intelligence as an aggregate of abilities. This idea became popular in 1908 when psychologist Alfred Binet invented the IQ test.

Putting Children in Boxes

Binet was commissioned by the French government to develop a test to identify children who weren't smart enough to learn in regular classrooms. He decided to try out a variety of tests on children at different age levels. After computing averages, or "norms," for each age level, he developed a "battery" of several tests which seemed most closely related to children's success in school, and thus, presumably, to their intelligence. Comparing individual scores with Binet's norms enabled testers to assign any child a "mental age." To compute IQ, the mental age is divided by chronological age and multiplied by 100. For example, a superior child aged four who performed at the level of a five-year-old would have an IQ of 125 (5/4 × 100). An "average" IQ at any age is 100. Since more is expected as a child gets older, the tests get harder and the IQ score should remain stable throughout life. Of course, some allowance for error must be made; it is assumed that a Binet IQ might be in error by 5 points in either direction.

The Stanford-Binet Intelligence Test, which has been used for years, still contains subtests similar to those of the original. Here are some examples of skills expected at various ages:

Age 2: Placing three geometric shapes in a form board
        Naming common objects from pictures
        Finding an object after a ten-second delay
Age 6: Giving opposites: "Fire is hot; ice is ———."
        Telling the differences between two objects
        Finding the shortest path in a simple paper-and-pencil maze
Age 10: Giving definitions of abstract words
        Counting the number of cubes in a three-dimensional picture
        Giving reasons for certain types of laws
Average adult: Doing mathematical word problems
               Giving the meaning of proverbs
               Telling the differences between two similar concepts

A brand-new revised version of the Stanford-Binet is rapidly becoming popular because it gives a much broader picture of both verbal and nonverbal abilities and can be used all the way from age two to adulthood. Some of the skills tested include:

—Defining vocabulary words

—Remembering patterns of colored beads

—Telling what is "silly" about a picture (e.g., someone ice skating on a sidewalk)

—Copying patterns of cubes

—Answering questions about everyday situations ("Where do we buy clothes?")

—Figuring out what a piece of paper would look like when folded and cut in certain ways

—Remembering a series of digits or sentences

—Figuring out math equations

"We've Found the Answer!"

Binet's idea was immediately embraced by educators, who began to develop categories, cutoff points, and labels such as "mentally retarded." They were firmly convinced that the tests could tell how well a child should do in school. Those who did better than the test indicated were termed "overachievers," almost as if they had done something wrong! Few dared to suggest that maybe the test was incorrect.

The use of tests skyrocketed and soon "group" intelligence tests that could be administered to roomfuls of children became popular. These pencil and paper tests departed considerably from Binet's original concept, yet they proved to measure something closely related to children's success in school. Was it intelligence?

Dissenters soon began to object to test score infatuation. How, they asked, do we know that the tests are really measuring what they claim? Maybe the ability to do well in school and basic intelligence are not the same thing. Have educators been too eager to put children into mental boxes? Despite its critics, the philosophy of testing has permeated American education, with IQ scores, as in Meg's case, often used as the final determinant for special educational placement on both ends of the ability scale. As a parent, you may want to know about some of the issues involved in their use.

Are IQ Tests Fair?

One of the biggest questions concerns how much IQ tests are influenced by previous learning and school training. Children with different cultural backgrounds may lack the experiences of those on whom the norms were based. Concerns about fairness have grown to the point where some states have discontinued use of all school IQ tests.

Other critics fear that the tests encourage "convergent" thinking: the child must come up with one particular answer instead of getting credit for novel or creative approaches. A child who is imaginative, they complain, might even be penalized for answers that are "too clever." One psychologist I know is still chuckling about a response that a very precocious seven-year-old produced. When asked, "What is a diamond?" the child replied, "Oh, a diamond is just like a dog."

Baffled, my friend asked, "Can you tell me some more about that?" This is the only question the tester is permitted to ask.

"Well," said the child, "a dog is a *man's* best friend." She got full credit even though this answer wasn't in the manual. On a group test, or with a less patient tester, this child would have been marked wrong.

Thoughtful educators also worry that a test score may become a self-fulfilling prophecy. They point to studies in which teachers were given falsely high or low IQ scores for their students. By the end of the year in a few classrooms, the children's level of achievement corresponded to the incorrect scores. For this reason, teachers are often not allowed to see the results of IQ tests. Unfortunately, they are missing out on some information that might help them teach more effectively, for despite their problems, tests can be useful for those who understand their limitations.

Why Should a Child Be Tested?

Parents should never authorize any important educational decision about a child on the basis of a group IQ test. An individual battery gives a fuller and more accurate picture, but still should be considered only as part of a full appraisal of ability.

Most parents will never confront the need for individual IQ testing, which usually arises because teachers and parents are puzzled about a youngster's achievement. A few schools routinely use individual IQ tests to diagnose learning style, strengths, and weaknesses —information which is far more important than the total IQ score. Since children don't come in tidy intellectual boxes, looking at only one score is far too simplistic and not very helpful. Tests should not be given unless someone is willing to take the time to use the results constructively.

Individual IQ testing is expensive, because of the time involved. Sometimes parents must request it. If the school is unable or unwilling to make the arrangements, a private psychologist or clinic may be used.

PARENT GUIDELINES FOR IQ TESTING

1. An IQ battery should be used only as part of a total evaluation of a child's ability and achievement. Teacher comments, school records, or other tests may be used to supplement the IQ report.

2. You should request individual testing if:

—Your child's achievement in school is lower than might reasonably be expected or there is any other reason to suspect a learning problem.

—Your child is chronically unhappy in school and other efforts to discover the reasons have been unsuccessful.

—You have good reason to believe that your child is intellectually superior and is becoming bored or "turned off" because of a lack of challenge.

—Your child is unusually slow to master "readiness" skills in kindergarten or first grade.

3. The test should be administered by a trained psychologist who understands current interpretation of learning profiles.

4. A one- or two-page report should be part of the finished test. It should comment on the child's:

—Attitude and motivation during testing.

—Ability to pay attention, think problems through, and control impulsive answers.

—Response to difficult items and ability to handle frustration.

—Ability to follow directions.

—Auditory and visual processing strengths and weaknesses, with implications for teaching.

5. The psychologist should meet with you to explain all the

results and make specific recommendations. Some also meet with older children to share useful information (not IQ scores!) and make constructive suggestions.

The test now most commonly used, the *Wechsler Intelligence Scale for Children, Revised* (WISC-R), has twelve subtests which provide a diagnostic profile of each child's learning strengths and weaknesses. This test was chosen to determine whether Meg would enter the gifted class in her school.

Meg Takes the Test

When Connie agreed to have Meg tested, she signed a consent form for "psychological testing" because of the requirement in their state that all individual intelligence testing be done by a licensed psychologist. Some parents ask me if they should try to test their own child with commercial books or kits. I recall the time when I was learning to give the WISC and decided to practice on one of our sons. Despite my careful training, both mother and son ended up in tears. We cared too much! Maybe you and your child can remain coolly objective, but it's not usually a good idea to put this kind of pressure on a youngster.

Before signing the consent form, Connie made an appointment with the principal, who assured her that Meg would not be embarrassed or singled out by this procedure, and that she would not miss any important classroom work while she was being tested. At the principal's suggestion, Connie told Meg that a lady would be coming to work (for younger children "to play some special games") with her sometime soon, that she hoped Meg would try hard and enjoy the activities, and that she was proud her daughter had been chosen. Then she dropped the subject. Cramming information or "motivation" into a child before a test does not work! Pressure or anxiety can even cause a child to forget things she normally knows.

During the week of the test, Meg's regular schedule of bedtime and morning routines was kept so that she left for school each day rested, fed, and as happy as possible. Had the child appeared sick, Connie would have kept her at home. Individual IQ tests are more or less stable even during minor illnesses, but there is no reason to make important decisions on information gained when a child isn't feeling up to par.

On Thursday morning Meg's teacher told her she would be going to the testing room with Mrs. Joseph instead of to recess for the next two days. When she got there, a friendly young woman immediately put her at ease. Part of a psychologist's training is to establish a good rapport before starting the test and to encourage each child's best efforts. Meg was an easy child to test, because she was friendly and cooperative, and had been looking forward to the challenge. It is much harder to get good results from children who haven't been told what is happening, who are very shy, or who have difficulty following friendly suggestions. Meg was also a persistent worker; when one puzzle did not go together the way she had expected, she sat back, chewed on her finger for a moment, said, "This one's a hardie—I'd better try another way," and succeeded. When children give up easily, it is difficult to find out how capable they really are since the examiner is not allowed to ask leading questions or help the child do any of the problems.

Mrs. Joseph started by asking Meg some simple questions. Here are examples of similar questions for different age levels, although none of these is actually on the test: How many ears does a rabbit have? What continent is the United States part of? This section is usually a good predictor of school success, since it reflects the information available in the home environment and the child's ability to remember it. If this first subtest score is obviously lower than the rest, it may be a sign of nervousness.

Meg then took alternating *performance* and *verbal* subtests. The verbal tests, like the first one, are mainly oral questions which start out easy and get increasingly difficult. When a certain number of consecutive items are missed, that test is discontinued. A child who isn't panicked at the idea of a wrong answer can often get additional points by making sensible guesses. The verbal tests measure several different abilities: seeing relationships between words (How are a train and a bus alike?), doing mental math problems (If John had four apples and gave away three, how many would he have left?), defining words (Tell me what ———— means), and responding to common practical situations and rules of society (What should you do if you break a friend's toy? What are some of the advantages of a two-party system in government?). Memory for a series of numbers read out loud may also be tested.

The tests on the performance scale minimize the need to understand or use language. They require identifying items missing in pictures, arranging different types of puzzles, copying a "code," putting picture stories in order, or solving pencil and paper mazes. Most of these tests are timed, and some children run into trouble when the stopwatch is brought out. They either rush and make unnecessary errors, or they get paralyzed with fear.

Meg, however, thoroughly enjoyed the whole procedure. Every once in a while she would look up and ask, "I'm doing good, aren't I!" In her report, Mrs. Joseph described Meg's excellent ability to concentrate, to come up with varied solutions to problems, and to respond positively to a challenge. Here are some other qualities which help children score well on traditional IQ tests:

—A large fund of practical knowledge and life experiences; older children who read widely have an advantage on verbal tests.

—A good vocabulary; they know the meanings of many words and are able to formulate good definitions for them.

—The ability to size up a problem quickly.

—A good immediate memory and understanding for oral directions, sentences, or a series of numbers.

—The ability to understand and talk about relationships (how are things alike? different?).

—An enjoyment of a challenge; and a willingness to try something that looks "hard."

—The ability to risk; a willingness to make a sensible guess.

—Persistence; the ability to try different problem solutions.

—The ability to accept failure and get on with the next problem.

—A lack of impulsivity; the ability to stop and think through a problem and to go back and check the results even under time pressure.

Meg did very well on all the subtests compared to other children of her age. Does that mean she is intelligent? You may have to decide for yourself. Meanwhile, let's look at the way this test, and others, can best be used to learn about children.

Using IQ Scores

Here's how to understand IQ scores. Meg's total IQ was 133. It comes from her scores on the verbal and performance scales: Verbal —137, Performance—125. On the WISC-R, and many other tests, we use the average IQ of 100 to determine how unusual she, or any other child, is compared to others of the same age. One way to see how IQ scores are distributed is to imagine piling up all the children in the United States according to their IQ scores.

A graph of those scores would look like the illustration on page 182. You can see that most children (68 percent) are piled up between IQ 85 and 115. Anyone below 70 or above 130 is very unusual, and only about 2 percent at any age level score as far away from 100 as Meg did.

In Meg's school district, an arbitrary cutoff for the gifted program was set at 130, and any child with an IQ under 70 was placed in a special classroom for slower learners. These cutoff points may differ depending on how much money a district has for special programs.

Subtest scores tell a lot about a child's individual style of learning. For example, even though Meg is well above average on both scales, her verbal score is noticeably higher than the performance one. She tends to learn better when she can use words, rather than visual solutions to problems, and when she can analyze elements rather than having to take in the whole situation immediately. She may become confused if she has to look at a lot of information all at once, so she should be given time to analyze and talk her way through maps, charts, graphs, or visually complex workbook pages.

Recently trained psychologists may know how to interpret IQ tests in the light of research on brain functioning. For example, the entire verbal scale with its emphasis on sequential, analytical processing, could reflect left-hemisphere functioning. Conversely, the performance tests demand more of a wholistic, visual, right-hemisphere style. Most normal children show variations in these two types of ability, but dramatic differences of more than fifteen points between the verbal and performance scales may suggest potential learning difficulties.

Unfortunately, some school psychologists do not know about the wealth of diagnostic information that is concealed in IQ test subscores and continue to use only the totals as a means of consigning children to categories. If your child has been given an individual IQ test, try to find someone familiar with current interpretation to explain to you—and to the teacher—what the results mean in practical terms.

Looking into the File

Parents have a legal right to see all permanent records on a minor child. When Connie attended the report meeting in the principal's

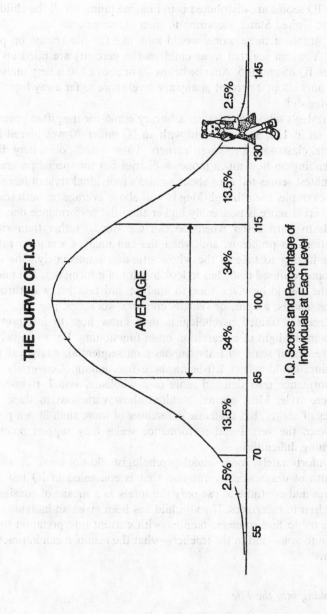

THE CURVE OF I.Q.

2.5%

13.5%

34%

AVERAGE

34%

13.5%

2.5%

55 70 85 100 115 130 145

I.Q. Scores and Percentage of
Individuals at Each Level

office, she was amazed at the size of the file that had already been assembled. It contained four types of records:

1. Report cards and teacher comments since kindergarten.
2. Results of achievement tests.
3. The results of a group-administered IQ test.
4. The WISC-R test and report.

Many parents are confused about the difference between achievement and aptitude tests. *Achievement* tests are designed to measure what the child has been taught in school. They are usually given once a year in each subject—reading, math, etc.—and are a fairly reliable estimate of a child's progress from year to year as well as a comparison with other children at the same grade level. High school students trying out for competitive colleges also take college board achievement tests in subjects they have studied.

Aptitude tests, such as IQ tests, should reflect the child's basic learning potential and do not need to be given more than once or twice. They do not tell how a child is doing in reading, math, or other school subjects, but as children grow older, almost all tests become increasingly dependent on the quality of previous education. The infamous SAT (or ACT) tests for college-bound students give scores for verbal and mathematical aptitude, but results are highly dependent on the math courses completed, vocabulary, and the reading skill developed through years of English courses and independent reading.

Making the Decision

Several weeks after Connie's last visit, she burst into my kitchen again. "Meg is going to be in the gifted program! Everyone agrees it will be the best way to challenge her, and the teachers think she needs the creative emphasis. I really appreciate the time they took explaining it all."

Wouldn't it be nice if all quick little minds could have exciting new territory to explore! A test such as the WISC-R or the Stanford Binet which gives a profile of at least ten scores is a reasonably effective tool for identifying such special needs. As we learn more about individual patterns of ability and brain functioning, we may expect to see some new viewpoints, however.

A Newcomer on the Testing Scene

The *Kaufman Assessment Battery for Children* (K-ABC) is the first completely new individual intelligence test to be published since the 1930s. It was designed to get at pure "reasoning ability," following theories about the preferred learning styles of the right and left hemispheres: sequential and simultaneous. The *sequential* tasks require several variations on remembering series of words or pictures in order. *Simultaneous* processing involves seeing wholes or general outlines. For example, the child sees a partially completed picture of a common object and tries to figure out what the whole is. Another test of simultaneous processing shows the child a picture of a face which he must remember and pick out of a picture of a group of people. The test has received some criticism because many of the tasks are heavily dependent on short-term memory, and because the emphasis on visual instead of verbal challenges may be unfair to some children. Because its format is similar to that of the WISC-R, some think it is only a new version of an old idea.

Many parents like the K-ABC because it provides insight into variations in children's learning. Although this approach to brain functioning may be oversimplified, it emphasizes that one style of reasoning is not necessarily more "intelligent" than another. If your child is going to be tested, particularly if you are concerned about achievement, you may find the K-ABC part of the battery. It could offer a different perspective on your child's ability to learn.

Perhaps you are beginning to understand why professionals disagree over definitions of intelligence and ways of testing it. Yet we haven't even touched on the most interesting—and controversial—questions. Where does mental ability come from and how early can we predict it?

MENTAL ABILITY: BEGINNING TO END

Where Does Intelligence Come From?

Current research makes it clear that some mental ability is inherited. Identical twins who have the same genetic makeup are more alike on measures of intelligence than are fraternal twins or siblings, who are not genetically identical. Adopted children's mental endowment resembles that of their natural parents—even when they were adopted as infants. Similarity seems to increase as the children get older and are able to make more choices of their own. Most experts feel that between 50 and 80 percent of mental capacity is inherited, and many agree that special styles of thinking and learning also run in families.

Does this mean that we should give up on children who seem to lack potential? Or that all progeny of bright parents will be super-smart? Not at all. One peculiar phenomenon in statistics, called "regression to the mean," makes it likely that individuals who are far out on the edges of that pile of IQs—either very bright or unusually slow—may have children with IQ scores closer to the middle of the distribution. Moreover, the home environment can change the way a child learns to use basic mental ability and possibly even the way the brain develops.

Children who have more contact and conversation with adults generally fare better on IQ tests. Those who have talked mostly with brothers and sisters have not had the same language stimulation as firstborns, only children, or those from small families. One group of specialists, testing the effects of early language stimulation, picked a group of disadvantaged children whose mothers had IQs around 80 —well below average. Ordinarily, these children would receive little verbal or intellectual stimulation in their homes, and the IQs could be expected to drop even though they started out around average. Half of the children were entered in a special program before they were one year old: language stimulation in a day-care setting where teachers read and talked to them, showing them how to use words for thinking and interacting with others. After they were three years old, simple activities in science, math, and music were added.

The experiment worked! When the children were retested at age four, their IQs had not dropped, while the scores of the nonintervention group had fallen about twenty points. Stimulation after age one proved to be the most important. Even if we agree that IQ tests don't tell the whole story, this kind of "preventive intervention" could make a difference in future school success for many children who are at risk because of environmental factors.

How Early Can We Tell?

The success of infant intelligence tests has been limited. Some tests administered at birth can identify children with nervous system immaturities, but IQ tests before eighteen months are unreliable predictors, possibly because the tests are inadequate or because environmental influences can influence later scores. Moreover, testing young children is an uncertain art at best.

The most commonly used infant intelligence test is the *Bayley Scale of Infant Development.* Its Mental Scale consists of 163 items for infants of two to thirty months, testing such things as accuracy of visual, auditory, and tactile (touch) perception, understanding and use of language, memory (e.g., remembering where toys are hidden), interaction with and imitation of adults. Even this well-standardized scale is not very predictive of later IQ until at least age two, and many doubt its accuracy even then. When IQ tests agree with each other, it means only that they are measuring the same thing—not that it is necessarily intelligence.

Several researchers are excited about findings which they think may open a new window on innate mental skills. Rather than trying to get babies to follow directions, they have found ways to measure natural responses, such as looking, sucking, kicking, or heartbeat speed to determine the child's level of interest. Several studies of this type have shown a surprisingly simple predictor of later intelligence scores—the infant's ability to pay attention to new things. When children are shown either a novel toy or one they have already seen, the babies who display more interest in the new item later show up with higher IQs. One study measured infants' reactions to novel sounds. Those who responded faster had higher IQs at age six. Whether these apparent links to intelligence involve superior memory, accuracy of perception, attention, speed of understanding, or some other factor is not entirely clear. Is this the mysterious "g factor"?

Preschool Testing

I have done plenty of testing with four-year-olds, and I can guarantee that children's answers don't always reflect their abilities. "I don't know" may actually mean she doesn't have the information, but it may also mean:

"I'm tired of this silly game and I want to play by myself." or

"I have to go to the bathroom but I'm embarrassed." or

"Why should I answer these questions, anyhow?" or

"Mom told me not to talk to strangers and you look pretty strange to me!"

Some psychologists like to have parents stay in the room when they test preschoolers. You can suggest this if you think your child will respond better and *if* you promise to stifle the inevitable urge to prompt. ("But you know *that*—don't you remember. . . .") You're sure to get an interesting new perspective on your child.

Why should a preschool child be given an intelligence test? Usually because someone suspects a dramatic difference from the average range, which might call for intervention or a special educational plan. Handicapped, highly gifted, language delayed, or "late-blooming" youngsters all fall in this category. Some very selective schools use IQ tests to screen applicants, but few responsible educators judge a young child on the basis of only one test. Many school districts test kindergartners with borderline birthdays for early entrance—but wise parents ask for an honest assessment of social and emotional maturity in addition to intellectual ability.

Preschool Intelligence Tests

Here are the most commonly used intelligence tests for preschoolers:

—*Stanford-Binet:* This classic was heavily weighted toward verbal ability and previous learning, but the new version gives a broader picture and includes a memory score.

—*Wechsler Pre-School and Primary Scales of Intelligence (WPPSI):* The preschool version of the WISC-R; has both verbal and performance scales.

—*McCarthy Scales of Children's Abilities:* Similar to the WPPSI but also includes tests of motor development (e.g., throwing, hopping) and a memory score.

—*Kaufman-ABC:* Gives a profile useful in diagnosing learning style rather than an IQ score.

All of these tests include activities which are colorful and fun for the child. In the hands of a sensitive examiner, each can reveal a great deal about a child's educational needs.

In the Long Run

You might be interested to know that IQ scores, although closely related to how well children fare in school, do not predict career success. In the United States, members of higher socioeconomic groups tend to have higher measured IQs—perhaps because professions with more status attract people with better grades. Once a person has chosen a career, however, other qualities become important. If you want your child to aspire to managerial success, for example, cultivate talents that aren't directly measured by IQ tests: ability to communicate with others, persuade and influence people, focus on the important aspects of a problem, take responsibility, and enjoy the satisfaction of a challenge. Careers in the arts tap a different set of abilities which are particularly difficult to measure.

The limitations of IQ tests confirm the suspicion that practical intelligence may be too complex to measure easily. Two big components that are particularly hard to boil down are *memory* and *motivation.* Let's glance at some research on these important topics.

MEMORY

Memory provides the framework for both intelligence and learning. Researchers are just beginning to draw practical ideas from their mountains of data on this complicated phenomenon. Here is a summary of what is currently known about how memory works, how it develops, and how we can help children use it more effectively.

Where Is It?

If you were to roam around in the brain searching for a special room labeled "memory," you wouldn't find it. Human memory calls upon widespread circuits as well as on specialized areas. Likewise, if you asked me, "How's your memory?" I would have to respond, "For what?" Most people don't realize that the thing we call "memory" is a group of separate abilities. Each has its own neural circuitry, and all but one must be learned.

The simplest kinds of remembering are handled by lower, subcortical brain structures which are not unique to human beings. My dog becomes wildly excited every time I put on my coat because she associates this action with taking a walk. Does she remember previous walks? More likely this type of learning is simply a reflex connection between two events that have occurred together many times. People also experience such stimulus-response learning. "Conditioning" is very effective in training people to behave in certain ways, and most parents use it instinctively. Your baby approaches the stove, you shout "Hot!" and pull the child away. Eventually, a connection is made, even though Baby doesn't understand the logic. Babies can "remember" other things too, such as flash cards, if they are trained to do so. But encouraging learning at this level might almost be considered an insult to the human brain!

The most irritating parent conference I had this year was with the father of a six-year-old who was doing her best to learn to read but failing to meet his very unrealistic standards. Angry at both his daughter and the school, he shouted, "All you people need to do is give her more *training!* It's your job to *make her remember.*"

I nearly shouted back at him, "This isn't a school for animals, sir. We're in the business of *teaching,* not *training* children." I settled for trying to explain the difference between remembering for meaning and merely reciting something that has been pushed in from outside. I know he didn't understand.

Most everyone agrees that human memory goes beyond the level of mere association. Parts of the limbic brain, so closely tied to emotion, are involved in the formation of memories, and hormones and chemicals associated with emotional states are part of the "juice" that fuels the circuits. At an even higher level, the cerebral cortex is the key to meaningful memory—not training!—as it receives incoming information and associates it with previous experience.

Different parts of the brain handle memory for things that have been seen, heard, and physically experienced. Memory for general knowledge is separate from recall of specific data—understanding what school is for and how one acts there as opposed to remembering a list of dates, for example. Children use many channels to store many little pieces, but meaning is the cement for the system.

How Children Learn to Remember

Meaningful memory is a five-stage process:
1. Sensory memory: registers input for a fraction of a second.
2. Attention: sorts out what goes into the system.
3. Short-term memory: keeps it alive for up to thirty seconds.
4. Long-term memory: stores it from minutes to a lifetime.
5. Retrieval: gets it out of long-term memory.

The only part of the memory system which operates as efficiently in young children as it does in adults is "sensory memory," which registers input for a brief fraction of a second. To keep the brain from being continually overwhelmed, however, a selection process must be perfected. The brain's attention gatekeeper decides what should be admitted to the next level; the rest decays immediately and is lost. If a child can't pay attention, there is little hope that material will be retained. Guidelines for dealing with attention problems are given in Chapter 4.

The next level is short-term memory (STM). If you look up a telephone number, your short-term visual memory can hang on to it only for brief seconds unless you do something to keep it alive longer. One way is to say the numbers over and over; this process, called *rehearsal,* is a good technique because it adds an auditory trace to the visual one. Rehearsal is also one way of getting the stimulus past the next step, or inside the doorway of long-term memory (LTM). Once inside, it may be kept for minutes or for years, depending on its personal importance and the amount of mental effort expended on keeping it there.

Although the ability to register sensory information is present from birth, the rest of the memory system develops as a result of experience. Children must literally learn to remember, and parents who show them how and require them to use memory increase their ability. They need special practice at two different levels:
1. Storing information in LTM
2. Recalling, or retrieving, it when necessary

Getting It into Long-Term Storage

As memory pathways form, they make physical changes in the brain. Although there is a limited amount of space in "working memory" at any one time, a vast reservoir of past experience and learning always lies just under the surface. Most people don't have conscious memories of events before they were about four or five years old, probably because their level of understanding was too limited at the time, but the traces may still remain.

The importance of a child's level of understanding is shown by some experiments in which children were asked to remember patterns of blocks. Young children could not copy some hard patterns, but eight months later they remembered them perfectly. New mental growth enabled them to look back and understand—and thus remember accurately. Likewise, adults' memories of childhood events are probably structured by current understanding.

Practice with simple memorization may be valuable for rote-level tasks such as lists, telephone numbers, or math facts. Get the child actively involved and try to attach some meaning. Interesting or funny poems and songs are appealing and also build language skills. Memorization is facilitated by rhythm, melody, and lots of repetition. Likewise, repeating patterns of movement—finger plays, dance, simple exercises—builds motor memory pathways.

Adults use a number of strategies for hanging on to things they want to remember. You may need to show a child how to implement them:

—*Giving new material a meaningful form:* rephrasing it; saying "What does that mean?" "Why should I remember it?"

—*Using a different sense to practice remembering:* writing down spoken information, making a mental "picture" of a series of dance movements.

—*Organizing, seeing patterns: putting words into categories:* "I need to remember 5 fruits and 4 vegetables;" "Three of these names begin with *m*, three with *b*, and two with *w*." "These numbers are each 2 larger than the one before;" "This number has a 6 on each end and three 4s in the middle."

—*Rehearsing:* repeating or mentally going over the material several times and then periodically going through it again to refresh the memory.

—*Elaborating:* hooking the material together in some way—making up a story using words that have to be remembered or making a mental picture linking items together; using tricks such as acronyms (the first letters of the Great Lakes spell HOMES).

—*Using visual memory or imagery strategies:* "seeing" yourself following a series of directions; imagining a "mental movie" of the events in a story.

—*Associating material with something already known:* "That new word reminds me of my friend's last name." "That number is my house number turned inside out." "That reminds me of the idea we studied last week in science class." This is probably the most effective method, but it requires a mental scaffolding with lots of "hooks," which are acquired only through active thinking and learning about the world.

Parents Teach About Memory

All of these strategies become more automatic as the child gets older. One reason is that practice improves them. A second is that children only gradually learn what memory is all about. If you read a pretend shopping list to kindergartners and ask them if they think they can remember it, most will blithely assure you that they can. When they get to the "store," they are surprised that they don't know what to ask for. An older child will immediately start to employ strategies ("Let's see, there are meats, canned goods, and bread on the list; eight things altogether. . . .") because they are familiar with how to make memory work. Even most adults can't remember more than about seven items unless they use some strategies. Recent studies on the way parents teach children about memory show that using the words "memory" and "remember" and suggesting ways to practice it help a lot.

Children's memory banks are only as good as the deposits of mental schemas which have been made in them. Semantic networks help associate ideas. To help your child develop the best long-term storehouse, review the suggestions for cognitive and language development in earlier chapters.

I Know the Face, But . . .

Once something has been stored in memory, the next step is to be able to "retrieve" it, or get it off the hook, when it is needed. You may be asked to do this in two different ways: Given a roomful of people, can you *recognize* the ones you have seen before? Can you *recall* their names? Quite different problems. Recognition is usually much easier; to aid a child's recall, give a choice to trigger the connections. If he can't remember the name of your street, for example, give him three names from which to choose. Children in school have to take tests which make demands on both recognition (matching, multiple choice) or recall (essay questions, fill in the blanks). If they know about the test in advance, they can study accordingly. Recall is more of a challenge. A child with a large, well-organized base of knowledge has the best chance of digging around and finding what he's looking for.

Growing Memories

Memory changes as children's minds grow. Some abilities are age-related:

By 3 months: Most infants have recognition memory for mobiles, toys, and common objects. They can remember long enough to distinguish between objects they have seen before and unfamiliar ones, and can imitate actions.

8–12 months: Babies can look at masks and recognize the ones that are more like human faces, showing they can hold information in their minds and compare it with something new. Now they begin to show fear of unfamiliar people or objects because they know that they are different. They also learn to remember where a toy is hidden —a sign that mental development is guiding memory growth.

Preschool years: "Eidetic imagery," the ability to hold a visual picture in short-term memory, is stronger than verbal memory at first but diminishes as the child learns to use words. By age two, children show a natural propensity to use rehearsal by repeating things they want to remember. Preschoolers also do a lot of "incidental learning"—they remember things which were present when they were learning something else, and they do not restrict their attention very effectively. The preschooler remembers things with which she has direct experience and still doesn't understand much about how to make memory work. If a four-year-old is shown twelve pictures of familiar objects, she can recall three or four of them and recognize ten or eleven if asked, "Did you see this one before?"

Elementary School Years: By age six, children begin to understand reasons for remembering things and develop memory strategies. They instinctively rehearse material, and by age seven should be able to see patterns and organize groups of things to be remembered. They should be able to remember and retell a story with the events in reasonable order. Ability to focus on relevant material should improve, but children with attention problems continue to take in so much incidental information that they have difficulty remembering what is important. By age ten, most children shown twelve pictures can recall eight and recognize all twelve.

Adolescence: This is the age for making connections between different subjects and ideas. Memory becomes a mechanism for abstract thinking as the adolescent learns to retrieve two or more bits of information and hold them in his mind while evaluating new thoughts. The more things fit together, the better memory works. If insufficient groundwork has been laid for understanding material presented in school, now is the time to rebuild. Teenagers should have reached the adult short-term span of seven items they hear, and should have numerous strategies for memorizing longer amounts of material. They can differentiate between recognition and recall when studying for tests if someone explains the difference.

Freedom to Remember

Research shows that personal interactions, praise, security, and self-confidence are powerful factors in children's memory development. If a child of any age is anxious or overwhelmed by interfering thoughts, the information may not even get by the first checkpoint. Many who have "memory" problems in school are actually distracted by worries or fears. Encouraging a child to express emotions honestly helps all learning.

Helping Children Build Memory Circuits

Here are some activities that are helpful at different ages, if they are kept unpressured and *fun:*

—Devise games to build visual, auditory, and motor short-term memory. Let the child take turns being "teacher" so the situation doesn't become one-sided. You can vary the amount of input according to the child's age.

—Teach children to use language to help them remember. Having a child rephrase stories or factual information in his own words is a good way to get it into long-term storage.

—Teach children to rehearse by repeating material over and then reviewing it periodically.

—Ask young children questions about events that happened in the near and distant past. Children of mothers who ask this type of question become better rememberers than others.

"Can you recall where I got those cookies you liked so well?"
"Who were the guests at Pete's party last week? Can you remember the presents?"
"Let's tell about what we did at the farm last summer."

—Show children how to use recognition cues to trigger recall.

"Leave your skates by the back door so you'll be sure to remember them."

Tips for Elementary School Children

—Memory for visual material is a powerful hook. Show them how to put "mind pictures" to work for remembering.

"Would you please go into the kitchen, put this apple in the yellow bowl, and then close the window? As I say it again, try closing your eyes, and making a picture in your mind of each thing I say."
"While you are reading, try to 'see' what the girl is doing in the story."
"Let's pretend you have a chalkboard in your mind. Write the spelling word there in a special color."

—Let children make choices about what and how they will remember. Personal involvement activates "association nodes" in the brain.
—If your child has trouble remembering something, help her associate it with an event, person, object, or idea that she is familiar with.
—Use as many senses as you can at one time. For example, have the child write multiplication facts with a finger on a rough surface (rug, pant leg) to feel them while saying and looking at them. Draw pictures of historical events with dates prominently attached. Use color whenever possible.
—Encourage the use of strategies for classifying, grouping, and making information meaningful. Have the child make stacks of flash cards in categories (all I know, all I want to learn; all 5s, all 7s, etc.).

Put states in categories (size, location, main occupations, etc.). Label the categories. Count the number in each.

—Dramatize or act things out. Make them funny, surprising, or absurd.

Tips for Older Students

—Remember it is easier to relearn material that is already familiar. When a test is coming up, make a review schedule to go over the material regularly for a period of several days.

—Don't underestimate the value of sleep in building memory circuits. Going to bed directly after learning something cuts down on interfering memories and firms up the new learning. This strategy is good for routine memorization of vocabulary drills, rules, lists, etc.

—Similar subjects should not be studied at the same time. Instead of doing Latin homework right after French, separate them with math and English.

—The "slight stress" of a high level of motivation seems to improve the ability to remember.

—The more thoroughly something is learned, the better you will be able to recall and apply it. You may need to "overlearn"—practice more than you think necessary, keep recalling and rehearsing it—if you have trouble with tests or remembering things in class.

—Ask your parents if they will drill you on factual material from a study guide you have made of the things you need to remember. If they get on your case, back off and find a friend with whom you can study.

—You will recall better if the situation is similar to that in which the material was learned. If you have to write an essay on a test, study for the test by writing practice essays. If it is a short-answer test, make up some questions for practice. Don't study orally for a written test. If possible, study in the same room where the test will be given.

—You will not be able to remember material if you do not understand why it is important or how it is related to the subject you are studying. Get your teacher to help you make study guides that show the main ideas and relationships in the material.

Genius or Fool?

A few individuals show prodigious memories for specialized kinds of material. One phenomenon which has never been explained is "calendar calculation," in which a person, given any date in history, can immediately tell the day of the week on which it fell. Singular memory skills have been found for mathematics, music, and other special fields. They show up in childhood, yet surprisingly, they are often associated with severely impaired intelligence. It is curious that children with highly developed skills in one narrow channel may be mentally deficient overall. The name used for this rare condition is "idiot savant," literally, "wise fool," and such memory abilities are called "splinter skills."

There is little danger of mistaking idiot savant memory for that of a normal child, since it usually goes along with peculiar behavior and other signs of abnormality. I mention it mainly because it underscores the bottom line: Intelligent memory is only as good as the whole mind that contains it. Focusing on "splinters" fragments the process of learning to remember.

WHO'S IN CHARGE? A QUESTION OF MOTIVATION

Motivation isn't yet measured by intelligence tests and is still something of a mystery, but it has a great deal to do with your child's success in using his mental ability. One piece of it that parents influence is called "locus of control." This term refers to the location of personal responsibility—either inside or outside. People with an *internal* locus are able to take responsibility for their own behavior. They can be objective about the reasons for their failures, but they are also able to take credit for their successes. Such children tend to be better students than those with an *external* locus, who are inclined to blame someone or something else for what happens to them.

"It's Not My Fault"

One year I was asked to work with a special group of students who were labeled "underachievers." They scored high on IQ tests but had abysmal academic records and were on the verge of failing eighth grade. As the year went on, I became more and more frustrated. I was having little success teaching them, and I couldn't figure out what the trouble was. Finally, one day, a girl came into class complaining bitterly about an injustice she felt she had suffered from her math teacher. Deciding to use this incident as an example for problem solving, I presented the issue to the class. What would they do if they had a problem with a teacher?

"I'd tell the principal."
"I'd tell my mother."
"I'd tell my father and he would tell that teacher off for sure!"

Not one student suggested personally assuming any responsibility in this situation. Bing! The light dawned. These children weren't admitting they were in charge. I remembered some of the year's other comments:

"That teacher is too hard. No one should be expected to do this."
"I can't concentrate in class. Amy keeps looking at me."
"How can we learn anything when it's so cold in here?"
"My mother says that this book is too hard for eighth grade."
"I don't like grammar and I don't see any reason to learn it. My dad says he hated it too and he never needed it after he got out of school."

Unfortunately, my little group was also missing the joys of accomplishment. Even when they did something well, they had trouble taking credit for it.

Meanwhile, I heard a delightful story from the mother of a second grade student who had been struggling to complete a science project. In desperation, the mother finally ventured, "Perhaps I should call your teacher and ask if she'll give you some help in school tomorrow." "No, Mom," replied the child, surveying the disaster. "I want to try and tough this one out for myself." I'll put my money on that child!

Research shows that children with learning problems tend to have an external locus of control, but no one knows which came first. If a child suffers defeat day after day even when trying his best, he may certainly start to blame outside forces. Nevertheless, the ability to meet challenges may be the distinguishing feature that enables children to overcome such problems. Locus of control is at least partially learned by example in the home. Here are some parental statements that encourage different attitudes toward responsibility:

EXTERNAL	INTERNAL
"I'll call Johnny's mother and tell her he didn't play nicely today."	"Let's talk to Johnny and you can tell him how you feel."
"I don't know why these things always happen to me."	"I wonder what I can do about this problem."
"Oh, I must just have been lucky."	"I'm really proud of myself!"
"We can't do anything. We're just ordinary people."	"Let's write a letter to our representative and try to get some action."
"I really shouldn't go through this stop sign, but no one is looking."	"I feel responsible for obeying the safety laws even if no one is looking."
"How dare the school bus driver threaten to throw you off the bus! We could sue them!"	"I'd like to know just what your part in this is. I expect you to follow the driver's rules."
"That teacher isn't fair. He shouldn't have picked Sue for the part. I'll call the school."	"I guess you have two choices. You can accept the decision or go and tell the teacher your honest feelings. I'm sorry you were disappointed, but sometimes life just isn't fair. We have to learn to keep trying."

Although locus of control can't be tracked down in the brain, it is an important adjunct to your child's mental equipment.

NEW DEFINITIONS OF INTELLIGENCE

It becomes increasingly apparent that current definitions of intelligence may not accommodate all its facets. Many believe it is time for some new viewpoints. At a recent three-day conference, an influential group of educational rebels agreed on several points:

—New brain research indicates that traditional views of intelligence are too narrow.

—Motivation and ability to take responsibility can be more important to success than a high IQ.

—Intelligence tests measure some useful skills, but they are more related to success in school than in life.

—IQ tests and schools neglect wholistic, intuitive thinking in favor of logical analysis. Both are needed in a productive society.

—Society is losing some of its most creative minds by defining intelligence too narrowly and penalizing those who do not fit the mold. One speaker declared that the most intelligent thing a child could do when confronted by an intelligence test was to walk out of the room!

How do these innovators suggest we approach redefining intelligence? Here are two viewpoints.

Modifying Minds

Reuven Feuerstein, an Israeli psychologist, refuses to accept the notion that IQ is a fixed commodity and insists that mental ability can be dramatically improved at all ages. When we test it, we should not look at how much the child knows, but the ability to learn something new. To test "learning potential," Feuerstein teaches each child for several hours. He then recommends an individual program of "cognitive modification."

This approach was tried with 200 low-achieving Israeli teenagers who had IQs between 55 and 85. Half received 300 hours of instruction in reading, writing, and arithmetic, while the other half got the same time in a program of mental exercises called "Instrumental Enrichment." Two years later, there were dramatic differences in test scores between the two groups. The Instrumental Enrichment group had gained in measured intelligence, while the others had not.

Using these techniques requires special training, but several of their principles provide practical guidelines for parents. According to Feuerstein, the roots of intelligence are developed by adults who help children make sense out of the world. They *do not teach directly,* but "mediate" experience for the child. For example, a mother could simply tell a child to go to the store and buy a can of tomatoes

—or she might also explain that she needed three cans to make spaghetti sauce and only had two on the shelf. Such simple ways of interpreting everyday events make the child a partner in the adult's thinking process.

Although Feuerstein does not use the term "locus of control," he states emphatically that the major problem of poor learners is passivity. They wait for information to be poured in, but take little responsibility or action in solving problems. *Intelligence grows not by acquiring facts, but by learning how facts are acquired.* Here are some of his major suggestions on enriching intelligence:

—Providing a stimulating environment is not enough; the child must get personally involved.

—Make the child an active partner rather than trying to "pour in" learning.

—Help the child see the reasons behind everyday events. (Instead of just stopping at a stop sign, point out what might happen if cars came from four different directions at once.)

—Guide the child toward an understanding of relationships whenever possible. Some examples from Instrumental Enrichment are:

1. Parent and child look at pictures of a stove with a pot that is first full and then empty. The child tries to figure out what caused the change. (The water was poured out, or perhaps it boiled away.)

2. The child looks at pictures of a woman cooking and a man gardening. He is asked, "What is similar about these activities?" (They are both working, etc.) "What is different?"

—Help the child get the feel of his body in space. Use the terms "right" and "left," but move with him as he masters them. ("Which way should we turn to get to Mary's house?" "In which direction is the library from here?")

—Gifted children may be hard to guide because they easily become impatient. Don't give up.

—Show your child that a deliberate plan of behavior is better than jumping in with random solutions to problems.

—Help your child identify inconsistencies ("Why do you suppose your teacher asked you to bring a raincoat on this sunny day?"), and see cause and effect relationships between events.

Some inevitable controversy has followed Feuerstein's claims that he can change intelligence. Nevertheless, studies in the United States show some promising results. In Venezuela, the minister of education became so excited about Instrumental Enrichment that all teachers are now receiving the training, and the government has embarked on a long-term plan to increase the level of all children's intelligence through a program of parent education. Experiences in the home may be the key to modifying our children's brains!

Seven Intelligences

Neuropsychologist Howard Gardner also believes we have neglected the spectrum of human intelligence and have unfairly slotted children into a system where their greatest talents may go unrecognized. In studying brains damaged by accidents or illness, Gardner observed separate abilities which function so independently that damage to one often leaves others completely intact. He identified seven separate intelligences which lead to different types of adult accomplishment:

1. Linguistic (poet, writer)
2. Logical-mathematical (mathematician, scientist)
3. Visual-spatial (architect, sculptor, pilot)
4. Bodily-kinesthetic (dancer, athlete, surgeon, instrumentalist)
5. Musical (composer, performer)
6. Interpersonal (understanding other people)
7. Intrapersonal (knowledge of self)

Gardner believes that individuals have a natural affinity toward one or more of these abilities, probably because of inherited neural tendencies. Each intelligence may have a memory of its own; a musician might have a prodigious memory for musical scores but not for spelling words. Gardner believes that we should term children "at promise" for different types of abilities and should encourage their natural gifts. He, too, thinks schools tend to force students into a traditional linguistic/logical-mathematical mold, and urges that we stop diminishing the importance of artistic and personal skills. It is difficult, says Gardner, to excel at two widely separated talents—art and literature, for example, and it is a mistake to neglect one in favor of the other. It is up to adults to help build children's skills in areas where they are less "at promise."

Adult models, or mentors, play an important part in encouraging children to fulfill their promise, and early experiences which excite a child about one field may galvanize choices for life. One question that another group of innovators asks is, "How early?"

Engineering Intelligence

Attempts to stimulate children's intelligence before and soon after birth raise a new issue for young parents. Playing tapes to babies in the womb or exposing infants to special teaching programs are options which are intriguing but confusing alternatives to natural development. Definitive answers about these programs' success are not yet available, partially because it is difficult to do research on human infants. How would the child have turned out without the special treatment? No one knows. The National Institutes of Health are directing substantial funding into prenatal investigations in an attempt to clarify some of these issues, which have implications far beyond an immediate goal of making kids "smarter."

Attempting to engineer intelligence implies value judgments about the particular set of abilities which compose it. A decision to teach an infant to recognize numerals, for example, occupies both time and neural capacity. There are numerous reports about children stimulated both before and after birth with cards containing letters, words, numbers, and colors. In one case, the parents also bombarded the baby in the womb with constant conversation.

Continued aggressive stimulation after birth reportedly produced a child with an IQ over 230 who entered high school at age five. Clearly, parents who choose this course have made a value judgment about what is important to them, and they no doubt feel satisfied about producing a child who meets their standards of quality.

Most of us who study children's minds are less confident of our ability to understand what is important in developing intelligence. If we mold the young plastic brain around current learning fads, what might be sacrificed? I personally question the wisdom of engineering specialized parts of a whole which, as yet, we can't even define. The concept of training children to be more intelligent has alarming similarities to computer programming. Someone has to decide what information to put in. What is left out?

Implementing mental ability calls for factors which defy programming into a machine or a brain. Artificial intelligence can't comprehend the nuances of human language and thought, the joy of humor, self-awareness, or altruism. Computers cannot imagine or leap conceptual chasms. These qualities also elude IQ tests, but they may be, after all, those upon which expanded definitions of intelligence should focus and which we, as parents, should prize most in our children.

LEARNING APPLIED

Children Read
with Their Brains

PHILLIP STARTED TO READ WORDS ON LABELS AND SIGNS WHEN he was two and a half years old. By the age of three he could read out loud from simple children's books, and soon began to spend hours reading anything he could find. One day when he was five his mother was surprised to find him perusing one of her nursing journals—and even more amazed at the skill with which he pronounced the complicated medical terms. Now, at age eight, Phillip is waiting at the breakfast table for his special school van. While he waits, he reads an article from the New York *Times*. He is so engrossed that his mother must remind him when the van arrives. Phillip reluctantly leaves the newspaper, grabs his coat, and runs down the driveway.

"Good morning, Phillip," calls the van driver.

"Good morning," intones Phillip, settling himself in his usual seat. He picks up the ends of his seat belt, regards them with a puzzled expression, and attempts to fasten them—behind his back.

"Here, let me help you," offers the driver, rebuckling the belt across Phillip's lap. "Remember, I tell you every day that the belt holds you and the seat together. You'll get it someday."

The van starts up and Phillip is off to school—his special school for children who are mentally retarded.

No, I am not making up this story. Phillip is a real child, although his name has been changed. I didn't believe it either until I met him and several others who changed my preconceived notions about early reading. Children who learn to read early are smart. Aren't they? Early reading is a sign of giftedness. Isn't it? Children can't read things they don't understand. Right?

Wrong. Phillip, and others, are "hyperlexic," literally, reading too much and for the wrong reasons. Although they develop reading at unusually early ages and perfect their "word calling" to a remarkable degree, that's all it is—calling out words without associating them with meaning. Some specialists call it "barking at print." This type of reading is a "splinter skill" which is compulsive and abnormal, like some of the other behavior of these children. Hyperlexic children have trouble relating to the world around them. They have serious problems with language development and social interactions, and some are even diagnosed as "autistic." Fortunately, hyperlexia is rare, but it raises important questions about what constitutes "good reading" as well as when and why children should learn to read.

Parents have been besieged by conflicting advice about teaching their children to read and helping them after they enter school. You can help your child become an enthusiastic and skilled reader, but not in some of the ways you may have heard. This chapter will challenge many common assumptions by looking at the way the child's brain learns to convert printed words into a meaningful message. Let's start with Phillip's story for some ideas about why children learn to read in the first place.

"A Weird Child"

"Yes, he was a weird child from the beginning." Phillip's mother pauses over her coffee cup as we sit in the living room of their attractive suburban house. "Don't get me wrong—I am crazy about that kid, but he never wanted to be cuddled, and he would never look us in the eye like most children do. That was just the beginning. His language development was so slow that he wasn't even speaking in sentences at age three."

"But you told me he started to read at two and a half." I was still skeptical, for this was only the first of twelve interviews that painted astonishingly similar pictures of children in a dozen differing environments.

"That's why I was completely amazed when I found out he could read. I had just decided to take him for a full evaluation—you know, to see what was wrong with him—when we were driving home from the library one day. He was sitting in the backseat and picked up a book and started to read some of the words. It took me a minute to realize what was happening, and then I almost crashed into a tree."

"How in the world do you explain it?" I knew that Phillip had, indeed, received several evaluations which placed his overall intelligence well below "normal." His language, despite intensive therapy, was still limited, and he had trouble understanding many things that are taken for granted with most children. Despite high-school-level abilities in word reading, his comprehension was below that of a second grader. Neurologists believed he had been born with some abnormal connections in his brain, although they were unable to find the specific source of the trouble.

"I don't know. Just to show you how weird he was, he was never interested in toys, never pretended, and never wanted to go out to play. Even in his playpen, he would push all the toys into a corner and lie there looking at books. For a while we thought maybe he was a genius, but obviously we were wrong. I often wonder what would have happened if we had gotten him to play more. We encouraged the reading, but I think it was a mistake. We thought that early reading was always a good sign."

After eleven more interviews and hours of testing these "weird" but engaging youngsters, I was convinced. A few children can teach themselves to read at very early ages even when other development is severely delayed. It is possible to read words perfectly but mechanically. For some reason which we don't yet understand, hyperlexic children manage to separate the words from the meaning. Perhaps they fixate on printed words as a sort of "anchor" because they have trouble getting patterns of meaning out of experience. They have excellent rote-level memories, but they live in a world full of things, such as toys, seatbelts, and people, which they are unable to understand. Yet without that ability to comprehend the world and the language used to talk about it, they cannot truly "read" even while flawlessly pronouncing the words on the page. Because they lack the foundations of language and thinking, they are unaware of the real purpose of reading—getting meaning from print.

What Is "Good Reading"?

Good reading involves more than learning to figure out, or "decode," the words. The perceptual channels of the eyes and ears are only the entry points into a huge system of meaning packaged in language that brings messages from the writer to the reader. Comprehension depends on a background of receiving language messages and connecting them with ideas—which come from personal experience with the world.

Studying hyperlexia has alarmed me about unbalancing normal children's early reading. I believe the lesson to be learned from these unusual cases is that only a base of mental growth takes reading beyond a hollow exercise. When that base is in place—and only then —children have the right reasons to read: to find meaning, to learn, and to expand their world. This is an important message for today's pressured parents. Let's now examine the natural course of reading development so that you can understand how children learn to read, when and how they should be taught, and the continuing role of parents during a child's school years.

HOW CHILDREN LEARN TO READ

Young Brains Look at Words

"Mommy, Mommy, there's McDonalds! Let's stop!" Is this four-year-old reading the sign? Not exactly, but she is following a natural process that starts children toward reading even before they enter school. You might not recognize these precursors because they are part of normal language development. The first reading lesson is mastered when the child learns that language carries messages from other people. The second comes when spoken words become symbols for objects and events ("Let's go to McDonalds!"). Eventually, they connect with "pictures" of words ("McDonalds"). Personal meaning meets printed symbol ("Let's stop!").

Brand names and logos are easy to remember because they come in interesting shapes and colors. Some children are able to take this visual skill one step farther and learn to remember printed words in the same way. The age at which this development occurs varies greatly—and *is not tied to intelligence.* Learning words by "sight," like remembering a picture or shape, is often called "the look-say method," and has been the basis for many early reading programs. Most adult readers depend heavily on "sight" words, too. How do you recognize the word "through"? You certainly didn't sound it out, but you can read it because you have seen and used it many times.

Young brains are particularly well adapted to simple sight-word learning because their right-hemisphere skills of visual picture recognition are usually stronger than left-hemisphere abilities to "sound out" words. Before age six or so, children, especially boys, tend more toward visual, pictorial processing. Yet words in books are a lot harder than the colorful shapes on signs. They require sophisticated visual analysis, and may all look alike to a young child. If your preschooler does not show an interest in the words when you read to him—if he does not ask you, "What does that say?"—chances are he is not ready to distinguish one from another. Don't force the issue! He should continue to learn actively from touching, exploring, and figuring out the world, not from being frustrated by abstract verbal symbols.

Learning by sight-word methods is not right for everyone. Even adults vary greatly in their skills of visual memory and recognition. Some exceptionally intelligent brains can't hang on to the way words look. (Is it "thier" or "their"?) It is a real mistake to force early reading on such children. I have treated six-year-olds who were positively phobic about reading because they already associated it with failure. If only someone had waited until their brains were mature enough to approach reading through another channel! Children like this need a special tool: the systematic use of phonics—through circuits that are not available until around age six—and sometimes later.

Sounding It Out

How do you read "romchembulate"? Since you never saw this nonsense word before, you probably sounded it out, syllable by syllable, even if the process was almost instantaneous. If you tried to read it all in one "picture," by sight, you would miss some of the sounds or get them in the wrong order. Most unfamiliar words have to be attacked through putting letters and sounds together—combining auditory and visual analysis. Teachers call this method *phonics.* All children need phonics skills because the visual system alone can't read and spell long unknown words.

How are phonics learned? In the normal progression of reading, some children figure out sound patterns from the words they have learned by sight. They instinctively generalize the rule that *ph* says *f,* for example, because they can read "phone" or know someone named Ralph. Others need to be taught the basic letter-sound principles. First, the word has to be visually analyzed: Which letter(s) comes first? What sound does it have? Now the second sound, and the third. Now, look at them and say them in order. Now, keep the order in your head and blend them together (this is *tricky),* say the word, listen to it, and associate it first with something you've heard before and then with its meaning. Not so simple, after all! The meaning connection is usually the last to be made.

Sounding out words meaningfully calls upon a relatively late-maturing area in the left hemisphere of the brain. At an important junction of sensory areas in the cortex called the *angular gyrus,* sound and meaning get attached to the letter shapes. This area matures early in some children, but many wait until after age six. There is good evidence that families differ in the inherited timetable as well as the size and efficiency of this part of the brain. Meanwhile, the schedule for development of fibers that connect right-hemisphere visual picture recognition and left-hemisphere sound processing also varies widely. I suggest you refer to Chapter 6 for a more complete account of this important event.

Once phonics have been partially mastered, children often begin to depend heavily on sounding out words. Because they have trouble connecting sight, sound, and meaning, they may read slowly and comprehend poorly because they are working so hard on the "decoding" process. At this point, our goal is to get them focused on meaning as soon as possible, and they should not be hassled too much about accuracy in oral reading. Do not encourage your child to be a "word caller" who barks perfectly at the print but neglects the message. Gradually, good readers learn to combine several strategies, reading mostly by "sight" and letting the meaning carry them along until they must decode a word that looks unfamiliar. Good reading calls upon many areas in the brain working together, and a smoothly running system takes years of practice.

Mental Scaffolds for Reading Comprehension

A child's reading comprehension ability can be greatly affected by methods of instruction. Studies show conclusively that understanding should be emphasized from the beginning. Words should not be presented in isolation but integrated into sentences and stories that are important to the child. Moreover, it is clear that children cannot understand reading that exceeds their language comprehension. The best reading programs are those which emphasize vocabulary development and oral language understanding.

Language and thinking are all wound up together in a child's brain. Learning to talk about experiences builds scaffolds for thought, and active thinking adds new layers to language. Comprehension depends on the quality of the neural networks that have been developed. For example, a third grader reading a story about a trip to a grocery store will probably have little trouble with "They paid the lady at the cash register," even if she has never seen the words "cash register" before. If she has never been to a grocery store, however, or doesn't know the name of the "thing you put the money in," she may not be able to decode the words or understand them.

If you're willing to try an experiment, I'll show you the importance of your mental scaffolds. Try to read this sentence about a familiar situation:

> The pimmelator groked the ghipt that his thwest was flandolent.

Can you figure out what this sentence is about? What? You didn't understand it? Couldn't you pronounce the words? But you "read" them all correctly, didn't you? What is the problem? See if this helps:

> In the courtroom, the pimmelator groked the presiding ghipt that his thwest was flandolent.

Now can you read it? I find that most adults soon figure out the message—that a lawyer is telling a judge about his client's innocence. What made the difference? I opened up one of your meaning frameworks with the words, "In the courtroom." Where did the meaning come from? Certainly not from those nonsense words! It was in your head all the time. If you didn't know about a courtroom, however, you would still be in the dark. Reading comprehension depends on frameworks of meaning from prior experience far more than on decoding words. Earlier chapters in this book tell how parents help children build those frameworks through lots of firsthand encounters with objects, stories, ideas, and experiences.

In the previous example you had some other frameworks, too. Did you realize that the "pimmelator" was a person performing some sort of action, and that "groked" was a verb in the past tense? This internal understanding of the structure of words is a very important part of reading comprehension and one more reason for giving your child a good language foundation.

Learning to read words is only an access route to whatever lies inside the reader's mind. Reading can add to our wisdom and store of knowledge, but it must start with ideas which are related to something we understand. Give your child that base of understanding first —we'll worry about pronouncing the words on the page when the brain is ready to attach meaning to them.

Reading Risks

Some teachers in workshops refuse to try that silly sentence. They are afraid they won't get it right. Good reading, particularly rapid, efficient reading, requires some risk taking: Looking ahead, guessing what will come next, skipping over words as long as the text is making sense. Children who are hung up about making a mistake rarely become efficient readers. They cling to every word as if they were drowning in an unknown sea. Often they come to me for help with "speed" when what they really need is confidence that if they make an error the world will not end.

I once had a student in first grade who looked like a frightened little rabbit when she came to the reading table with her group. She was off to a slow start, but her good language abilities made me confident that she would soon catch up. As the year went on, however, I was increasingly frustrated by her faltering progress. Whenever she was called on to read, she gazed up at me with large pleading eyes and a quivering mouth. Children do not ordinarily find me scary, so I puzzled endlessly about what the problem might be. Finally, one day, I took her aside and confronted the issue.

"Elizabeth, I have been wondering why you find reading so scary. You are good at so many things, it makes me sad to see you look frightened. Can you tell me what happens inside when I call on you in reading group?"

Elizabeth gulped and her chin quivered. "I hate reading!" she blurted out. Gradually, the story emerged. "When I was little, Mom had all these word cards pasted all over the house and then she would take them down and see if I could remember them, and I never could and I made mistakes *all* the time. I think I'm really stupid about reading. When you call on me my mind just goes empty."

Further investigation revealed that Elizabeth's mother, a former teacher, had indeed tried to teach her daughter to read at an early age. She genuinely believed she was doing the child a favor, but unfortunately, Elizabeth was one of those who have trouble remembering words by sight. The effort was a disaster despite Mother's best intentions. Moreover, it was evident that this was a household where mistakes were barely tolerated. Elizabeth was afraid of playground days when her clothes might get dirty, and she was so worried about perfect handwriting that she was often behind in her work. While I'm not recommending that you roll your child in dirt on a regular basis, I would suggest at certain ages there is as much to be learned from mud and water as from the alphabet!

Understanding the problem enabled us to help this little girl, but she will always be a slow, overly careful reader. She loses important meanings and rereads a lot because she is still concerned about missing a word or a detail. To be good readers, children must be able to take intellectual risks. Parents (or teachers!) should not shackle their intellectual energies by unreasonable demands—either for performance or for perfection.

Reading Development in a Nutshell

To help you sort out some of these important ideas about how children become good readers, let's summarize the main issues so far:

—Decoding words is only the beginning. Comprehension must come hand in hand for good reading.

—Children who develop early habits of "barking at print" may never become good readers.

—Learning words in isolation (e.g., on flash cards) removes reading from its normal context of getting meaning from real language.

—Children without a good base of language and thinking skills have trouble understanding and applying what they read.

—There are two main ways to recognize words: by "sight" or by "phonics." Most young children who learn to read by themselves start with a sight approach and gradually generalize the idea of sound-letter relationships.

—Some intelligent people do not easily remember words by sight. They need to depend on phonics in order to learn to read.

—Most children do not have the brain development required for successful phonics instruction until around age five or six. For some, especially boys, it may be considerably later.

—Reading comprehension is built on mental networks formed throughout childhood from real experiences with the world. Parents who provide interesting activities and talk about them with their child are laying the most important foundation for reading skill.

—Comprehension arises more from information stored in the reader's brain than on the printed page. Children can add to their information store by reading *if* they start with a base of understanding. Much reading failure results from inadequate foundations of experience with the ideas presented.

—Good reading requires intellectual risk taking. A perfectionistic environment where mistakes are barely tolerated may inhibit a child's reading development.

—Early reading is not always a sign of giftedness. If it replaces other activities which are developmentally appropriate (playing, talking), it may be a danger signal. If your child shows symptoms of hyperlexia, delayed language, and extreme difficulty with interpersonal relationships, do not encourage reading. Obtain a complete evaluation of mental and language development and work on activities more appropriate for early cognitive growth.

WHEN SHOULD CHILDREN LEARN TO READ?

Is Earlier Better?

Many parents mistakenly believe that encouraging early reading will get their child onto the "fast track" even before school begins. Since good reading is such an integral part of academic success, this attitude is not surprising. Lately, our parental insecurities have been heightened by people advocating that infants be taught to recognize words. Will these children be farther ahead? Will they grab up all the places at the good colleges because they are such academic stars? Let's look at this serious question in the light of research in mental development.

Yes, even babies can be trained to recognize words. Babies, however, cannot *read,* tapping into a vast personal storehouse of language and knowledge that takes years to build. Most preschoolers, likewise, can be trained through a stimulus-response type of teaching. The human brain can be trained to do almost anything, if the task is simplified enough and one is willing to devote the necessary time and energy. Yet the brain power—and possibly the neural connections—are stolen from the foundation of real intelligence. Reading becomes a low-level skill, and there is a danger that it will remain at the level where it was learned and practiced.

I believe that teaching reading to preschoolers is a serious intrusion on natural mental growth. Only a few, who *spontaneously,* motivated by their own curiosity, teach themselves to read *because they want to find out the meaning* are true early readers. Pushing others to call out words is a grossly oversimplified version of a complex intellectual feat. If we get children to "read" words before they have ideas, thoughts, and language to make reading interesting, we hand them a key to the door of an unfinished garden.

The Unfinished Garden

"Look, child, there is an exciting garden of adventure called reading behind this gate. It is important for you to get inside. Here's a key. Let's work on opening the gate so you can enter this wonderful place." The child labors diligently to fit the key into the lock. This is taking lots of time. Is it worth it?

"Of course it's worth it. Entering the garden of reading is the most important thing you'll ever do. You'll be ahead in school and get into a good college. Try a little harder." After hours of effort, the key begins to turn. More hours, and the door opens a crack.

"Whew!" thinks the child, "Now for the goodies! Hey, wait a minute! This is just a big bare place with some little sprouts coming up. This is *boring!*"

"Sorry, kid, I guess your mental garden isn't quite ready yet. If you wait a few years, those sprouts will turn into interesting ideas and then you'll be able to use your reading key to have a lot of fun. I promise you'll love it."

One of the biggest problems in schools today is that children do not like to read. They complain that it is "boring." Is it possible that we have turned them back at the doorway by forcing the key on them too soon?

A True Story

"Stop worrying," Carol told herself as she watched five-year-old Paul intently constructing an intricate block highway system. "He's obviously intelligent and you're just overreacting. So what if Marge is bragging that Erna can read." Still, she found herself reaching for the box of plastic alphabet letters. "Here's a *G*, Paul," she exclaimed with calculated enthusiasm, laying it on top of his newly designed garage. "*G* stands for garage. It says 'guh, guh.' "

"Grrrr!" shouted Paul joyously, accelerating a toy car into the garage and knocking the letter onto the floor.

"Look here, Paul." Carol's voice became insistent as she pushed the letter in front of her son's eyes. "Look at the *G* and say 'guh.' "

"I don't wanna!" wailed Paul, seizing the letter and flinging it across the room. "I hate those dumb letters!"

I know this is a true story because it happened in our home. How well I remember my panicky feeling when our eldest son—at the advanced age of five—wasn't interested in reading. I remember my gentle—and not-so-gentle—prodding, the attempts to teach him letter sounds, and my worry that he wouldn't make the top reading group because he was behind. To be honest, I was also worried about how he compared with my friends' children. I wish someone had given me the facts:

—Many bright, even gifted, children do not read early. Please let them enjoy stories without an underlying aura of expectation which they cannot fulfill.

—Truly gifted early readers are insatiable in their desire to learn to read. They do not have to be taught, and they make instinctive connections with thought and language. If you have one of these children, share the joy of this natural experience. The way they usually learn is from adults or older brothers and sisters reading to them.

—Early readers do not always win the race. The slower starters, with a wide base of experience and problem solving, often pull ahead when thinking skills and application become more important around fourth grade.

—Reading problems can be created by forced early instruction. Many authorities believe that age seven is the right time to begin formally teaching reading. Studies in different countries have shown that when five- and seven-year-olds are taught by the same methods, the seven-year-olds learn far more quickly and happily than do the fives, who are more likely to develop reading difficulties.

—Reading requires an *active pursuit of meaning.* Children who pick up the idea that it is something *done to them* are being programmed as passive readers who will neither enjoy reading nor pursue meaning effectively.

—Forcing or overloading neural circuits may cause the brain to go into "idle" because it cannot handle the load. Don't let your child associate reading with an idling brain.

Fortunately, my personal story concluded happily. I mustered up enough sense to back off after a few such incidents, and our son had an unusually skilled first grade teacher who repaired most of the damage. Still, it took several years before he discovered that reading was delicious fare for his keen intellect. Now I look back and wonder, "What was the rush?"

I told this story to one mother whose five-year-old is intellectually gifted but not yet ready to read. "I feel so relieved," she sighed. "I just needed some ammunition. I knew I was pushing her too hard, but you hear all these things. . . ."

Hold on to your good instincts about what is right for your child. Don't join the crowd of hucksters who sell keys to the garden of reading before children are ready to use them. There is no justification for turning a treasure into a boring commodity.

Another True Story

Ronee arrived on the first day of kindergarten clutching a worn book which she couldn't wait to show her new teacher. "This is my favorite story," she confided. "It's *Cinderella.* I just love *Cinderella.* I'll read it to you if you want."

The teacher, enchanted by Ronee's soft brown eyes and masses of electric pigtails, soon discovered that the child could, in fact, read— not only *Cinderella,* but every book in the room as well as the ones in the first, second, and third grades. Moreover, she could understand them. When Ronee read, she got so excited about the story, that she carried on a personal dialogue:

"Oh, no! They're not really going to do *that!*"
"What's going to happen? I'm scared!"
"Oh, that's so funny!"

As she read out loud, her voice got softer and softer until she was reading silently, like a mature reader going after meaning in the quickest way. This reading was definitely not a splinter skill!

Ronee's teacher referred her to the reading specialist, whose tests confirmed that the child could read and comprehend above third grade level. Most of her reading was based on sight recognition of familiar words or word parts, but she was instinctively using phonics as well. Curious, the specialist asked Ronee's mother what she had done to make her child such a good reader.

"Oh, not much. I always read to her a lot. She just loved her stories, and about a year ago she started bugging me to tell her what the words meant. I showed her how the letters went together to make words. She did the rest herself."

What kind of a kindergarten program should this child have? Some schools put children like this into the standard reading readiness program, where they drill on letter sounds. We should all object strenuously to such pedagogical absurdities. Ronee needs an enriched program where she can use her reading skill to learn about interesting topics and share stories with classmates. She can learn to write stories and plays of her own with "invented spelling" (see Chapter 10), and make books and illustrate them. She can extend her learning by tackling factual topics and reporting on them. If the teacher is overburdened, a volunteer or an older student might spend individual time with her.

Fortunately, Ronee's teacher views her gifted student as a delightful challenge and has arranged a special program that includes plenty of interaction with other children. Ronee may be unusual, but she is still five years old. Right now she is working hard, learning about dinosaurs and also writing a play for her classmates to perform —a dramatization of *Cinderella*.

If you have a child like Ronee, rejoice, but keep an eye on what is happening in the classroom. Gifted children represent a special challenge which many schools are only starting to address. Giving a child like this "reading readiness" worksheets reminds me of pulling the wings off a butterfly.

PARENTS HELPING CHILDREN READ

What Is "Reading Readiness"?

Does caution about early pressure mean that parents should have no part in their child's reading development? Quite the contrary. Parents lay the groundwork which enables the child to activate the system. Above all, children should be shown—by example—that reading is fun. Homes where books, magazines, and newspapers abound, where adults read and talk about ideas, produce the best readers. There are dozens of books with suggestions for parents, but in order to evaluate them you need to understand the underlying principles of reading "readiness."

To be truly "ready" to read, a child must have accomplished some important groundwork. First, visual development must be adequate for focusing at the proper distance, distinguishing letters and words, tracking in a left to right direction, and keeping the place. There is a serious question as to whether many preschoolers have this basic physical ability for reading. Second, thinking skills must be adequately developed. Some believe that a child must understand "conservation" to get beyond the physical appearance of words, understand that they have abstract meanings, and connect those meanings to ideas. Many parents are surprised to learn that object manipulation and play are major foundations for good reading.

Language is the third cornerstone. In addition to lots of conversation and vocabulary building, parents can have fun with one special aspect of language readiness. Before they read well, children must develop what experts call "linguistic awareness," meaning that they know some of the conventions of reading, including what a "word" is.

Developing Linguistic Awareness

—Show your child that a book has a cover, a title that tells what it will be about, and pages that go in order from front to back. Discuss the pictures and their relationship with the story.

—Let your child see that you are reading from the top to the bottom of each page.

—Help your child understand that words have interesting and important meanings, and that you enjoy reading them to get information or to have fun (e.g., use newspapers, magazine articles, recipes, directions, or comic strips).

—Young children may be unaware that words have spaces between them—both in speech and on the printed page. With a child older than four, call attention to what words look like when you are reading. Without making an issue of it, occasionally trace your finger under the line so that the child sees you moving in a left to right direction. Do not quiz or force the child to try and read the words.

—Learning to pay good attention to visual information is important for preschoolers. Encourage your child to look for details of pictures and objects and see how they are related to the whole, as preparation for visual analysis of letters in words.

—With children of four or older, sets of plastic alphabet letters can be made available, but not forced on the child. Remember that "uppercase" (capital) and "lowercase" (small) letters may mean the same thing to you, but they look completely different to the child. Do not expect a child to know that *H* and *h* are the same thing.

—With children of five or older, play games of counting words in short phrases or rhymes. You can clap for each word to keep track. Children will tend to clap for each syllable. The purpose is to show that a word is a unit of meaning, not just a sound.

—If children spontaneously start to ask about written words, tell them. When youngsters are really ready to read, they become real pests. Take the time to satisfy their curiosity.

Experiencing Written Language

One practical way for parents to capitalize on a child's spontaneous interest in reading is by encouraging him to create his own stories, which you write down for him. Termed "language experience stories," these creations provide an excellent tool for teaching reading; they are used in many schools and can be fun at home if the child is interested. Take a large piece of paper and tell the child that you will be the "secretary" for a story. Reserving the top half of the paper for a picture, write down the child's words *exactly* as he dictates them. Don't dress up the grammar or vocabulary; this story belongs to him. If you can't resist the urge to take over, or if the child acts bored, quit. Use uppercase and lowercase manuscript letters, not all capitals (if you have any doubt, consult your local school for models of the writing system currently in use), or type the story.

Encourage the child to draw a picture with each story, and soon you will have a collection to staple together into a book: "Charlie's Stories." Reread each out loud for the author as often as he asks for it. Some children enjoy trying to reread for themselves, and this is one of the best ways to start reading since children's own words have the most meaning for them. Don't force it, however. While you read, point to each word as you go along. Don't quiz the child, and don't be surprised if he can't remember any of the words in the story. Compliment him on his wonderful story, even if it says, "I sat on the grass." It makes his language seem very important—which it is!

Children vary in their fluency with storytelling. You may have to provide some ideas ("Would you like to tell about our walk to the park? What did you see on the way?" "I would love to hear a story about the castle you made in the sandbox. Could a little king be in there?") I would not start language experience stories until at least age four.

Incidentally, sometimes we get fooled by a youngster's good memory for familiar stories. Children can look and act as if they are reading when they aren't. For this reason, parent and teachers sometimes disagree about whether a child can read.

Parents Teach Story Scripts

Children pick up a special kind of knowledge base if they live in a home where a variety of reading is part of daily life. Sampling rhymes, poems, stories, fables, and folk tales builds mental frameworks for the structure of literature. A child who has learned what to expect from the structure of a story—a "story script"—will find reading much easier and more enjoyable. For example, if I told you we were going to read a fable about a fox, the words "sly" or "crafty" would be easier to figure out, and you would expect a moral at the end. Instinctive awareness that a story has a main character, that there is usually some problem, a climax, and an ending, facilitates comprehension. Likewise, a child who has been exposed to picture dictionaries and children's encyclopedias has a good start on using reference sources.

Try telling some stories, too. Don't be embarrassed—you will be surprised that your simplest attempts will enthrall your young audience. All children love to hear stories about when they were babies or tales of their parents' childhood experiences. One father who didn't particularly enjoy reading made up stories about children involved in a wonderful variety of adventures—finding caves in the woods, seeking hidden treasure, or even being chased by wild animals. Eventually he began stopping at the most exciting moment and inviting the avid listener to continue the story. His children loved the power of solving these problems, but soon learned to create a new climax and hand the storytelling reins back to Dad. Now grown, they still recall the fun of trying to invent the most improbable dilemma for the hero.

The Wiggly Ones

Some children seem to have come from a different programmer. They don't like to sit still and be read to. Capturing one like this is a challenge, and you may need subversive methods. Sometimes postponing bedtime for reading or storytelling works wonders. Look for books with lots of pictures or a subject that is especially interesting. Follow the child's lead—even if she wants to read the toy catalogue —and make sure your own vibrations are positive and fun to be around. Our wiggliest one eventually chose to be an English major in college, and "discovered" the joys of listening to Shakespeare. It took a little longer for him to get his time into joint—but it was worth the wait!

By the way, reassure your child you will keep on reading out loud even after she has learned to read for herself. One study suggested that some children may resist learning to read independently because they fear they will lose the close contact of story time with their parents.

Raising children who read well means raising children who have been encouraged to think well. The following list summarizes the characteristics of homes which produce good readers and good thinkers. You may be surprised how few have to do directly with reading.

HOMES FOR GOOD READERS

—A nonpunitive but structured atmosphere where children are encouraged to express ideas and feel part of decision making.

—Absence of unrealistic restrictions, demands, or inappropriate pressure.

—Encouragement of independent problem solving. Preschoolers are encouraged to be self-reliant in zipping, tying, setting table, etc. Older children are expected to think through problems.

—Tolerance of reasonable mistakes.

—Focus on praise rather than criticism.

—Emphasis on expanding rather than correcting child's conversation.

—No forcing of early reading.

—Adult models of reading for a variety of purposes. Pleasure in reading is evident. Boys and girls see both parents reading, since children tend to copy the attitudes of the same-sex parent.

—Regular time for reading to the child; reading is associated with relaxed and loving contact.

—Availability of books, newspapers, magazines, and interesting children's books.

—Regular trips to the library, where the child is encouraged to select books that are personally meaningful.

—A broad range of experiences, and conversation about them is a regular part of family life.

TEAMING WITH THE SCHOOL

Helping the Beginning Reader

A parent's supporting role does not end when a child starts school. The first months of formal reading instruction, usually in first grade, are a time of unrecognized stress for most children. Acutely aware of everyone's expectation that they will learn to read, they may secretly worry they will fail. Youngsters who have been victims of premature expectations are particularly vulnerable. Parents can do much to allay this natural anxiety, even to the point of articulating for the child how "scary" this new experience must be.

MOTHER: I remember when I started first grade it seemed like everyone thought I should learn to read and I felt scared that I couldn't.

CHILD: Yeah?

MOTHER: It took a while, but I learned. It takes a long time for children to learn to be good readers. Some children start out real fast, but that doesn't mean they're smarter. Everybody has their own special way to learn.

This last message is especially important if your child is in a class with children who are faster out of the gate. We must emphasize the message that slow starters are often just as smart but on a different learning track for a while. For "lumpers," who favor a wholistic approach to incoming information, splitting words up into sound sequences is not natural, and they have trouble remembering in which direction they are going. They would much rather start in the middle than analyze pieces in order. Thus, "was" and "saw", "on and no" may be confused. Letters may get turned around—*b* and *d, g* and *q*—because, if you're not into left-to-right sequence, they *are* alike. This confusion is usually not caused by problems in the eyes, but by the immature brain's difficulty registering and retaining symbols in order. Most children learn to straighten letters, words, and numerals out by the end of second grade, when their left hemispheres take more firm control, and they should be reassured that these normal errors do *not* mean that they are "stupid." Nor do some reversals mean that the child is necessarily going to be "dyslexic." There are other symptoms which accompany dyslexia, to be discussed later in this chapter.

Parents can become too concerned about the normal ups and downs of early reading. Please try to protect children from your own level of anxiety. If early reading becomes associated with stress, fear, or tension, it may retain that negative aura long after any initial problem has been overcome.

Reading with a School-Age Child

To help the teacher develop your child's reading ability, continue daily story time, express interest and enthusiasm about school progress, and let the child read to you at home every day. Your job is not to teach, but to reinforce good reading habits. Here are some guidelines:

1. Set aside a regular time to read to your child. As she learns to read, add ten minutes a day when she can read to you. Continue regularly until silent reading ability is gradually established.

2. Make sure that the child is reading from books that are easy

and enjoyable. This is called the "independent" level of reading. If you have any questions, ask the teacher. The purpose is not to teach skills but to practice fluency and learn to enjoy reading.

3. Let the child choose the books, as long as they are at the independent level. Children sometimes try to please their parents by selecting "hard" books, but this is a self-defeating exercise.

4. As the child reads, listen to determine if she understands the meaning. Clues are found in the way she phrases, observes punctuation marks, or makes comments about the story.

5. Insert an occasional question that will challenge her thinking and to which there is *no one right answer.* "Why do you think John wanted those shoes?" "What do you think will happen next?" "Let's guess what they could find in the old barn." "What might have happened if he had stayed home from the picnic?" Don't focus on literal-level questions like, "What color were the shoes?" "What did they take on the picnic?"

6. The most common error adults (including teachers) make is helping too much. If the child mispronounces a word, remain silent. Listen to the rest of the phrase or sentence to see if the mispronunciation changed the meaning. For example, if the phrase "a little dog" is read "a little doggy," I recommend you leave it alone. For beginning readers, confusion of "a" and "the" may also be ignored. If the child makes errors that change the sense of the story, wait for her to realize that meaning has been lost. You want her to monitor the meaning herself. If she continues, stop her at the end of a sentence or paragraph. Ask, "Did that make sense?" Encourage her to listen and reread for meaning. If a word is too difficult, have her read to the end of the sentence and try to figure out the missing word. If not, supply it.

7. Remember, perfection is not the goal. Comprehension is. Accuracy will follow if understanding leads.

8. When the story is finished, ask her to retell it *briefly.* Help her find only the main ideas and important parts and recall them in order. This process of synthesis is difficult but important. Encourage quality rather than quantity in retelling.

9. If you are both interested, extend your discussion of the story. You could imagine another ending, a different main character, or a different setting. Children enjoy creative projects: acting out scenes, making models of the setting in a shoebox, or even rewriting the plot from another point of view. Such projects can be taken to school and

shared with the class. They are far more interesting than the standard book report!

10. You can help your child with one of comprehension's greatest tools if you encourage mental imagery. Practice making "mental movies" of what is happening in the book. Try drawing pictures of what you each "saw" in the story. Use books without pictures or cover them up so that you can get your own ideas. Research shows that good comprehenders instinctively make mental pictures when they read, and that poorer readers' comprehension can be improved by direct instruction in this important strategy.

11. If your child resists reading to you at home, reflect on the amount of pressure in the situation. Are the sessions too long? Should you get easier books? Are you expecting perfection? Are you giving enough praise? Do you take a turn reading now and then? If a real problem seems to exist, go to the teacher or the reading specialist with your questions.

12. Encourage habits of independent reading. Extending bedtime is still a good inducement. Turn off the TV and let the whole family read together. Despite all our efforts, children learn to read by reading.

Neurological Impressions

Some children have trouble picking up the rhythms and patterns of oral reading. Halting, labored reading may result from material that is too difficult or from immaturity in the brain's word-processing systems. One way that parents can help nonfluent readers is called the *neurologic impress technique,* which sounds a lot more complicated than it is. Sit beside your child in a comfortable place. If the child is right-handed, you might sit so that your voice will enter his right ear to stimulate the opposite left (language) hemisphere. No one is sure if this is necessary, but it shouldn't do any harm. The child holds the book (at his independent reading level), and reads out loud. Your job is to read right along with him at a normal pace, providing a feel for the rhythms and phrasing. The child's voice may start to trail off, but keep him going as well as you can. Your voice is the guide; he tags along until the sentences become more familiar.

This technique is appropriate *for children of school age.* Ten minutes a day builds fluency. Repeat each story several times until the child is confident with it. Studies show this type of practice with a teacher improves speed of word recognition. The warm, cozy experience of reading with a parent should be even more effective.

Never criticize a child's reading. Children do not make mistakes on purpose. If he has trouble keeping the place, a file card which follows his progress down the page can help. The latest theories also say that using a finger to keep the place is OK. Most children "subvocalize" (pronounce words out loud as they read) until they are well into second or third grade. We all have a natural tendency to subvocalize with difficult material. Even older children may need to read out loud when something is above their independent level.

SQ3R

One nifty technique that is helpful with textbook reading for students above grade three is called *SQ3R,* which stands for:

1. Survey
2. Question
3. Read
4. Recite
5. Review

If your child's teacher has not introduced SQ3R, you can show your child how to use it for history, science, literature, or other texts. Here's how:

1. **Survey:** Look over the entire assignment or chapter. Read the title. Read all the subheadings. Look at any maps, charts, pictures. How do they all fit together? Skim the first and the last paragraphs. Survey study guides at the end of the chapter. How does this chapter relate to the entire book? To the course? Assure your child that the time spent on this step is not wasted, but will cut down on total study time.

2. **Question:** Who wrote this and why? Why am I reading it (for fun, for a test, to learn about how to make widgets)? What will it be about? Think of some questions inspired by the title (e.g., *Building the Colonies:* What were the colonies? Where were they? What did the colonists need to build? Homes? Stores? Factories? Governments? How did they build them? Who did the work?). Try to guess how to answer the questions. This step gets the child personally involved, setting his own direction and reasons for reading. Turn all

the chapter topic headings into questions. Try to guess answers to these and to any questions given in the text.

3. **Read:** Now read the chapter carefully. Writing summaries of each section in the margin is a good habit for students in junior high or older. Most students tend to underline too much. Read first, then go back and highlight only the most important points.

4. **Recite:** Without looking back at the text, try to answer the questions you asked at the beginning. How do all these subtopics fit together? What are the main ideas in this chapter? What are the important facts and details? How are the pictures, charts, and maps related to the topic?

5. **Review:** Go back over the material after some time has passed. Refresh your memory of the important facts and ideas. Periodic review is the best way to create memory circuits. Make study guides of facts and ideas that must be remembered.

SQ3R is only one of many practical tools to help students' reading comprehension. Experts are concerned that teachers have focused too much on teaching children to decode words and spit back facts rather than understanding and relating what they read to important ideas. Keep this in mind whenever you have a chance to be a coach in the reading game. Check to see if your school is working on comprehension skills. Encourage teachers to keep up with these new ideas, which will help children read with their brains instead of only with their eyes and voices.

WHAT TO DO IF YOU SUSPECT TROUBLE

"Dyslexia," abnormal difficulty with reading, writing, and spelling, is a widely used term guaranteed to inspire terror in a parent's soul. Many good books are available about learning problems, so I will limit this discussion to an overview of preventive measures, symptoms you should be aware of, and ways to go about seeking help if you suspect a problem.

Preventing Reading Problems

By now you can probably guess that my main prescriptions for the prevention of reading problems are:

1. Delaying or altering reading instruction until the child has the

required neurological maturation, even if it means waiting until age seven. Find out if your school uses testing or some other means of determining the level of students' readiness. Listen carefully to their advice.

2. Building language skills before expecting reading development.

3. Providing a broad base of experience so the child has many frameworks for attaching meaning.

4. Presenting beginning reading in a way that will capitalize on each child's most appropriate channels for learning.

5. Emphasizing reading comprehension along with basic decoding skills.

6. Making reading an interesting and creative mental activity for students at all grade levels.

Experts are optimistic that many, or even most, reading problems can be ameliorated by careful early intervention and reading instruction flexible enough to accommodate differing needs. Parents sometimes find themselves at cross purposes with school personnel who force lockstep instruction on all students, but I also hear the other side of the story from teachers who say they get relentless pressure from parents demanding results.

Does Your Child's School Encourage Good Reading?

If you want to exert constructive pressure, ask these questions about your school:

At the Beginning

—Is language development stressed along with reading?

—Is beginning reading taught through language experience stories as well as with more structured basal reading programs?

—Do children use real books, not just workbooks or computers?

—Is an effort made to identify children's level of readiness and provide instruction for varying needs?

—Are they willing to hold back the bright "unready" child and develop a program to get him ready?

—Do they give children the tools of phonics for future reading and spelling proficiency without limiting the program to "The cat sat on the mat"?

—Is writing an integral part of the reading program? Kindergarten is not too early to start linking reading and writing.

In every grade . . .

—Is silent comprehension stressed rather than attention to accuracy in oral reading—"barking at print"?

—Are children allowed to move at their own pace in reading, making sure that each step is comfortably mastered before imposing new demands?

—Conversely, are children encouraged to move on to more interesting uses of reading once skills are mastered?

—Is instructional grouping ("reading groups") flexible enough to accommodate a child's sudden spurt or emerging need? Is discrimination against the "bottom reading group" minimized?

—Is drill and textbook instruction supplemented with a wide variety of "real" reading: quality paperbacks, newspapers, research materials?

—Is reading instruction integrated with writing, poetry, drama, and other creative uses of the language arts?

—Is there some system of reporting the child's progress to parents in regularly scheduled personal conferences in addition to report cards?

—Is reading instruction fun?

Skilled instruction that is planned around each child's level of neurological development and learning style can prevent reading problems; patience and skill from both family and school are required.

Recognizing Problems

How do you know when to be worried? Danger signals differ depending on the age of the child. Here are a few signs to watch out for:

Early Signs

—Repeated ear infections; hearing impairment or loss.

—Language delay or problems at any age. Experts now think most reading problems are caused by a language disability, with visual reversals a symptom of the brain's underlying difficulty in processing language symbols (letters, words, and sometimes, numerals).

—Problems with paying attention.

—Uncorrected vision problems. Be sure to have your child checked early for amblyopia (lazy eye).

—Family history of language, reading, spelling, or writing problems.

—Left-handedness or ambidexterity, *if* there are other signals. (Many left-handers are fine readers.)

—Protracted difficulty telling time, learning telephone numbers or addresses, tying shoes, following directions. All require sequencing, handled in the area of the brain that also puts words and sounds in order.

During School Years

—Reversals or confusion of letters, words, numerals, directions, or ideas that persist after age seven or eight and are accompanied by other symptoms. All young children reverse letters. It does not mean they will be dyslexic. Please don't make an issue of this with your child!! Tension can make normal developmental errors into real problems.

—Unhappiness in school; physical symptoms (stomachaches, nightmares, worries) that can't be otherwise explained.

—Eye problems or headaches. Although most reading problems are in the brain, the eyes get blamed because they are the window onto the difficulty.

—Schoolwork brought home that is consistently too difficult for the child to do.

—Labored oral reading and difficulty with comprehension on material that the school sends home.

—Difficulty getting the meaning while reading silently after grade two.

—Problems with writing or spelling. Bright children may be dyslexic without showing severe reading difficulty. Their problems with language symbols show up when they have to write them down. You will learn more about this topic in the next chapter.

A parent's main job is to stay attuned to the school's ability to meet a child's special needs. If you find yourself forced to teach reading, rather than just reinforcing it at home, something is wrong. I can personally vouch for the fact that most parents are too emotionally involved to do a teacher's job with their own children! The parent-child relationship is too precious to clutter up with pressures from inappropriate school demands. If trouble is brewing in your house, go to the school and try to get at the source of the trouble.

How to Seek Help

As a part-time college professor teaching teachers to teach reading, I know that most teachers are in the business because they care a lot about their students. When a child is having trouble, they often welcome parental support, but like all of us, they don't take kindly to criticism. Some, unfortunately, may not be aware of the current research which has inspired this chapter, so you may have to tread lightly when presenting new ideas. Remember that your shared goal is the child's well-being, not an adversarial relationship. Here are a few suggestions if you are forced into the role of troubleshooter. As with any suggestions, filter these ideas through your own common sense about your child's best interests.

—Be available for conferences with teachers. Keep a careful eye on your child's progress.

—If you suspect trouble, do not delay too long before you make an appointment with the teacher.

—Present your problem calmly. Describe what you have seen in your child without laying a trip on the teacher. Assure her of your desire to help. Suggest looking for solutions you can work on together. Ask the teacher bluntly if she thinks you are putting too much pressure on the child. Listen to her answer.

—Your most important evidence is (1) your child's negative attitude toward learning, and (2) schoolwork which is clearly beyond the level of her current skill development. Bring in the messy, inaccurate, or incompleted pages. Do not accept—or believe for *one minute*—that your child is "lazy." Children are not lazy! They have an intense desire to achieve and please you. When the demands are too great, children look "lazy" because sometimes it is better to believe that you didn't try than that you are a failure

—Don't accept, "He can do it when he tries." I could run a marathon if I tried hard enough, but I sure couldn't do it every day! Moreover, one of the hallmarks of a child with a learning problem is inconsistency. Some days things connect and other days they don't. Your mutual goal must be to teach the child at a level where the payoff for trying is sufficient to inspire the effort. Failure does not inspire further effort. Success does.

—Try to work with the teacher to develop a plan of attack which will help your child start to feel successful. This may mean scaling back your mutual demands. Bite the bullet. If your child can't do the work, there is no point in trying to keep up with anyone else. Children learn nothing from work they don't do except how to avoid doing work.

—If your mutual efforts fail to get the child back on course, you should request an evaluation by (1) the school reading specialist or (2) a school psychologist at the earliest possible time. You can ask the reading specialist for diagnostic reading tests and an assessment of visual and auditory processing skills. If there is still doubt, request an individual IQ battery and learning disability testing from the school psychologist.

—In the meanwhile, ask if there is any individual help available through the school from a reading specialist, a tutoring program, or a special teacher.

—If the school is unable to provide testing or special teaching, seek help from a clinic or private educational psychologist. Ask your pediatrician and check with the local branch of the Association for Children with Learning Disabilities to get the name of a good one. If the problem has continued for more than six months in a young child or more than a year in an older one, do not delay. Ask these professionals to work with the school in planning a program to meet the child's needs after they do a thorough assessment.

—If a suggestion is made to hold the child back a year—especially in kindergarten or first grade—don't fly out the window. The reason you are here is that you have a problem, and this may be the best of several alternatives. When you have a problem, no alternative is perfect. Consult Chapter 4 for specific guidelines on holding a child back.

—Once you have gotten some help, expect your child to do his part. Having a problem must not be viewed as an excuse for giving up. If the demands are reasonable, you and the teacher may have to provide some structure to undo old habits of avoidance. ("You have a problem, which we understand now. It doesn't seem fair, but I guess that means you'll have to work a little harder than some of the other kids for a while to catch up, but we're all going to help you.")

—A child needs extra emotional support at home if there is trouble at school. Fill up his little spirit with praise whenever you have an opportunity. Many poor readers are whizzes at mechanical things, good artists or designers, fine athletes, or just plain wonderful people. Sympathize with his problems. "I know this is hard, but I love you, and you're OK, and I expect you to keep trying" is the message.

Since children come into the world with different brains, it is not surprising that reading comes more easily to some than to others. If your child is one of those whose talents lie in different areas, do your best, but don't decide that you are a failure as a parent. Some very talented people are simply not facile with the printed word. Reading is not the only important human talent.

REFLECTING WISDOM

Parents are important partners in reading development. They help build frameworks of language and thinking and encourage life-long attitudes toward reading. They can model and support good reading during school years, and be advocates for a child's particular needs. They should protect children from pressures to read too soon or for the wrong reasons. Above all, they can encourage use of this versatile tool to learn, to imagine, and to probe unlimited horizons.

One of my favorite quotations neatly sums up all the current theories. "Reading is like a mirror: If a fool looks in, you can't expect a wise man to look out." A child's reading ability is truly a mirror reflecting the background of mental development and interest which he brings to it. Learning to decode the words is only part of the process; understanding and applying them for learning is what good reading is all about.

Thinking on Paper:
Writing and Spelling

FOR MANY CHILDREN, WRITING AND SPELLING TURN OUT TO BE thorns in the academic rose garden. Parents get stuck trying to help without being very clear either on what the school wants or what they should do about it. Sometimes they feel they are expected to do the teacher's job at the risk of jeopardizing the relationship with their child—who most likely resists their help whenever possible. Other families, not impaled on these problems, are concerned about reports that schools are not teaching children to express themselves well in writing.

Their concerns are justified. Until recently, no one looked very closely at these skills, and teachers still know little about the best ways to develop them. The natural result has been neglect; many students graduate from high school after countless hours of instruction in reading but very few in the skilled writing that should have a central role in every child's education—as a tool not only for communicating ideas to others, but also for clarifying his understanding of a topic, experimenting with ideas, or simply enjoying the landscape of his own mind.

For those of us who were brought up to view writing and spelling as boring old educational staples, new techniques come as a surprise. Can you imagine kindergartners eagerly penciling stories and poems —without any help? Would you expect to see a fourth grader working intently over the fifth revision of a piece of creative writing? How about a high school student asking a computer to alert her to all the spelling errors in a term paper? For schools who have kept up with current research, times are changing fast in the writing curriculum, and your child may well be affected. Moreover, we now realize that some kinds of parental help are really not helpful. In this chapter I will try to bring you up to date on the latest ideas, on reasons why some people have trouble with spelling and writing, and ways to avoid the pitfalls.

THE WHAT AND WHERE OF WRITING AND SPELLING

What Are They?

"Writing" means several different things which span the range of mental functioning. First, there's *handwriting,* which I regard, quite frankly, as a lower-level skill. Writing itself runs the gamut from copying all the way up to getting original ideas down on paper, certainly one of the highest-level processes demanded of children. Original writing requires integrating several mechanical skills (handwriting, spelling, punctuation) with sequentially organized thought and language. No wonder it causes trouble!

Defining "spelling" is confusing. Until recently, we regarded it as a routine skill, but recent research suggests it may reflect a child's ability to use high-level conceptual processes. Research also emphasizes the interrelationship of all these skills with language development. Let's look at the way the brain organizes such varying demands.

Separate Circuits

Neurologists have been amazed to find that a few patients suffering brain damage from a stroke can write down an idea but cannot read what they have written. In other cases, people with damage to certain neural areas talk fluently without making sense or read words without understanding them. Damage in another area leaves understanding intact but destroys the ability to express ideas in words. These phenomena occur because the subskills of expressive language are housed in different parts of the brain. Researchers call them "separable processes."

Studying language processes in young brains is a lot different from looking at brain-damaged adults. Children's brains can bend themselves around different tasks in so many ways that deficits may not be obvious. Moreover, many variations in the way children learn are due to inherited patterns rather than to brain injury. Nevertheless, the idea of separate neural circuits for different aspects of reading and writing explains why children may be terribly good at one thing and terribly bad at another. It's not necessarily because they aren't trying, but because those separate skills have different systems of wiring.

In the early years of my teaching, I was baffled by some bright students' difficulty with handwriting, spelling, punctuating decently, or getting ideas down onto paper in some orderly fashion. If they were reasonably smart, I figured, they ought to be able to learn these elementary skills with a little bit of effort. Sometimes these same children were also excellent readers, which only made me more impatient. When I began to study the brain organization that underlies all these "simple" abilities, however, I realized how complicated the situation really is. One way to sort it out is to deal with each ability separately.

HANDWRITING

The Mechanical Copybook

Once upon a time, everyone knew what children should learn: the basics of mathematics, reading, spelling, geography, and history. Above all, any educated person needed to practice a "fine hand." Schoolwork consisted mostly of memorizing, and hours were spent over the copybook. Soon, however, society became more complex, and so did the demands on education. Now it isn't so easy to make decisions about what children should learn. In the midst of an information explosion, teachers are haunted by the probability that many things they choose to teach may be obsolete within ten years. Memorized "basics" are only the entry points into knowledge—and what are the "basics" of science, anyway? Of world history? Of philosophy? How can we shovel everything important into those little brains?

Educators agree that children should not spend too many precious hours practicing mechanical skills. Since the fate of the world probably does not depend on handwriting, they now set a more pragmatic goal—legibility. Yet some children fail to achieve even that, and researchers continue to search for the most effective way to teach handwriting. They have found it has early beginnings.

From Scribble to Manuscript

Preschoolers who are around adults soon pick up the idea that writing is something important and interesting. By the age of three, most children can distinguish between pictures and written symbols. Often they try "writing" themselves; they scribble exciting—if illegible—messages, and act surprised when no one understands them. This "scribble writing" is important evidence of linguistic awareness. Eventually, some children begin to identify where the scribbled "words" start and stop by putting spaces in between. Experts believe that scribble writing should be encouraged because it gets the child in the habit of linking ideas, pencil, and paper, without getting caught in complex mechanics. Some parents dignify scribbled stories by encouraging the child to draw a picture on the same page and hanging the masterpiece in a place of honor—on the refrigerator, for example. A young child in an environment which values attempts at written expression has a good chance of excelling later at real writing.

Another important preschool development is copying one's own name, a good example of learning driven by personal involvement. As with any skill, it is wise to wait until interest develops. Some children, whose perceptual or fine motor (small muscle) development is delayed, find this job too taxing. A sensible parent does not make an unpleasant issue about any aspect of writing! Movable plastic letters can create that all-important name without negative associations.

One problem for young children who are encouraged to write at home is the development of a faulty pencil grip that later is hard to correct. The best way to hold a pencil is to grip it between the thumb and first finger of the writing hand, with the middle finger underneath, supporting the pencil. Have the child make "pinchers" to grab the pencil, then add the "shelf." For some children, a larger pencil is easier, but many do better with the standard adult model. One big help is a small plastic slip-on holder called a "grippy," which can be purchased at stationery stores. Its shape makes a correct hold much easier. If your child can't hold the pencil correctly, he is better off not writing. Poor pencil grips are a major factor in later problems, causing fatigue and inefficient letter formation. Stick to crayons, chalk, paintbrushes, fingerpaints, or a stick in the sandbox.

Children under the age of six should not be expected to copy sentences. Meaningful copying requires integrating two or three modalities (looking, feeling, moving, and sometimes even hearing a word) and is not developmentally appropriate until certain areas in the brain have matured. Little ones can copy at a rote level, but they're probably not using the circuits which will connect with meaning. Let it wait. Children of this age should not be sitting at desks doing academic tasks. Get their busy brains out *doing* and *learning,* not practicing low-level skills.

Perceptual Learning

Current theories of perceptual learning tell us interesting things about the way children differ in mastering visual information such as letter formation or spelling patterns. Those who are best search actively for visual clues and details, extracting information from the environment. Some of this ability may be attributed to inborn brain organization, but much of it results from practice with nonliterary materials. You probably didn't realize that helping your child identify details in pictures or examine an ant or a blade of grass built handwriting skills! Any activity which promotes the ability to sort out details and make sense of what is seen helps. As always, the key word here is *active,* as the child must make the connections. Good perceptual learning abilities depend heavily on motivation and the desire to be "in charge" of sorting out information that comes into one's brain.

Practice is the key to perceptual learning, but rote copying or tracing letters is not very effective. Here's an example of a parent helping a child to be actively involved at higher levels. This youngster wants to learn to write her name, "Maria."

PARENT: Here's what your name looks like when it's written down. [Takes large piece of lined paper with colored crayon.] Watch me as I write it. [Names each letter as it is written.] Each one of these squiggles is a letter. Let's point to each one and count them. [Shows child how to identify five letters.] Now, let's see if any of them are alike. [Helps child see the two *a*'s.] Would you like to try writing it yourself? What color would you like? [Child selects colored crayon.] Oh, that's a lovely color! Which lines will you choose to write on? [This gets the child to organize the perceptual field of the paper.] Show me which letter you think comes first. [Helps child identify *M*. Covers up the rest of the letters so only the *M* shows.] Before you start to write, can you tell me what that *M* looks like?

CHILD: Well, it has two sticks and two pointy things on the top. They come together and there's another point looking down.

PARENT: You really looked carefully. Why don't you start by drawing the first stick *from the top to the bottom.* [Children are inclined to go "bottom-up"; try to encourage top-down strokes.]

This is the beginning of a lesson that gets the child involved in visually analyzing and organizing the stimulus *before* doing anything with it. Can you sense that this child feels "in control" of the situation? That she is learning, not only to copy a letter, but to use skills of analysis in perceptual tasks? That she is "verbally mediating"? This learning will help her remember better and avoid difficulty sorting out details of similar letters in reading (e.g., *m* and *n).* Most schools still do not teach writing in this way, so it is one place where parents can really help. Please wait, however, until your child is old enough (probably around age four or five) so that you will both enjoy a successful experience! Getting a copy of the school's letter chart showing how the letters are formed avoids relearning later. I suggest you start right off with uppercase and lowercase letters rather than teaching words in all capitals.

If you find that your child is spending a great deal of time tracing letters in school, take this book in and suggest that there is good research evidence that passive learning is relatively ineffective. I have listed some current references at the end of the book which might be useful for teachers as well as for parents.

Handwriting and the Older Child

The principles of perceptual learning can also be useful for older children who have missed out on good handwriting habits. Some very able brains have difficulty becoming automatic on letter formation, and many children in upper elementary, or even junior high, are still agonizing over such details as how many bumps are on the *m* and the *n*. If you stop to think about how these particular letters differ in manuscript (print) and cursive writing, in uppercase and lowercase, some confusion is not too surprising. Most children manage because their perceptual skills carry them through, but "visual memory" for letters and words varies widely among people. It affects writing and spelling just as it does sight-word reading.

Accepting this natural variation without criticism for "dumb" mistakes can make the difference between a child who is willing to keep trying and one who starts to "lose" assignments and devote her creative energies to alibis for avoiding work. If trouble shows up, go back to the beginning and rebuild her knowledge of what each letter looks like. The first tool is visual analysis, as described above; the next is adding as many senses as possible. "Feeling" letter shapes in sand, in cornmeal trays, in clay, on sandpaper, or on rough-textured clothing helps embed them in the brain. Near the end of this chapter I will also suggest an electronic remedy for handwriting difficulties.

Handwriting problems may stem from a poorly tuned fine motor apparatus, causing trouble remembering and executing the motor patterns for the letters. The selectivity of neural programming confuses everyone by enabling some of these youngsters to be terrific in sports which require large muscle movement.

Interestingly, the part of the brain responsible for hand movements in writing is very close to the one which organizes the mouth and tongue around speech. Problems with articulation and handwriting often go together. Professionals who do not suffer from the problem are able to pronounce its name—the "articulatory-graphomotor" syndrome. One of the classic indicators is poor pencil grip; the child clutches the pencil at the base of her thumb, or wraps it in a contorted fist, a habit which persists even after more mature neural circuits are in place. No wonder writing is laborious and boring! This child needs a "grippy," and someone who can help her reprogram handwriting from the beginning. It is a difficult job which may call for professional help if the problem is seriously interfering with school success.

Still another difficulty that some children face is combining perceptual and motor tasks. Copying is particularly difficult for them. If your child has a copying problem, you should distinguish

between near-point (close-up) and far-point (e.g., blackboard) copying, which may operate independently of each other. Since it has
been estimated that in some schools seven-year-olds spend as much
as 20 percent of their time copying (horrors!), either problem calls
for assistance. Using a marker, such as a card, can help keep the
place for near-point copying. Saying the words to be copied and
writing them from auditory rather than visual memory often provide
an effective strategy. Helpful adults regard such breakdowns in normal skill development as real problems for the child, accept them
without hurling accusations or put-downs, and work for solutions
that keep some responsibility in the child's court. Variations in brain
organization—not cussedness—are the most likely objects for the
Blame Game.

A Crumpled Six-Year-Old

When our middle son was about halfway through first grade, he
began complaining of stomachaches every morning before school.
After several weeks I became sufficiently concerned to take him to
the pediatrician, who ruled out physical problems and suggested this
reaction might reflect some difficulty at school. When I quizzed Jeff,
however, he stoutly claimed that everything was "OK."

The stomachaches vanished at the end of first grade, but it took
several years for the source of the problem to be unearthed. One
evening, as the boys exchanged stories about first grade, Jeff recre-
ated a situation that, even in retrospect, made my own stomach
queasy. Unknown to us, his "veteran" first grade teacher had been a
leftover from a more unenlightened era. When children trustingly
offered up the smudged, uneven products of their attempts at writing, Miss S. would sneer and fling their papers, crumpled, into the
wastebasket while the epithets "Messy! Disgusting!" rang through
the classroom. When an earnestly clutched pencil slipped below or
above the lines, she affixed large red X's to the spot. Only a few
technicians made the grade; Jeff's gifts for invention, his creativity—
all of his mental abilities—were ignored!

Even today when I think of that woman's assault on those tender
intellects, I would like to wring her neck. With a six-year-old's im-
plicit faith in teacher as God, our son took her judgment to heart and
decided he was a failure in school. It took years to repair his self-
confidence. Now an honors graduate of an Ivy League college, he

still remembers the unrelenting misery of that first grade year—which he was too innocent to complain about!

I wish now that I had possessed the confidence to unearth the truth and march on the principal's office. Parents can intervene if they suspect that a young child is being brutalized by inappropriate demands from a teacher. Insistence on neat, perfect penmanship from all six-year-olds certainly falls into that category! I wish all adults could look first at the product of the child's mind, and only secondarily at the output from his fingers.

SPELLING

When a Fish is a GHOTI

Spelling our language presents inherent difficulties. Although our alphabet contains only twenty-six letters, we use some forty different sounds in speaking; thus some letters must do double, or even triple, duty. Children who are poor spellers might be delighted to learn that a computer, programmed with all known spelling rules, could score only 50 percent on a standard spelling test! The inconsistencies are illustrated by spelling the word "fish" as "ghoti." How? Take *gh* as in "rough," *o* as in "women," and *ti* as in "nation." Don't ask why some kids have trouble!

As in reading, there are two basic ways to approach spelling. One is through visual analysis and memory, which is needed for irregular words such as "says" or "could"; the other is through auditory analysis, or phonics. Knowing phonic and basic spelling rules (change the *y* to *i* before adding a suffix beginning with a vowel, *i* before *e* except after *c,* etc.) can take care of about 80 percent of the words that children need to spell if, unlike the computer, they have had experience reading and writing real language. Yet most successful spellers also have a good visual memory for verbal symbols. When in doubt about how to spell a word, do you write several versions in the margin and then use your visual memory to choose one? Some children lack that equipment, and as a result, spelling is difficult for them. We do not know exactly where in the brain this ability is located, but it is separate from visual memory for places and things —at which poor spellers are often very adept.

How They Learn to Spell

The natural progression in spelling is opposite from that in reading. Children first tend to spell mainly with sounds. As maturation speeds the interchange of messages between the visual right and the verbal left hemispheres, sight and sound are integrated. Simply, children learn to spell by spelling. In addition, the more they read, the more experience they get with the patterns of letters in words. Since children with poor spelling skills are often unmotivated readers and writers, disuse of visual-verbal memory circuits compounds their problem.

Some good readers, too, have trouble with spelling. This apparent inconsistency can be explained by the fact that reading is a recognition skill; the printed words are the clues. Spelling, on the other hand, demands pulling something out of memory with no visual cues. When you write those words in the margin, you make the job easier by changing it from recall to recognition memory. See how specific these abilities are? The first step in trying to help is getting the child involved in solving the rule mystery.

Rule Detectives

Traditional approaches to spelling have settled for rote-level drills such as writing a word ten or twenty times, hoping to fix it permanently in the mind. This technique may work if the child spells out loud while writing each letter, but it has its drawbacks. Children can dutifully practice an incorrect version because they copied it inaccurately in the first place. Others already know the word and find this exercise deadening.

Other drill formats give lists of unrelated words at the beginning of the week for a test on Friday. Unfortunately, the words are often learned without meaningful context and the students turn around and misspell the same words in their writing. Current research suggests there are better ways of learning to spell. Even if your child's school is still stuck with these outdated methods, you can help at home with more current techniques.

We now assign spelling a higher rung on the ladder of cognitive skills. School children must absorb and generalize rules that govern spelling patterns in words just as two-year-olds learn the rules of language. Both must observe many individual examples before internalizing them into rules. When children induce rules, they do not forget them because they did the detective work. For example, I have endlessly taught first graders about the "silent *e*" at the end of a word making the vowel "say its name." Sometimes I feel like bashing my head against the blackboard when each class keeps forgetting it. Are these children stupid? Not at all. I have inadvertently encouraged them to remain passive while I tried to do all the work! In a minute I will tell you about a new system which makes it easier and lots more fun for all of us.

Children who have good skills for perceptual learning, who can pick out patterns, tend to become better spellers. To prepare your child for this type of learning, check back to suggestions in earlier chapters for building visual reception and association skills. One neuropsychologist says that good spelling is built on "cumulative knowledge about the world," which creates a database for figuring out rules. As with all learning, the active thinker is the one who gets the prizes. If you start by pushing words in, don't be surprised if you end up with a passive child who regards correct spelling as something for which others are responsible.

"Wnsupnatim Thr Wz a Monstr"

I often get a shock these days when I walk into the kindergarten and first grade of our school. Among whirlwinds of active learning there is always a group of children bent earnestly over paper and pencil, writing original stories. They don't ask how to spell the words, and they are so excited over their creations that they clamor to read them out loud to the class. But many of these youngsters can't read yet! What is going on?

This school, like many others, has discovered a system called "Invented Spelling," which may soon revolutionize early language arts experiences both at school and at home. Here's how it works:

1. Children are encouraged to write their own stories from the first day of kindergarten. They choose topics that are of immediate and personal interest to them. An adult also writes language experience stories on a large chart as a model for story writing. No one is pushed, but most children are eager to try, even if it is with "scribble writing."

2. The spelling of a word is "invented" by the child as it is needed.

First "words" are usually single letters or jumbled combinations, but it is astonishing how quickly sounds and the rules are mastered. Children can start writing when they know as few as six consonants.

3. Emphasis is on written language as communication. No comments are made about accuracy or neatness.

4. Adults do not supply correct spelling when the children are writing. If the child wants to "publish" a story for others to read, a teacher may write out "a way that will help people understand what you wanted to say." Gradually, the child moves toward the correct form. A typical progression for inventing the spelling of the word "liked" went like this in a single year: "L-LT-LKT-LAKT-LOKT-LIKT-LIKD-LIKED."

Experienced teachers have been amazed at the enthusiasm with which five- and six-year-olds take to spelling independently—and with the carryover into reading development. The success of this method has caused many to believe that reading and writing should be taught together from the beginning. Moreover, studies are beginning to show that this system, used in first and second grades, produces better, more accurate spellers in the long run.

Inventing Spelling at Home

This system is an ideal one to use at home if a child around age five wants to write. The most important hurdle to get by is worrying whether a word is "right." If the child knows what it says, it is right! *Do not supply spellings.* Say to the child, "Let's listen to the sounds in your word. What letter do you think comes first?" Of course, no wise parent would force this activity and create negative connections for future learning. Samples from five- and six-year-olds are shown on the next pages.

Poor Spellers

Despite our best efforts, some children seem destined to have trouble. Most people are not aware that "dyslexia" in bright youngsters does not always show up as a reading problem but as difficulty with spelling and writing. According to current research, poor spellers may have been taught before their brains were ready—or interested —in making sense out of letter patterns. Spelling remains an irritation to them. When they write, they make dozens of "dumb" mis-

NO
HO
HO
HO
IT RTS

THE   IRT

MY DAD FIKIT IT

NOO IT DIKS

NIT RT

The Hurt
Oh, oh, oh, it hurts.
My dad fixed it.
Now it does not hurt.

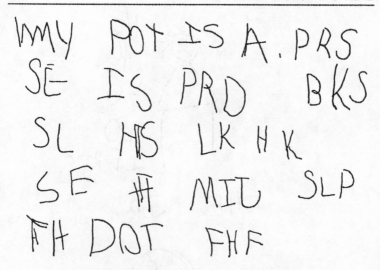

My puppet is a princess. She is pretty because
she has long hair. She has new slippers. They
don't fit.

---

takes and don't seem to care about correcting them. Sometimes it
seems as if they have given up completely.

The key to helping poor spellers is to let them know you think
they're smart enough to actively retool the right circuits. You can
start anytime, but a good opportunity often occurs around the onset
of puberty, when the growth of the fibers that connect the right and
left hemispheres makes it easier to put visual memory and auditory
analysis together. The key to success lies in getting the child involved.

Poor spellers can be divided into three groups:

1. Primary difficulty with visual memory. These children spell everything phonetically: "A gurl wud clime."

2. Primary difficulty with auditory analysis. These children can't
discriminate the sounds accurately or put them in the right order.
Long, multisyllable words are particularly difficult. "The gril is veay
eixsidot abot the plais." (The girl is very excited about the palace.)

3. Difficulty with both visual and auditory skills. "He sid youes a
befor a kosnest." (He said, "Use *a* before a consonant.")

Spelling problems are hard to cure, but here are some ideas for helping your child get through:

Helping the Poor Speller

Things that don't work:

—Assuming that spelling ability is a sign of overall intelligence. It isn't.

—Shouting or berating the child for errors.

—Telling a young child to "look it up in the dictionary." Poor spellers often have a terrible problem with alphabetical order.

—Drilling in only one sensory modality (i.e., parent says word out loud, child spells word out loud *or* child copies list of words without saying them out loud).

—Insisting on perfection in spontaneous writing. This has the unfortunate side effect of corking up written expression.

—Putting emphasis on mechanics instead of the quality of the child's thought.

Things that might work:

—Praising the child's good ideas before starting in on errors.

—Looking for patterns and rules in spelling. A source of useful materials is given in the Selected Bibliography.

—Using visual analysis: "Is it 'bad' or 'bed'? How are 'chip' and 'check' alike? Different?"

—Encouraging auditory analysis by saying the sounds in order *before, during, and after writing the word.*

—Encouraging visual memory with this five-step procedure:

1. Examine the word for any recognizable parts (roots, suffixes, prefixes). Relate letter patterns to words already known.

2. Cover the word.

3. Visualize the word. Imagine writing on a blackboard in colored chalk or a big piece of white paper with crayons.

4. Ask the child to spell out loud while writing the word. If an error occurs, stop immediately. Don't practice wrong spellings.

5. Have the child check the spelling.

6. Repeat steps 2 to 5 several times.

—Get the senses of touch and movement involved in spelling using the same techniques suggested for handwriting.

—Play spelling games. Commercial games are available, and old standards such as Anagrams, Hangman, and Ghost get everyone involved.

—To help children with auditory analysis, play with rhyming, tongue twisters, Pig Latin, or Hinky Pinky.

—Older students who are constitutionally poor spellers need a dictionary chained to their belts. Get a "Poor Speller's Dictionary," which helps them find the words. Don't expect this much motivation until late junior high.

—If your child's school offers Latin, grab it. On the other hand, be wary of French, which often causes horrendous problems for poor spellers. Spanish is a better choice for a modern language.

—Get a word processor. More about this later.

Entymology Etymology

This week I wandered into a classroom and found a teacher and a six-year-old bent over a pile of large, colorful pictures of different types of insects. The little girl was sorting the pictures into piles according to categories she had selected. She first made two piles: "insects that suck blood and ones that don't," then she resorted them into "with and without wings," and then "skinny and fat." As I watched her analyzing and categorizing visual details, I suddenly realized this child was building skills for spelling! As with letter patterns in words, she was learning to pick out, classify, and derive rules from visual details—not low-level skills at all! Parents who encourage this kind of active perceptual learning are laying a far better foundation for intelligent spelling than those who encourage passive copying.

WRITING

The Topmost Skill Starts at Home

Having to express ideas in writing is the final test of a child's background of thought and language. A writer must: (1) understand and pull together ideas or information; (2) formulate an original statement; (3) find the right words; (4) get them in order; (5) call up the mechanical skills while remembering the ideas long enough to (6) get them down on paper. A child's ability to perform this sophisticated exercise depends on three abilities: comprehension of ideas, expressive language, and facility with mechanics. If you have read the preceding chapters of this book, you know that parents have a major role in the development of all three.

Children first begin to write stories about their own experiences. Later they tackle imaginative stories, poetry, and "expository writing"—reports, essays, and research papers. Only a few master formulating an original thesis statement and supporting it with research, or writing satire, drama, or short stories. Children who have been surrounded by reading, storytelling, and involvement in conversation with adults have a head start, but many teachers are concerned that students' level of language use is declining. A child who cannot easily express ideas when speaking is almost sure to have trouble when he tries to write them down. No amount of teaching can make up for an impoverished language environment!

Too Much Lost Time?

Toni was a skinny little eight-year-old who came closer to making me cry than any child I've worked with. Her first six years of life had been shaken by her mother's serious illness, frequent hospitalizations, and eventual death. Her father, sincerely concerned about the child, was so personally overwhelmed that most of Toni's upbringing had been taken over by housekeepers. Although competent, they had done little talking or reading with her. I worked with Toni one summer because her teachers were worried about her reading comprehension and appalled by her writing; although her handwriting was fine and she had learned to sound out and spell words, she simply couldn't write anything original. A psychologist had suggested that she might be blocking overwhelmingly painful emotions, which would not have been too surprising!

As I had anticipated, Toni was enthralled by my personal computer and responded excitedly to a suggestion that she tell a story while I typed it. We settled ourselves in front of the keyboard, and I asked the standard question, "What would you like to 'write' about?" Instead of the usual barrage of words and ideas, silence reigned. Toni stared helplessly up at me. "Would you like to make up a story?" I prodded.

Large eyes searched my face. "How?" she asked.

As the summer wore on, I became more painfully aware of the

gaps in Toni's learning. She had been taught the mechanics at school, but the purpose, the structure, and the intimacy of written language had been left out of the package. We worked many hours that summer, but I knew that one thing was missing; I could never provide those lost years of snuggly story times. Is it too late? Toni's dad and new stepmother are trying hard; perhaps she may yet be able to write a happy ending.

Encouraging Children to Write

Don't lose time for your child if you can help it. Here are some suggestions for starters:

—Read aloud on a regular basis, even with older children. Delve into poetry, literature, essays, and good journalism. Don't be afraid to broaden your own tastes. Your librarian can advise you. Do not waste time on watered-down versions of classics with "pop" language. You'll be surprised how much children can understand and enjoy (even Shakespeare!) if it is read to them dramatically in a pleasurable atmosphere.

—Encourage clear expression of ideas at all ages. After you read a story, ask, "Can you tell about what was important in the story? How would you put Peter's feelings into your own words?" Practice describing pictures and daily events. Check for more suggestions in Chapter 7.

—Write notes and letters to your child. When he is old enough, encourage him to write back—first with pictures and scribbles, then with words. Don't criticize. Enjoy the message.

—Create a writing environment. Equip a "writing table" with lots of paper (lined and unlined), pencils, felt-tip pens, crayons, a stapler, wallpaper samples and cardboard for book covers, a hole-puncher, scissors, paste, a wastebasket, and a bulletin board. Encourage ideas by clipping pictures from magazines, cartoons, or items from newspapers. Get excited over any writing that is produced. Praise your child for wanting to exercise his creativity.

—Suggest starting with experience that is personal and meaningful. Drawing a picture or brainstorming works for some. Try Rico's technique of "writing the natural way" (see the Selected Bibliography).

—Suggest the child use a tape recorder to talk about the topic and write the ideas after the tape is played back.

—Always have a dictionary and thesaurus (synonym dictionary) on hand. Both are available in editions for younger or older children. A thesaurus is particularly useful for building vocabulary. A child can use it to learn new words and "dress up" the language in his writing.

—Sometimes children try to use fancy words they don't understand—and end up sounding ridiculous. Help with new words by showing how they sound in sentences.

—Develop the habit of mutual storytelling. Tell a round-robin story with all the family members. Accept the child's ideas and have fun. You don't have to be a teacher. Enjoy!

Writers Need Readers

Personal journals are a great way to "turn on" a child of almost any age to writing, once the language and thinking foundations are in place. Some preschools have initiated a delightful exchange in which a child carries the journal between school and home. There is no pressure, because parents and teacher do the actual writing. If you and your child's school are interested, here's how it works:

Staple several pieces of unlined paper together into a book. Once a week or so, help your child choose a topic, draw a picture, and dictate a language experience story following the guidelines in the last chapter. Ask the teacher if she would be willing to let the child share it with her and then dictate one at school, too. Some topics for starters can be: "Friends at Home, Friends at School"; or "Halloween at Home, Halloween at School." Preschool teachers and parents who have used this idea are enthusiastic, and children love to feel that their own words and ideas are important.

Journals are effective tools for developing writing at any age. One unusually persuasive mother, concerned that her daughters' school was neglecting writing in the primary grades, instituted a lasting tradition of journal writing on their frequent family trips. Every morning after breakfast, wherever they are, the whole family sits down to write in their journals (spiral notebooks). A child too young to write draws a picture. Even Dad, who had to be cajoled mightily at first, admits that he began to enjoy this time for reflection, and he loved hearing the different perspectives each family member brought to a situation. Now that the girls are teenagers, they still reread these

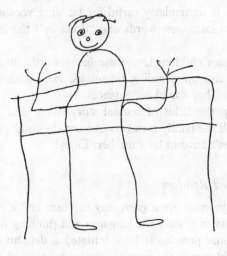

Play at School

I like to play in the
sandbox. I like to play with
the thing you put the sand in
and then it all comes out.

often hilarious records of their times together and are convinced that
the effort was worthwhile.

Cluttered Thinking = Cluttered Writing

Children who have avoided practice or who have an actual disability in writing often lack automatic use of the mechanics, a deficit
which impinges on expressing even the best ideas. I have often seen a
child get a fantastic thought, start to write it down, then get trapped
by some mechanical problem. By the time she returns to her idea, it
has fallen out of her head. Reread the section on automaticity in
Chapter 5 if you want to understand this issue better.

Likewise, parents and teachers wail, "He spelled it perfectly on the
weekly test and then turned right around and misspelled it in his

Play at Home

I LIKE TO PLAY ON OUR
SWING SET WHEN I AM AT
HOME. I LIKE TO SIT ON
THE TOP.

report. Careless!!" Not necessarily. Stop and think for a minute about the demands on working memory in a spelling test—where all attention and higher-level reasoning is focused on the words alone. Then compare these demands with paragraph writing, when higher brain centers must focus on ideas. This child may not be purposely careless; his spelling is not sufficiently automatic to free his cortex for thinking about content and organization. There are three constructive approaches for such problems.

1. Encourage children to get their ideas down in a *first draft* without emphasizing mechanics. "First draft" writing is an often-neglected process that forces the writer to discover what he really knows (and doesn't know) about the topic, to organize and clarify

ideas. Allow enough time for successive drafts to tidy the work up and produce a piece of writing of which a child can be proud.

2. Parents can serve as proofreaders for students who have problems with mechanics. Some suggestions follow for ways to assist without taking over the job.

Helping Your Child Proofread

—Always start by finding something to praise at the beginning and the end of the session. Be sure to express more interest in the ideas expressed than in the mechanics of handwriting, spelling, and punctuation. Then offer to help polish the work so it will be "even better."

—Encourage the author to make the corrections. You might develop a system of marks in the margin which indicate a certain type of error in a line (e.g., "sp." for spelling, "p" for punctuation). Work with the child to help him find the error and correct it.

—If the child has trouble with wording, have him read it out loud to see how it sounds. If he thinks it sounds fine, suggest another form. Have him listen to the difference. Suggest reading it into a tape recorder. Play it back. How does that sound?

—If you are unsure of writing rules, ask the school or a bookstore for a style manual. Your interest in informing yourself will be a powerful example for your child. Never be embarrassed about seeming "ignorant." Figuring out the rules together will make them "stick" for both of you.

—Remember that good writers make many drafts before they are satisfied. An original draft must "become messy before it becomes clear."

3. Consider the use of a word processor to increase fluency, organization, and accuracy. Our entire view of learning to write may soon be changed by the advent of electronic secretaries for children.

Electronic Secretaries

Word processing on a computer is one of the most significant changes ever to hit writing, and your child is sure to be affected by it. Here is what you need to know.

Typing words into a computer's memory eliminates many of the demands on the human brain that make writing difficult for some people. Needs for visual memory and automatic motor programs are eliminated. The part of the brain mainly responsible for the physical act of typing is the cerebellum, a low-level reflex responder which can carry out these automatic programs and leave the cortex free for organizing ideas and getting them into words. Moreover, spelling correction systems now serve as automatic proofreaders. Once the child has finished writing, the program scans the text and highlights any word that is not in its dictionary (e.g., "sed"). Systems in which the child must then check and respell the word are a powerful inducement for first-round accuracy and also reinforce correct spelling. Computer printouts look wonderful—a real blessing for a child whose own efforts create instant nausea in readers. The pride children feel spurs them on to correcting, rewriting, and struggling for a better word as it frees them from laboriously recopying each corrected draft.

A question still exists about when children should learn word processing. I feel personally that until students have microcomputers to take to class, they must still learn penmanship. Many authorities agree that children should learn touch typing before starting word processing. If they begin with "hunt and peck," they program an inefficient method into their neural circuits (some skilled hunt-and-peckers disagree). Vision is a dominant sense, and visually searching for keys not only is slower but leaves less cortical energy available than does touch typing. Current studies show that even first graders can learn touch typing, so I suspect this trend may become an issue before long.

Any categorical statements in the midst of a bona fide technological revolution are risky, so I recommend you keep your eyes and your minds open. In the meanwhile, if your child has trouble with any aspect of writing, consider investing in a computer with software for teaching touch typing, word processing, and spelling correction. If the school has computers and printers, you might save the cost of a printer by getting a computer that can "interface" with the school's printers. If a computer is too expensive, start with a typewriter. Let's capitalize on a development that can free up many bright minds handicapped by a difficulty with automaticity.

Bringing More of the Brain into Writing

Some people write better when they combine language with the visual, wholistic approaches associated with right-hemisphere processing. One interesting new technique encourages children of all ages to start writing by drawing pictures and describing them. This simple technique sparks ideas and forces some preliminary organization. It is especially effective with a young child who has trouble finding something to write about or with an older one whose learning style tends to be more visual than auditory-verbal.

Gabrielle Rico is a brilliant writing teacher who believes her technique brings right-hemisphere visual creativity into the process. She has achieved impressive results by the use of imagery and free association with adult writers who were "blocked." Here's the way Rico's system works: A web of personally associated words is developed for one special word or phrase; the writer relaxes, lets his mind come up with connections, and then maps the ideas around the kernel idea. Once the visual outline is created, writing begins immediately; the goal is to let ideas flow rather than to worry about form or even content. I have seen extraordinary results from adults trying this system for the first time, and was anxious to try it with some students. Here are some examples from eighth graders who thought they "couldn't write."

A parent and a child can try this system together. If you can free your mind from remnants of copybook experience, you may be astonished at your own networks of creativity!

Donald Graves is another teacher getting great results from children's personal involvement in creative writing. If you recall the importance of appealing to the limbic brain, you will see one possible explanation for the success of Graves's method, which gets children willingly to write, rewrite, and polish as many as six or seven drafts. An integral part of the process is having the young authors read their writing to the teacher or other students in the class for suggestions. One parent whose child was taught by Graves's approach told me that her son was transformed in one year from a child who hated writing to a budding author who now keeps daily journals *because he enjoys it!* You can encourage your child's school to keep tuned in to such new developments. Making writing a stepchild of the curricu-

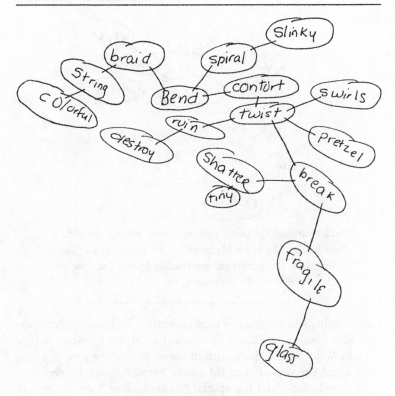

It twisted like a pretzel,
Broke like china.
It swirled into many colors,
Shattered, as of fragile glass,
Was contorted, then destroyed.
With the wind, the shattered pieces
Blew into the sunset.

lum cheats every student and may ultimately rob us all of our cultural voice.

A Writer's Voice

To write well, children must learn to carry on a personal conversation inside their own heads. Good writing has a unique voice that is different from "talk written down." The only way to pick it up is

Circling around the pond, cutting crisply into the ice with its silver blades. The sharp blades of the ice skates are like knives cutting steel. Its circular pattern steadily follows the same pace until the blades hit the ice once again.

---

from reading and listening to quality writing. To illustrate how parents give children a chance to develop a "writer's voice," author Eudora Welty recalls the wealth of language and the love of books with which she was surrounded during her childhood. Immersed in their sound, she found her special "writer's voice," which she still uses as a guide. I often worry that writer's voices are becoming scarce commodities as I work with youngsters who lack even a basic sense of what sounds good on paper.

Proficiency and pleasure in reading and writing evolve from the foundations of listening and speaking. If your child is young, don't miss the opportunity to enjoy poetry and good literature together. Make writing a part of everyday life—a lively, personal mental adventure. Even for older children, it is not too late to turn off the TV and hang up the telephone for a while and venture now and then into the treasurehouse of the literate mind.

Parts into Wholes:
Building Math Skills

RECENTLY I MET MY NEIGHBOR STEVE IN THE CHECKOUT LINE OF our local supermarket. Enthroned in his cart, four-year-old Deborah joyously clutched a new workbook filled with number facts and simple equations. Knowing my interest in math learning, Steve was delighted to point out that he was getting his daughter off to a good start. I wanted to share his enthusiasm, but I hope after he reads this chapter he realizes that the supermarket contained raw material infinitely more important to Deborah's future math ability than her new workbook.

Mathematics causes parents more anxiety than any other school subject. It is the only area of the curriculum with an identifiable "phobia" attached to it. Math homework takes the prize as a cause of family shouting matches and parental feelings of inadequacy. What can be done to demystify this topic of ever-increasing importance in our technological world? How can parents help when they feel less than competent? Good news! Even if you can't compute the Pythagorean theorem or calculate when two airplanes will meet over Chicago, you can help your child build a foundation for excellence in math. Understanding two ways in which the brain processes mathematical information is the key.

RULES VS. REASONS

Most people think of math as arithmetic, the study of numbers and the rules or operations, such as addition and multiplication, that we use to manipulate them. Guess again! Mathematics is a much greater science of relationships, which uses numerical symbols to describe fundamental truths about our universe. The numbers on a page represent powerful abstract concepts—but they are rooted in concrete experience. Mathematicians of all ages begin by asking questions about the world: soap bubbles, pendulums, swings, pretzels, patterns of spider webs, springs, seashells, and the leaves on tree branches are all raw material for brilliant mathematical minds.

What does this mean? For success in math, the child must develop two separate abilities which are linked throughout the study of arithmetic, algebra, geometry, trigonometry, and calculus. First, and probably most important, is the ability to comprehend relationships, to reason abstractly, and to solve problems. The other side is the ability to follow the rules, to analyze, and to compute accurately.

Recent research suggests that these two types of abilities are mediated by the two hemispheres of the cerebral cortex. As we saw in Chapter 6, these two sides of the brain process information in distinctive ways even while they continuously interact. The right hemisphere, which is good at seeing the whole puzzle, may contribute much of the understanding of the *reasons*—the big, global concepts which are rooted in a visual-spatial understanding of relationships. The left hemisphere, on the other hand, enjoys following rules—analyzing the pieces, doing equations in an orderly manner, and understanding the language, or sequence, of math. This sounds like a pretty complicated business, especially since the hemispheres must learn to work together efficiently. Let's look at some examples of how these thinking processes develop, and discuss specific steps that parents can take to ensure that both sides of the brain do their part in making math learning an exciting adventure for a child.

FINDING THE ROOTS OF MATH

Active Explorers

What can we learn from thirty-two boys and girls, ages two to three and a half, who are allowed to explore a room in a museum or follow a route through a specially designed playhouse, about the way children develop math skills? Some provocative findings came from a study which measured these youngsters' exploratory behavior and their visual-spatial abilities, or how well they could relate their own bodies to objects outside themselves. The children who explored more actively proved significantly better when they had to reverse their path back through the playhouse; their "cognitive mapping abilities" were superior to those of children who were passive explorers or depended on a parent to guide them. Researchers were surprised that children this young could hold a mental image of the route they had taken, apparently by associating it with their own body movements. The key was not how much movement they made, but whether the children themselves were the initiators. This study is one of many showing a link between early behavior patterns and later ability with spatial relationships, one of the best predictors of math ability. The right hemisphere, working together with lower brain centers, is probably the one which enables us to get this feel for a "whole" problem and to size up the relationships of the variables involved.

Reasoning Spatially

There are practical reasons why a child's active physical exploration builds important spatial skills. Concepts of the physical universe which we, as adults, carry around in our brains and use continually, depend on getting the "feel" of objects and their relationships in space, distance, quantity, and direction. For example, if you were asked to describe the route from your house to your office, you would probably use both your visual "mind's eye" and some slight body or head movements to get the directions right. Similarly, if you are asked to subtract 57 from 321 in your head, chances are you will employ similar strategies to form a visual image, borrow, subtract down, go back up to the 10s column, go down, and then back up again, although some mathematicians have such a good feel for these numbers that they can get the answer in quicker ways (e.g., subtract 57 from 100 and add 221). An individual who has trouble with the spatial aspects of this challenge may find mental computation very trying.

Children in school who have a poor sense of spatial relationships have difficulty with place value, directionality (subtract down, but multiply up), the relationships in fractions (which is on top and which on bottom?), estimating (which way do I go?), and geometrical problems, and may be baffled by charts, graphs, and maps, all of which require some intrinsic notion of the relationships gained through the experience of our own body in space.

Toys may play a great part in developing these important concepts. Large blocks, mechanical toys, and carpentry tools are effective, as are sand, clay, and water play. A child building with wooden unit blocks, boxes, spools, or other objects which have shapes of varying sizes is also building the concept of *seriation,* the ability to make a "stairway" out of graduated-size objects. Why is seriation important? It implies an understanding that a block, or number, can be bigger than one neighbor and smaller than the other—all at the same time. This seemingly simple idea is usually not fully mastered until after age five or so, yet is prerequisite to a true understanding of counting.

Feeling and figuring out how parts go together helps budding reasoning abilities. A child taking apart a castoff clock or radio with a screwdriver may be learning more math fundamentals than one doing a pageful of sums. Never underestimate the value of "junk" as raw material for learning.

Children need to climb, crawl through things, and explore new paths, increasing those "conceptual mapping skills" and firming up notions of direction and relationships in space and distance by physical means. Making mud pies, believe it or not, is a readiness activity for algebra—the science of describing relationships of quantity. Measuring or comparing distances and sizes of objects is also important. During school years, team sports encourage an understanding of position on a field and relative movement of players. Remember once more that the child's active physical involvement, linking subcortical and motor areas with higher reasoning powers, is paramount. For most of us, learning comes from doing it, not from watching it happen.

Are Girls Different?

Some theorists have suggested that the selection of toys and play activities may account for the fact that boys invariably score better on tests of spatial relationships than do girls. One study showed that mothers of girls who later excelled in math had allowed them to actively explore and solve problems themselves; they had been encouraged to play with "boys'" toys as well as with more traditional female ones. Both boys and girls with low math scores were more passive in play activities and tended to be dependent on their parents.

As we saw in Chapter 6, the finding that girls tend to score lower on visual-spatial abilities and higher in verbal tests has caused some researchers to believe that their right and left hemispheres are arranged differently from those of boys even from before birth. In mathematics, they do not score as well as boys, but these differences don't become evident until junior high school. It is likely that parental expectations and early learning experiences have as much to do with lower math scores as does intrinsic brain organization. Several studies have shown that parental expectations for girls to have trouble with math tend to be a self-fulfilling prophecy, and that some girls may avoid it because they believe it is a "boys'" subject. Messages such as "That's OK, I always hated numbers too and girls aren't supposed to be good in math" are all too common.

Parents who want children of both sexes to do well in math could help them by providing manipulative toys and encouraging active exploration, avoiding stereotyped ideas that those of either gender should always be "good," conforming, and quiet. Continual worry about muddy clothes or docile behavior can deprive a youngster of the opportunity to build right-hemisphere skills, encouraging a "helpless" student and a passive problem solver.

When Steve takes Deborah home, will she be encouraged to sit quietly with her new workbook or to explore and play actively? Does she always ride in the shopping cart or sometimes navigate the grocery aisles herself? Does Steve ever ask her to find her way back to get a box of cereal or a certain number of apples? These challenges are more important at age four than learning to write numerals or recite the answer to $2 + 3$.

SKILLS THAT AREN'T IN THE BOOK

Authors of textbooks try hard to convey all the basic skills that will produce good math students, but they get frustrated because they know that some of the most important abilities resist encapsulation on the printed page. These are the attitudes and problem-solving skills that children have developed before they march, creep, or get dragged through the classroom door on the first day of school.

Taking a Risk

Several years ago a worried father came up to me after a parents' workshop at a school in an affluent neighborhood. The discussion that evening had focused on problem-solving skills and the fact that children who learn to meet challenges and develop strategies are frequently good math students. As I often do, I had used the example of climbing trees as one natural way to develop these skills, as well as those of relative distances, cause and effect, and other important concepts. This dad was worried about his daughters' problems in math. "They've never climbed trees," he lamented. Then his face brightened. "I'm going to buy some trees tomorrow!"

What do you do when you don't know what to do? These are problem-solving skills, the focus for the 1980s of The National Council of Teachers of Mathematics. These teachers are concerned that students at all grade levels have difficulty figuring out what to do when confronted with a math problem even when they are adept at subtraction, division, and other types of computation. When given story problems, they have trouble developing strategies or understanding the relationship of the numbers involved. Dutifully finding the "right" answers to a page of equations may get you through elementary school, but those who excel are also able to try new solutions and to approach problems from different angles instead of relying only on a set of rules. Children who are locked into the "one right answer" mentality tend to fall behind in junior high school math courses. For example, good mathematicians use the technique of estimation frequently, either to establish a problem-solving stategy or to check the sense of an answer. Some children are so fearful of making a mistake that they are unable to estimate.

HELPING CHILDREN SOLVE PROBLEMS

1. Encourage questions, particularly those which have more than one possible answer, and preferably ones to which *you* don't know the answer. ("I'm not sure why leaves have different shapes —let's collect some and try to figure out some reasons.")

2. Ask open-ended questions and welcome innovative responses. ("What do you think these woods will look like a hundred years from now?" "What would children do if there weren't any schools and everyone stayed home and learned from a computer?")

3. Encourage divergent approaches to everyday situations, within reason. (If the child can think of a reason for setting the table in a new and different way, why not?)

4. Help your child to tolerate some uncertainty—mathematicians must delay the best solution to a problem until they have tried out several hypotheses.

5. Provide toys and games that encourage a variety of types of play which the youngster must create himself; praise and admire innovative uses of play construction, or game materials.

6. Show your child how to estimate. ("You have 9 pennies in your bank—that's close to a dime." "We have to drive 295 miles to Grandmother's house—that's almost 300 miles.")

7. Practice "guess and test." ("I'm not sure what will happen if we put lemonade in the jello instead of water—let's guess some possibilities and then see what happens.")

8. Avoid using the words "right" and "wrong" unless a moral issue is at stake; take time to listen to the child's ideas before passing judgment. Try out the phrase, "That's an interesting idea —tell me some more."

9. Work hard on helping your child feel secure enough to take sensible risks.

One study of school subjects found that children who tended to feel "helpless," needing to depend on an adult for guidance, were particularly put off by math because it usually seems more confusing than other subjects at the beginning of a new topic. Children who were described as "mastery oriented," feeling capable of meeting a challenge, did much better. Early experiences which develop feelings of safety, assured love, and protection from a trusted adult give children the freedom to be active explorers. Although some children may come into the world with right hemispheres better equipped to master the visual-spatial challenges of physical exploration, each has a level at which parents can help build a base of security for this important assignment.

The Magic Chalkboard of the Inner Eye

"Mary has 36 apples in a basket. She wants to put them into 4 equal bags. How many will be in each bag?"

The largest chalkboard in my classroom is an imaginary one which soon becomes familiar to children who come to me for help in math. Repeatedly I find that these youngsters lack another skill which can't be taught in math books—visual imagery, the ability mentally to "see" something that is not actually in front of them. Not only do they have trouble with mental math calculations, but they are unable to create a visual representation of a word problem, to remember or relate the important elements. Instead of "seeing" Mary divide up her apples, they may take a chance and add 36 + 4. Often they do not remember the numbers in the problem.

When I teach math to children like this, I put aside the textbooks and "right" answers and go back to the beginning—what does this *mean?* Our first job is to imagine Mary and talk about what she is doing. If the child is unable to visualize the situation, we may draw a picture of Mary, the apples, and the bags. Often we act out the problem first, using paper clips or chips as apples, getting the body involved in this important step.

Next we try to figure out a mathematical sentence (equation) to connect with our story. What is Mary's problem? How does she get the apples into the bags? Oh, she needs to *divide* the apples! Show me on your paper how we say that in math (÷ or $\overline{)}$). And so on, slowly, until the equation is developed.

Once the facts and the process are understood, we go back to imagination. "What color is your chalkboard today?" I ask, as the child closes her eyes and selects from a delicious mental rainbow. "And what color is the chalk?" Then we "write" the equation in these wonderful colors, saying and imagining the numerals and the process. Repeated practice may form a habit which makes computation more manageable. The imaginary chalkboard with its vivid col-

ors also helps children who have difficulty remembering the "facts":
8 × 7 = 56 written in the mind in blue, purple, green, and yellow
sometimes sticks!

Any time parents encourage picturing ideas mentally, they are
building similar abilities. After Deborah has explored the cereal aisle
in the grocery store, Steve might devise a game in which they close
their eyes and try to remember what it looked like. Where were the
cornflakes on the shelf? What color was the box? Can they remember the picture or any of the numbers? Was the oatmeal above or
below the Pop Tarts? Now let's imagine a giraffe walking down the
aisle. Let's put three children on his back. What do they look like?
As long as the child is having fun, parents have many opportunities
to help develop the "inner eye," a big part of the "big picture" of
math ability, and as we have seen in another chapter, of reading
comprehension as well.

Concrete-Symbolic-Abstract

The ability to create and hold mental pictures is closely related to
a child's development of symbolic thinking. Remember the toddler
talking to a pretend grandma on a toy telephone? He has mastered
the first step in a natural progression from concrete to abstract
thought. First come seeing and feeling, then understanding that
things (or pictures or numerals or words) can stand for other things
(a toy telephone for a real one; a "pretend" grandma; a 1 for the idea
of a single object). Only after these stages are mastered can children
start to move to abstract thought.

Abstract thinking requires reasoning with symbols, or understanding that one symbol system (algebra, for example) can stand for
another (numerals). Since this type of reasoning isn't well developed
until at least teen years for most people, moving down a level on the
hierarchy makes a problem easier. For example, dividing up real
objects—counters, pennies, matchsticks—is a concrete task easily
understood. If we make these objects "stand" for apples, we have
entered the symbolic level. Likewise, the drawing (symbol) of Mary
and the apples is difficult for little children but helps those who are
teetering on the brink of abstract thought. Creating graphs and
charts to illustrate more complex problems accomplishes the same
purpose. Endless pies can be divided to master the idea of fractions—
first, real ones with a knife, then paper pies with scissors, then circles

THE BUILDING BLOCKS OF THOUGHT

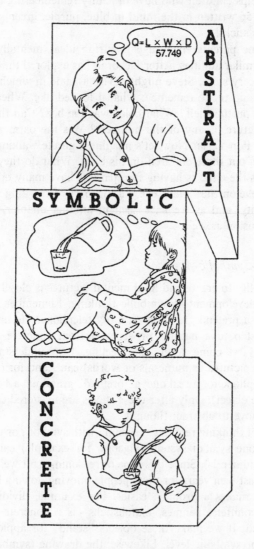

drawn on the real and imaginary chalkboards. Finally, the concept is internalized and the child is ready to use it for solving increasingly complex equations—with no pictures and no scissors!

If your child is having trouble with fractions, you may need to revert all the way to the real pie and start working up. Remember, things that can be seen also link the visual reasoning of the earlier-maturing right hemisphere with the more verbal left.

THE LANGUAGE OF MATH

Understanding the Puzzle

Even teachers get stuck with the idea that math consists only of numbers, forgetting about the important roles that words and language concepts play. Although experts have never agreed whether it is possible to engage in visual-spatial reasoning without using any words, mathematical learning definitely uses a combination of these two modes of thought. Much of language, as we have seen, is mediated by the left hemisphere, but some of the most important linguistic concepts in mathematics are probably still based in the right.

Language in math takes two forms: (1) words that describe abstract concepts, such as "equal," and (2) grammatical statements, such as "four take away two equals two." As in other language processing, the right hemisphere probably helps with the conceptual understanding of individual words, whereas the left is adept with the sequence and the grammar. Both skills are an important part of your child's mathematical background.

Many of the words that are used in math stand for abstract concepts, but the way that the child learns them is—guess what!—through physical experience with objects and events in daily life. Some of these concepts are: equal, greater, less, more, bigger, smaller, plus, take away, multiply, divide, when, until. Steve might ask, "Which box is bigger/smaller? Which holds more/less cereal? Let's see if these oranges are *equal* in size/weight. I have too many cans of tuna—let's *take away* some. Do you think we can *divide* these cookies into two equal bags?" Prepositions are important words when learning about relationships. How many ways can you expose your child to the ideas of up/down, before/after, above/below? Any time such ideas can be tied with language to everyday experiences, they seem interesting, and understandable.

Because Why?

Even larger mathematical concepts are also represented in language. One of these is "because." Most children do not grasp causation until well after the age of entering school. In order to understand cause and effect relationships, one must grasp three related ideas: (1) events have causes, (2) causes precede effects, and (3) there is a link between cause and effect. While we adults take this knowledge for granted, a child experiences many causal situations before getting an intuitive notion of its meaning. You may have noticed that, in the meanwhile, their understanding of "because" and "why" are quite unique. Once more, we see the value of active experience, and of a parent who will ask the right questions, such as "If I pull out the bottom block from the pile, what will happen?" "What made the light go on?" "Why do you suppose Mom got angry?" (Be prepared for "Because she's a mean mom.")

Piles of Ideas

Abilities to categorize and classify also underlie math learning. Parents have ideal opportunities to develop these skills at home between the ages of three and seven. After Steve gets the groceries home, he and Deborah can sort them into all kinds of categories—boxes, bags, cans; square, round, rectangular; large, small; heavy, light; vegetables, meats, fruits, grains; things Deborah likes and doesn't like; things for breakfast, lunch, dinner. Here the child is developing a basic understanding of "sets"—groups of similar objects. They might put cans and boxes, for example, in separate piles, and then draw a picture diagram using small circles and squares to represent them, finishing off with a big circle around each set. For older children, the idea of overlapping categories (intersecting sets) can also be illustrated—fruits and vegetables, for example, with the two circles intersecting around "ones I like."

You can classify leaves, flowers, insects, or other items found on walks. Adding a chart or graph in some simple form will build visual organization skills as well as the notion that symbols can stand for concrete objects. You might make a bar graph by coloring in a square on large graph paper for every leaf you find, using a different color bar for each type. You might trace different leaves and record the number found. If you also let the child think up new and interesting ways to create charts, you may get a creative surprise. If it isn't perfect, wonderful! It's better to figure out what doesn't work, and why, than only to be shown what does. Classifying objects also offers a good opportunity to discuss likenesses and differences, shapes, and symmetry, all concepts that will be needed later. Practicing these visual discrimination skills will eventually contribute to the child's ability to recognize the form of numerals.

ANALYZING THE PIECES

Where are the numbers? So far we have been concerned with math skills that are predominantly right-hemisphere-type abilities. Another, quite different set of abilities are especially important in the first stages of arithmetic learning. Counting, learning basic math facts, and calculating are probably handled by the sequential, orderly, and analytical left hemisphere. Left hemisphere skills produce accuracy in computation and help with understanding of the "grammar of math": the order in which propositions are expressed, such as "two plus three equals five."

Can He Really Count?

Counting is one of the first elements of arithmetic which parents consciously teach. "Billy can count to twenty!" exclaims an excited mother of a three-year-old. What she means is that Billy has learned, by rote, to recite the numbers from one to twenty. She would be surprised to learn that he cannot actually count, since there are several aspects of this skill which he will not master for another year or two. Did you ever stop to think about the steps in actual counting?

1. Reciting numbers in order.

2. Pointing to a few objects in a row and saying a number while touching each object; starts around age three.

3. Accurately counting, or enumerating, an array of objects; this ability is called rational counting with one-to-one correspondence; it does not usually develop until at least age four and often later.

4. Mentally counting a number of objects without touching them; the child has internalized the idea of number.

5. Understanding the difference between being fifth in a line and representing the quantity "5."

Most children between ages three and five have some definite ideas about what counting is; they believe that it is necessary to go from left to right, start at the end of a line, and go in order. Only later do they begin to grasp the concept of numerosity so that they can size up an array of objects that are not in a row or tell you how many marbles you are holding in one hand. In fact, although children twelve months old were able in one study to tell the difference between three and five objects, the abstract notion of number is slow to develop. Incidentally, although many parents were taught in school that the word "number" means the printed symbol on the page, we now call them "numerals." The era of my education is apparent, unfortunately, as, despite years of teaching, I repeatedly use the wrong term.

The "One" Idea

What does "one" mean? Think of one pencil, and then of one world, and you will begin to understand why grasping number concepts takes a certain level of mental maturity. As in all other learning, children gain these ideas from lots of practical experiences with sets of objects. You can help your child by not only teaching numbers in order, but also by asking, "Please bring me 3 pencils." You might have a scavenger hunt outdoors: 6 acorns, 8 leaves, 3 stones, etc. Again, a trip to the grocery store offers innumerable chances to count objects and money. Once the child masters one-to-one correspondence up to 10, you can start asking questions such as "If you take away 4 of those acorns, how many will be left?" and encourage the child to use the objects as "counters." Such activities are infinitely more valuable than trying to teach answers to written equations, because the child develops a working understanding of what the number facts mean.

Teachers use various objects which they call "manipulatives," such as rods, cubes, or beads, to build numerical understanding. If your child's school has young children glued to workbooks without hands-on experiences in math, you should probably ask a few questions. You may avoid incidents such as the one in which a first grader, when asked what he had learned in school one day, replied, "I learned that 3 + 4 is 7. What's 7?"

Once most children have enough concrete experiences at a sensory-motor level, ideas of numerosity will be internalized, but the ease with which this happens varies widely. I have worked with bright elementary school children who still do not have a "feel" for such ideas as the relative size of numbers ("Which is bigger, 28 or 32?"), or the fact that 13 means 10 + 3 rather than a 1 and a 3. We get out the manipulatives to build the missing concepts with games and problems. Anything that can be counted works; things that can be put into bundles of 10, such as straws, will help with *place value*. For example, 2 bundles of 10 plus 3 single straws equals 23. Such grouping helps the child see why different numerals go in different columns—a difficult abstract idea.

Don't be surprised if your child has trouble with the notion of "zero" or the "empty set" until at least age seven, and perhaps later. It is especially hard to understand when 0 is used as a place holder, as in 107, although we adults take it for granted. The child's reasoning abilities are simply different from ours.

Parents always wonder if children should be allowed, or even encouraged, to count on their fingers. As a teacher, I am convinced that (1) they will do it whether we like it or not, and (2) fingers represent the original manipulatives. Eventually, however, the number facts must be mastered automatically for success in higher math. Most children need help at home, and some never learn them. One young lady, a high school junior whose abysmal score on the math SAT test may keep her out of her preferred college, confessed to me that she never learned to add or subtract without using her fingers. She recalls sitting partially under a blanket in the classroom during "number fact drills" so that her "digital" system was hidden from the teacher's eyes. Was she learning-disabled? Not quite! This girl had been identified early as "gifted" in math and placed in a program so accelerated that she was working in a fifth grade math book when she was still in third grade. What happened? Why does she now "hate" it and get failing grades in algebra? Her mother blames the school for pushing her ahead. She laments, "The ordinary kids ended up way ahead. They did what kids are supposed to be doing in those early grades."

Aiming for Automaticity: Drilling on "Facts"

How do we get computation out from under the blanket? Despite the advent of calculators and computers, quick and accurate mastery of the basic "facts" of addition, subtraction, multiplication, and division demands hard work. Yet one reason some children have trouble learning these combinations is a basic lack of comprehension of the relationships involved; if you don't understand adding and multiplying, it is hard to sort out + and ×, or to figure out that 4 × 3 really means four 3s added together. Without meaning, isolated drill will be of limited value, and "memory" will be undependable. As we saw in Chapter 8, the human brain tends to remember material that (1) it is ready for, (2) has meaning, (3) can be arranged in patterns, and (4) can be linked to some previously learned information. Thus, Deborah's new workbook of equations may actually be counter-productive until she has gained more understanding, and drilling a first grader on 3 + 4 = 7 seems silly if he doesn't understand what 7 is!

Number facts are a good illustration of a skill requiring automaticity, also discussed previously. To foster any automatic skill, four things are important: (1) motivation and involvement by the learner, (2) repetition, (3) novelty, and (4) presentation through different modalities. How can a parent help? To increase the child's involvement, it is important to allow for some choices, and to keep the task manageable. With flash cards, for example, the child might choose which set of combinations to learn first, grouping the cards in bundles of "known," "not known," and "next to learn." Parents may have to decree a specific time each day for flash card work, but the child needs to "own" some of the process. Personally making the flash cards is one of the best ways for the student to become involved.

Repetition is important, as is reinforcement of previously learned material every few days or so. The neural path through the woods, once made by repeated journeys, needs only an occasional trip to clear out the underbrush. Quick review on written fact sheets (time tests) is helpful, especially if similar tests are given in school. Time spent riding in the car can be used to repeat multiplication facts forward and backward. Computer programs for drill and practice are useful because they blend novelty, which appeals to attention-regulating brain areas, with repetition through several senses. For additional novelty, the child might make flash cards in different colors or with pictures on them representing each fact (8 pizzas + 7 cokes = 15 [stomachaches?]). Pictures link drill both with meaning and with a visual image.

Presentation through different modalities involves looking, saying and hearing, touching, or body movement. For example, the child might say $7 \times 8 = 56$ while writing it on a rough surface (living room rug, corduroy pant legs, sandpaper). Singing works for some. Writing it in the air with the foot, head, or shoulder gets the motor cortex involved. The more senses that can be activated simultaneously, the better the fact will stick. Some experts have even recommended gustatory experiences, if you feel like baking cookies in the shape of multiplication facts!

LEARNING THE RULES

Finally, we reach the point at which most people think math begins—computation. Adding, subtracting, multiplying, and dividing are skills that are learned through sets of rules, called algorithms, which can be memorized. It is possible, simply by following one rule, such as subtracting with regrouping (borrowing), to do pages of problems without understanding the process or the reasons. Many children perform math in this manner, but the minute they have to switch approaches or apply the knowledge, as in a story problem, they become confused. They also find math "boring." Many school programs, in fact, have been criticized for allowing this kind of "mindless computation" to substitute for mathematical reasoning.

It is probable that the left hemisphere's analytical, linear style lends itself particularly well to routine computation; you may notice that many children verbalize steps as they go ("You can't take 7 from 3, so go to the 10s column. . . ."), which also engages the left brain. Such verbal strategies are good for children who have difficulty remembering the steps and can also help with directionality. ("The sign says subtract, so I will start at the top and go down.")

"Seeing" the Problem

The right hemisphere gets into the act with computation, too. Visual organization is needed for lining up numbers, keeping answers in the right column, and manipulating decimal points. Some children need to write problems on graph paper with large squares in order to keep columns organized. Spatial skills are tapped by distinguishing similar signs (+ and ×, for example). Many children reverse or invert numerals such as 6 and 9 until they are about seven years old and may become frustrated if too much pressure is applied before they are neurologically ready to see the difference. To build these skills in the young child, specific work with numerals may be less important than practice in getting meaning out of a mass of visual information. Games such as "hidden pictures," puzzles, mazes, or any activity which involves making sense of an array of dots, for example, help visual organization and discrimination. Looking for constellations in the night sky is one natural example. Math has been defined as "a search for patterns"; in this area, parents are important teachers.

Workbook pages, which are probably the most common method of drilling on the "rules," also require certain visual organization skills which may cause trouble. When looking at books with your child, you might occasionally discuss the way the pages are organized ("Why is this line here across the middle of the page?" "Let's look to see how many activities are on this page." "How many pictures are here, and how many captions—what can you tell about the way they go together?").

Too Careless or Too Careful

Some children seem to understand the reasons, but have trouble with computation. They are inaccurate and have difficulty putting an orderly equation alongside an idea. Such youngsters often know the answer but can't tell you how they got it. Recently, we have begun to understand that such students may be more global thinkers who intuitively size up the problem, but have difficulty with the analytical, sequential skills. They are often called "careless" by teachers, as they tend to be impatient with the details of accurate computation. Such students are often highly creative. It is helpful for them to learn that their style of learning does not mean they are "bad" or unmotivated, but that they need to practice steps in order if they are to succeed in a standard math curriculum. These children usually respond to movement or visual cues; acting out, drawing pictures, or making diagrams may help them identify the sequence of a problem.

For such students, mechanical aids to accuracy such as calculators or computers are very helpful, enabling them to use their fine conceptual abilities more freely.

The other end of the scale is occupied by children who are excellent technicians, love the detail, and compute accurately, but have a dreadful time when required to go up to the "big picture." Story problems and geometry are particular challenges for them. Activities that have already been suggested for problem solving and building the visual-spatial skills of the right hemisphere may be helpful.

BUILDING MATHEMATICAL BRAINS

Computation is only the tip of the mathematical iceberg. Clearly, for ultimate success in math, right and left hemisphere skills must be merged into a single working unit which can simultaneously perceive the overall problem, analyze it, and apply strategies for a solution. Parents' major role in math learning is to help build the concepts and the underlying skills with interesting and meaningful family activities. Here are some common examples; you can create many more.

Cooking offers a wealth of possibilities for understanding the important idea of quantity, measuring, sequencing steps in a problem, following directions accurately, and fractions. Here is an enjoyable, meaningful, and delicious mathematical experience!

Family games involving numbers or money promote an understanding of relative quantity and build computational skills. Games requiring visual organization or strategy are invaluable learning aids.

Shopping offers chances to compare prices, learn about decimal places, and practice computation in a meaningful situation. Catalogue shopping at home can become a math game—figuring out how many items can be purchased for a certain amount, for example. This type of experience is a natural antecedent for story problems.

Every child should have some sort of **allowance** to manage, even if it is only a few pennies, and real experience buying small items and getting change. Older children can learn about interest in a natural context if they need to borrow from the parental exchequer.

Travel games, such as license plate bingo, keeping mileage records, or even computing gas mileage can be fun. Working with maps builds graphing and directional skills and can make a child feel very important.

Measuring activities are appropriate even for very young children. Making diagrams of rooms in the house or maps of the yard or neighborhood is fun. You might try introducing nonstandard measurements, such as "How many Daddy-shoe-lengths wide is the kitchen?" The *Guinness Book of World Records* is a rich source of relative measurements.

Following directions is one of the most important skills from the home. Taking steps in order, planning ahead, and talking about what to do before tackling the task can all be encouraged. Cooking, as noted above, treasure hunts and building models are all sequential step-following activities. For older children, map and compass skills are very helpful.

Calculator games, now becoming widely available, are a rich source of problem-solving situations with numerical concepts.

These are only a few of the multitude of activities which are the family's natural source of math learning. Mathematics is about the real world, which is the best place to learn about it.

Not long ago I was visiting a friend on the farm which she and her husband have worked hard to develop. At the breakfast table, I was struck by the rapt attention of her seventh grade daughter, whose head was bent with her father's over a page of figures that would have frightened most thirteen-year-olds. "Doing your math homework?" I inquired. "Oh, no," she replied, "Dad needs my help figuring out where to put the fences in the new pasture." I don't need to tell you that this child's brain is ready and eager for math. She has the reasons for learning the rules.

The Toolshed Muse:
Creative Minds in Process

WHEN TALKING WITH TEACHERS ABOUT CREATIVITY, I ALWAYS get their attention—not with words of wisdom, but with the jewelry I wear. My "creativity" necklace is an aged aluminum bottle cap suspended from a length of cotton string. Several lumpy knots unite the ends of the string with a rusted chain which started life on an anonymous piece of yard equipment. Embedded in white glue on the cap's inner surface is a wobbly heart made of dried kernels of Indian corn.

This treasure was ceremoniously presented to me many years ago by our eldest son, then eight, who found himself with nothing to do on a hot July afternoon except delve into the recesses of an old toolshed. It has become my personal symbol for the special muse of creativity which awaits discovery in the quiet corners of children's lives.

Parents tell me they are concerned about "developing creativity" in their children. They wonder how they can recognize early talent and worry about when they should start art, dance, or music lessons. Some have heard that schools neglect parts of the "creative brain," and wonder if there is any way they can help to keep it stimulated. When they ask professionals in education and the arts, they get conflicting reports and more questions. Can creativity be taught? Can it be tested? What is its relationship to "giftedness"? Are schools stimulating original thinking in mathematics, science, and philosophy?

Will today's students become "problem finders" who can come up with creative solutions for the world's needs?

Creativity—intellectual and artistic—is a timely topic, but studying it is somewhat like dissecting a flower. By the time all the pieces are examined, the essence of the whole has vanished. My favorite definition of creativity is a general one: *The ability to generate or invent, to approach problems in any field from fresh perspectives.* Creative brains seek out patterns of experience and new ways to put them together. A limited amount of available research suggests some practical questions and tentative answers for parents who would like to help with the search. The first question is, How do we recognize different forms of creativity in a child?

THE DIMENSIONS OF CREATIVITY

Gifted, Creative, or Prodigy?

Terms applied to talented children are confusing even to teachers. Here are some workable distinctions:

Gifted is a term most commonly used for those who score near the top 3 percent on IQ tests. Although some schools also utilize tests of creativity, most students labeled "gifted" are primarily adept at traditional verbal, school-oriented abilities; in fact, many do not turn out to be particularly creative. You may wish to refer back to the discussion of intelligence testing in Chapter 8 if you wonder why.

Creative children may also be gifted, but many escape this classification because their talents lie in areas which are untapped by traditional school tasks or standard IQ measures. One large study found that 70 percent of highly creative students were not identified as "gifted" by IQ scores. Such children often have several spheres of potential talent which don't show up in school. Highly creative adults tend to be similarly multidimensional.

My own bias is that *all* children are both gifted and creative. It is up to parents and teachers to uncover those abilities and help the child make the most of them.

Prodigies exhibit a high degree of specialized ability at an unusually early age. A large part of their talent is believed to be innate, but its fruition requires exposure and encouragement. For example, a potential chess prodigy who grew up in an environment with no chess sets would doubtless go unrecognized. Most experts believe it is impossible to make a child into a prodigy; an unusual degree of native talent and a characteristic drive to pursue it are needed, for the path is not an easy one. Almost all child prodigies undergo an intense period of questioning and self-examination during adolescence, and many abandon their field of early promise.

Some so-called "prodigies" actually display "splinter skills," a poorly understood phenomenon in which one extraordinary talent accompanies severe deficits in other abilities. In one famous case, a three-year-old named Nadia began to draw strikingly realistic pictures; by the time she was five, her sketches were technically comparable to those of adult artists. Nadia, however, was severely autistic and unable to communicate. After she went to school, acquired some language and began to socialize with other children, her interest and talent in drawing declined. Can we infer that her right hemisphere's visual capabilities were unusually advanced and dominant until she was taught left-hemisphere skills? This issue has been debated extensively but inconclusively. Perhaps most interesting is the latest information: As a teenager, Nadia is once more beginning to draw.

This case is an extreme example of the divergent quality of early prodigy. The majority of creative people are not prodigies, and many who have achieved eminence in artistic fields were not even regarded as particularly precocious. Most parents wish to focus on broader definitions of creativity for their children.

Testing Creativity

Many believe that creativity, by its very nature, is impossible to test. Dr. E. Paul Torrance disagrees. He has worked for twenty-five years to identify and develop tests of four characteristics of creativity:

Fluency: Different relevant ideas generated about a topic. For example: In two minutes, how many uses can you think of for an empty pop bottle?

Flexibility: Different categories or shifts in thinking (e.g., switching types of uses for the pop bottle from a holder for flowers or pipe cleaners to a doorstop).

Elaboration: Use of details in working out an idea. Embellishing a story plot, for example, or weaving unrelated details together in some interesting way such as designing a pop bottle with futuristic details.

Originality: Creative and imaginative ideas that others haven't come up with. One student suggested that a pop bottle could be a battering ram for a gopher.

Teachers who have worked to encourage creativity in students would like to add a fifth criterion:

Evaluation: Selecting and refining ideas. Rather than accepting anything that sounds unusual or clever, truly creative people are able to apply a sifting process to glean the best or most relevant ideas.

Torrance's tests have not gained universal popularity because they are difficult to score. How do you decide what is original? What is the difference between fluency or flexibility and silliness? One seven-year-old almost missed being included in a "gifted and talented" class the day she came home from school and announced, "Mom, you'll never guess what happened today! A crazy man came into our classroom and handed everyone a paper clip. Then he asked us how many things we could do with a paper clip. Isn't that the dumbest thing you ever heard!"

Antennae waving, Mom called the school. Yes, her daughter had "failed" the creativity exam because she didn't attempt to answer the question. Fortunately, reason eventually prevailed.

Identifying Creativity

It is clear why critics feel such tests don't always pick out the most creative students. Torrance himself acknowledges many signs of potential creativity. A child exhibiting several of these qualities may have unusual potential for creativity:

—Intense absorption in activities. Persistence in working or playing.

—An unusual ability to see patterns and relationships. ("Look, the legs on the picnic table and benches are all *x*'s—just like the lines on the kitchen floor." "Oh, I get how that gear made the other turn; just like on my bike." "Monique and Abby probably act the same way because they both feel shy." "See the triangles in the tree branches?")

—An ability to combine things or ideas in new ways. ("If I turn the gate on its side and put it against a box, it could be a ladder."

—The use of analogies in speech. ("I feel as bouncy as a ball.")

—Seeing things in a new or different way. ("What if the roads moved instead of the cars?") A sixth grade girl invented a unique wallet for the blind which is now being patented.

—A tendency to challenge assumptions or authorities because of a reasoned-out difference in opinion. One two-year-old boy informed his mother that he would like to wait until he was three to become potty-trained. A four-year-old girl dressed her kitten up in baby clothes and sat it in a high chair to circumvent the house rule that prohibited animals at the dinner table.

—Independent decision making and the ability to take action.

—An ability to shift from one idea to another.

—Strong intuition. "Seeing" answers to problems.

—An ability to go "out on a limb," take risks.

—Insightful observations or questions ("Where does the lotion go after you put it on your hands?" "What if we see different colors for the thing we both call 'red'?")

—A tendency to create and test hypotheses ("I put my broccoli in the dog's dish and I found out that dogs don't like vegetables.")

—An ability to tolerate ambiguity while exploring alternatives. Creative people don't always expect an answer to be immediately apparent.

—An interest in new ideas ("What if . . .")

To the extent that we encourage qualities such as these in our children, we encourage the ability to think and act creatively. Does it surprise you that no emphasis has been placed on skill development? Those who study creativity don't talk much about teaching specific skills to young children; in fact, they are seriously concerned that our culture is pushing them too hard too soon. One man's search for landmarks in creative development may help resolve the issue of artistic timetables.

STAGES OF CREATIVE DEVELOPMENT

Growing Creative Brains

Howard Gardner, perhaps the most insightful current observer of childrens' creative development, wondered what happens to the spontaneity of early creativity during elementary years and what would promote continued artistic development. Years of study and observation convinced him that creativity has distinct forms and different needs during three periods of a child's life. You may find it interesting to note their close relationship to the stages of cognitive development described in Chapter 3.

Preschool children, in the *first stage,* are instinctively creative, delighting in original music, art, drama, and language. Gardner observed that the expressiveness of their paintings and drawings had much in common with those of talented adults, much like their ability to use simple poetic language combining ideas or images in fresh, unusual ways. Preschoolers, however, are uncritical observers with little perspective on artistic accomplishment. They might believe that a painting is finished "when the paper is filled up," or that an animal like a tiger could be a painter because he could hold the brush in his mouth. They may prefer "inferior" art or music simply because of familiarity—a clear implication for adults planning a child's creative environment!

Around age seven, however, the pattern shifts. Children's imaginations appear to get stuck and they stop engaging in those delightful flights of fancy. This *second stage* is characterized by concentration on rules and practical ideas. Gardner observed eight-, nine-, and ten-year-olds searching for literal meanings rather than for metaphors. Many prefer to copy or collect pictures rather than create their own. What has happened? Have their creative spirits been crushed?

Some observers are ready to blame schools; they claim originality and imagination get smothered by inexorable demands for accuracy, rule learning, and convergent thinking. Many teachers reward conformity, not creativity, and the first item cut in a budget is often the art or music program. Sometimes parents join the anticreativity movement with pressure for output and doing things the "proper" way. Thus few individuals ever achieve the *third stage* of mature creativity; a convergence of the ability to plan a creative project, and implement and evaluate it.

Gardner is not convinced that schools and parents should get all the blame. The period of literal thinking, with its emphasis on following the rules, may be an essential way station for growing minds. After ranging widely in imagination, children must solidify understanding and mastery of the physical world and feel the security of operating successfully within stated limits before they can venture on.

The years of middle childhood therefore become ideal for lessons and practice in the skills of artistic achievement. Gardner points out that most successful artists in any medium must put in at least ten years of concentrated training before their talent can be fully expressed. Because he believes that different neural areas underlie various types of creativity, specialization and hard work are necessary—when the brain is ready.

If talent is thus specialized, should we expect a child to be good at everything? A potential artist, mechanic, dancer, or athlete may falter in school subjects. Can parents and teachers of such youngsters restructure their own value systems to accommodate nonacademic skills? Can we all believe that time and energy devoted to creative skills are important? Gardner says, "The ultimate flowering of artistry may require a society that has a genuine interest in its budding artists and values their creations."

Here are a few nodes in the budding process:

STAGE ONE: SPONTANEOUS CREATIVITY
Ages 1–2: Concrete mastery of simple artistic expression
> Making marks on paper
> Simple singing and musical chanting
> Imitation of voice tones and pitch

2–3: Beginning use of symbols
> Drawing geometric forms: circles, squares, crosses
> Words standing for objects
> "Pretend" play
> Gestures, movement linked spontaneously to music
> Awareness of and ability to imitate tunes

3–4: Beginnings of structure in creative efforts
> Attempts to reproduce whole songs
> Telling stories with simple structure
> Simple dance sequences
> Drawings of figures: human "tadpole" figures (circle and legs; no torso)
> Drawing a triangle

3–5: Beginnings of metaphor
> Creating metaphors based on appearance of objects and personal action ("The sunbeam is jumping.")
> Attempts to pick out tunes on musical instruments

5–6: Original combinations of ideas, sensory impressions
> Imitation of musical intervals; most six-year-olds can sing in key and pick up underlying musical rhythms

Grouping figures into scenes in drawings; shows
  sense of balance and color
Drawing a diamond
5–7: "The golden age"
  Love of drawing: may use art to express concerns
    and worries or gain a feeling of mastery over the
    world
  Spontaneous enjoyment of music, dance, and poetic
    language

STAGE TWO: LITERALISM

Ages 8–11: Craves competency, rules, feelings of mastery
  Ready to concentrate on lessons and skill practice
  Needs exposure to varied types of creative
    expression and quality models of good artistic
    forms
  Enjoys enrichment experiences in science, math, and
    other fields of special interest
  Ready to begin learning structure and forms of
    writing
10–11: Creative imagination beginning to broaden
  Practice making aesthetic judgments and evaluating
    creative efforts
  Appreciation of different types of literary forms
    (e.g., fairy tale, realistic fiction, opinion)
  Needs good teacher for development of potential
    artistic gifts

STAGE THREE: MATURE CREATIVE EXPRESSION AND APPRECIATION

Adolescence: Combining inspiration and execution
  Continued practice of skills
  Appreciation of others' artistic efforts
  Intense evaluation of own work
  Ability to create original artistic forms or ideas
  Needs a teacher of high achievement in chosen field
    and/or mentors to inspire choices

A PERSONAL LESSON ABOUT LESSONS

"Where Does He Take?"

When our son the necklace maker was completing first grade, his teacher held an afternoon program in which each child shared a talent or an interest. Some read original poems or stories, others displayed pictures or performed skits. At the end of the afternoon, Scott sat down at the piano and played a medley from *The Sound of Music,* for which he had arranged the chords by ear. As the program ended, I was surrounded by a clamor of mothers wanting to know my secret. "Where does he take?" they demanded. Somewhat sheepishly, I acknowledged that he didn't "take." His only instruction had come during the previous year when Scott pestered his father to show him basic chording. He did the rest on his own—and he hasn't stopped yet! I have heard many similar stories from parents of children who later excelled in a specialized field. When the right time came, the youngster became self-propelled.

Some programs in artistic expression are appropriate for preschoolers. Dalcroze, art enrichment, and Orff music training are a few examples that broaden rather than narrow creative bases. For most children, even talented ones, however, there is little reason to rush into skill-and-practice-oriented lessons before about age seven when the brain refines its ability to combine sequences from different senses. Reading music, for example, demands an integration of visual, auditory, and motor patterns, for which most preschoolers' brains simply are not equipped. Discriminating, identifying, sequencing, and playing notes from a staff are far different from experimenting with finger movements for a tune in your head. For most children, reading music should wait until after reading instruction is successfully under way. Even structured lessons without the demands of reading music, as on the violin, are very controversial among musicians who value "feeling" over mechanics for young children. They fear that forcing creativity may kill it.

Master teachers in the field of art tell us that presenting advanced practices or theory in the hopes of accelerating development is useless. Telling a child what to do to produce a pretty product will make him dependent on your direction and unsure of his own aesthetic choices. Children need to "own" all the steps of the learning process.

Trying to teach young children a structured set of "facts" about science, or any other topic, is another way to shut off the interest valves. One of the most creative physicists at MIT recalls that his parents never pushed early learning, but they always encouraged him to devise his own methods of playing with materials at hand. He laughs affectionately when he remembers his mother patiently sweeping up the kitchen floor after his favorite game—pouring her flour from the cannister and experimenting with different sizes and shapes of containers. Now he is experimenting with molecules that may someday lead to a treatment for cancer.

I'm glad our musician didn't "take" until he was ready and eager. When people ask me, "How did you get him to practice?" I have to admit it was the other way around. We couldn't keep him from practicing. Blessed with a talented child, we were happily too innocent of the dimensions of this treasure to steal the initiative from its rightful owner.

THE CREATIVE BRAIN

The Creative Brain Talks to Itself

Learning to think creatively is a process of making links: first between movement and the senses, then between ideas, and finally, between the human mind's most sophisticated achievements—inspiration and evaluation. At the heart of the system are the chains of neurons which make the connections. Although we have a great deal yet to learn about the brain's role in creativity, the gradual development of neurons' ability to "talk" among themselves probably explains a great deal about all intellectual talents.

In young children, the brain's inner communication systems are not well traveled. Perhaps because association pathways are immature, particularly in the left hemisphere and in the prefrontal cortex, preschoolers tend to react spontaneously, without careful analysis. Their approach to new situations reflects the first-strike capabilities of the right hemisphere. They can't evaluate details, put them in order, or plan ahead. They have trouble integrating the two sides of their bodies in complicated patterns. They enjoy creative activities that are restricted to demands on one or two sense modalities, such as spontaneous movement to music, free-form drawing, or dramatizing expressive poetry. Most need to use their bodies in creating; the motor cortex is one of the first high-level areas to mature in both hemispheres, providing children's first means of organizing their own brains.

For most children in elementary years, development is active in the left hemisphere, but perhaps because the bridge of fibers that links the two sides is still in the process of completion, eight-, nine-, and ten-year-olds have trouble linking imagination, free expression, and visual imagery, on the one hand, with demands for order, sequence, and analysis. Most schools emphasize these latter abilities because they are prerequisites for effective use of the entire brain. The best practical advice is probably to understand that children need to master the technical tools of thought and a large store of specific knowledge; meanwhile the all-important exposure to creative ideas and artistic expression may become the parents' responsibility.

It is impossible to separate the effects of millions of learning experiences from brain development; both contribute to changes around the beginning of adolescence. Integration of analytic and intuitive thinking becomes easier; an original idea can be analyzed and evaluated and its successful execution planned. Insight is followed by confirmation as the brain begins to move comfortably between wholistic and analytical processing.

Start with a general idea

Analyze parts, test, recombine

Synthesize an original whole

Plan, incubate

Execute

Evaluate

Divergent Hemispheres

You can see that both hemispheres are essential, but individuals have different balances in the knowledge-imagination equation. In one study, children between the ages of two and a half and five already showed clear inclinations to be either "verbalizers" or "visualizers." Some are better at analyzing, some at synthesizing. Many highly creative adults prefer wholistic and intuitive rather than verbal modes of processing. Isadora Duncan once remarked, "If I could say it, I wouldn't have to dance it." Picasso, who started painting realistically before he was in his teens, developed a mature style which portrayed figures as if he were looking at them from all sides at once.

Considerable evidence points to right hemisphere involvement in much artistic expression. Some believe this side of the cortex is also in closer touch with the emotional "feeling" centers of the limbic system; many studies emphasize the importance of a positive emotional climate for creativity. The right hemisphere may also generate characteristic brain waves called *alpha* rhythms, which are more laid back than the vigorous *beta* waves of analytical thought. If the left hemisphere is actively zapping an idea with beta waves, inspiration may not have much of a chance. Meditation, relaxation, biofeedback, and imagery techniques appear to be effective in activating alpha frequencies. Some parents are learning these methods along with children as young as three years, and some schools are trying them out in hopes of reducing students' levels of stress.

If these ideas sound too "laid back" for your taste, here are some other techniques that work for creative people:

Playing: Relaxation and enjoyment of spontaneous activities facilitates creative thinking, but many adults have forgotten how to play. Discarding the notion that a worthwhile product must lie at the end of every activity opens new mental avenues for adults and children together.

Humor: Invite humor to be a frequent visitor in your home—but be sure you laugh *with,* not *at,* each other.

Dramatizing: You can dramatize almost anything. Act out stories with your child. Pretend to be unlikely things. ("How would peanut butter act? Can you act like a pair of scissors?") Learn new vocabulary by acting out words ("Here's what 'vicious' looks like." "Do I seem 'tranquil' or 'perturbed'?") Help with school assignments by putting actions with ideas ("Can you pretend to be Magellan? Cortez? You be the king and I'll be the serfs. How might we act?") This type of learning lets all parts of the brain talk to each other.

Moving: Some evidence suggests that rhythmic aerobic exercise subdues the pressure of beta waves and opens new avenues between the hemispheres. Runners swear that it works! Even if you don't want to subject your child's joints to the stress of a running program, you might try it yourself when your patience is frazzled. Meanwhile, encourage spontaneous dance and creative movement. Invent dances in your living room for different types of insects, animals, birds, flowers, or objects. Dance to all varieties of music. For older children, you'll find material "studied" in this manner sticks better, too. Pretend to be molecules when your child studies science, or words representing grammatical terms (adverbs dance with verbs; adjectives with nouns, etc.)

Visualizing: The ability to "see" ideas in one's head is an important component of creative thinking. Start early, linking verbal ideas with pictures: First, read imaginative stories or fairy tales out loud while you show pictures; then let the children draw pictures of their own. After age four, suggest that they close their eyes and make a "mental movie." Say, "Tell me about the queen's dress. What did the troll's house look like?" Don't be surprised if it takes a lot of practice. Some creative children have excellent visual memories for faces, objects, events and scenes, but they bog down trying to link mental pictures with verbal material. Turn off the TV and the VCR and let the whole family make mind pictures instead.

Listening: Musical melody, processed by the right hemisphere, is a catalyst for creativity in many people, although whether music actually "turns on" or helps integrate parts of the brain is not proven. A background of baroque music has been claimed to facilitate creative learning and memory. You might want to experiment with different types of melody as a background for thinking or learning in your home.

Expressing: Children need time and encouragement to be able to attach words to images and ideas. Encourage your child to make intuitive discoveries and then talk about them.

Originating: Think up new uses for common objects (e.g., a sponge, a hair dryer). Approach household tasks in divergent ways; experiment with different food combinations. Some parents keep a "prop" box of common objects such as old hats, scarves, flowerpots, kitchen utensils, or household "junk" and encourage children to play imaginatively with them. Keeping an open mind to new ideas is important because intuition gets stifled by a "one right answer" mentality. One teacher asks students to tell their troubles to a bowl of yellow jello; he claims it loosens the imagination.

Incubating: Have you ever had a problem suddenly solve itself after you have "sat" on it for a while? Some of science's greatest discoveries demonstrate that intuition requires incubation time. Everyone needs time to be alone, to ponder, to contemplate. Sometimes doing "nothing" is the most creative activity of all. Likewise, allowing children to be "bored" now and then gives them a chance to investigate toolsheds or other unlikely places where inspiration may be hiding.

CREATIVE PARENTS

Parents who produce creative children show them how to be problem finders as well as problem solvers. Here are some specifics from recent studies:

PARENTS OF CREATIVE CHILDREN . . .

—Have full lives themselves and do not depend on their children to meet their emotional or achievement needs.

—Are not in awe of the child and do not defer to his demands or feel compelled to entertain him.

—Tolerate divergent ideas and mistakes made "in the service of learning."

—Provide discipline and structure to give children security to explore.

—Set realistic standards and encourage pride in achievement.

—Show active interest in a child's thoughts and creative efforts.

—Encourage a close relationship to nature and freedom of physical expression.

—Give children early responsibility for making choices and taking appropriate responsibility for their own decisions.

—Permit children to have solitude and develop imaginative thinking by daydreaming.

—Show children how to be curious and observant.

—Allow honest expression of emotion.

—Encourage children to feel intuitively as well as think logically.

—Do not put pressure on school for "competency" that excludes intellectual creativity.

—Expose children to a broad range of artistic and intellectual pursuits: you might visit practicing artists in studio, attend children's concerts and dance programs, go to museums together, obtain prints of interesting or important artistic works and enjoy them at home, read poetry out loud.

Sampling the Arts

What is the best way to get children interested in good artistic forms? One family planned a trip to a city with a well-known art museum, but the mother was worried because she knew her sons would be bored by a long tour through all the galleries. Before the trip, she identified three special pieces they would see, one sculpture and two paintings, and she obtained prints of these works. The whole family examined, read about, and discussed them. They went to the library to find out more about each artist. By the time of the museum visit, the excited boys had to be cautioned not to run through the galleries to find their "treasures." Once they had been located and savored, the family left the museum. These children could hardly wait for another visit! I suspect that a similar exposure to one single piece of music which has become familiar and understandable might be the key to preventing the "symphony ennui" learned from early concerts. A delicious sample is better than an overdose, especially for youngsters.

Complimenting Creativity

The way you praise your child's artistic efforts may be more important than you realize, both in encouraging creativity and fostering a feeling of internal pride of ownership. Compare these typical responses:

"That looks great; tell me about it," rather than, "What is it?"

"What an interesting cow!" rather than, "I never saw a purple cow."

"You certainly enjoyed using black!" rather than, "Why is it all black?"

"You must feel very proud of your project," as well as, "I'm proud of you."

This latter distinction is important for parents interested in starting children early on implementing and evaluating their own ideas. Learning to depend completely on external praise or an adult judgment about whether something is good/bad, right/wrong may block creative circuits. One father started saying when his daughter was two, "Aren't you proud of yourself," and teaching her to clap for herself while her parents stayed in the background. He says the credit and the pride should belong to the child, not to him!

A teacher suggests that children's artwork come off the refrigerator and into more "important" areas of the home. One mother who framed her children's paintings and stitchery and hung them in the living room got many compliments on her "modern art" while the children basked in the praise.

Evaluating "Creativity" at School

One question which bothers many families is whether children's creative needs are being accommodated at school. Many "gifted" programs make a particular point of stressing creativity. Although I am firmly in favor of meeting the needs of all creative minds, there are a few questions you might ask:

1. Is "creativity" defined by worksheet or one-shot activities that are artificially "cute" or divergent rather than meaningfully related to the child's needs or interests?

2. Are "creatively gifted" children singled out or made to feel awkward by scheduling of "pull-out" programs that may cause resentment by other children or even by classroom teachers?

3. Are children encouraged to share the fruits of their creative mental explorations with a wider audience? Sharing adds an important dimension of meaning and responsibility.

4. Does the "creative" teacher truly have a creative spirit? Can he answer challenging questions without feeling threatened or accept divergent approaches to his own lesson plans?

My own feeling is that a child who finds "creativity" class either boring and routine or aimless and undisciplined is better off without it. A creative classroom is not an excuse for mayhem or disorganization. Master teachers who focus on creative enrichment carefully plan and evaluate each activity. They realize, however, that an enriched setting and good plans are not enough. Creativity is a process that takes time, and often flourishes only after a process of trial and error. Does your child's school use any of these process-oriented activities?

—Hands-on science projects
—Creative writing of all types
—"Rap" sessions and brainstorming of ideas

—Studying "futuristics" (predicting what the future will be like and how to anticipate and solve problems)

—Simulation games (pretending to solve major challenges such as inventing a new civilization or planning a voyage to Mars)

—Thoughtfully probing philosophical or moral dilemmas

—Use of symbols

One teacher linked symbolic use to personal interest by asking each child to come in with a bag of disposable "stuff" which would characterize his family well enough for others to guess their main interests and personality characteristics. What would you use for your family?

Educators have a long way to go in resolving the contradiction inherent in *teaching* creativity—if it is even possible. They plead with parents to help them by not demanding a product from every learning experience. When the pressure is on from home for a picture every week from art class, or a test instead of a project, the process of creativity—and of learning—is shortchanged. Support your school's efforts to expand creative thinking, and don't underestimate the importance of your job on the home front. Let's seek our own creative synthesis by returning to the fundamental idea that an "enriched" home environment can have profound effects in your child's brain.

A LIFETIME OF ENRICHMENT AND THE BRAIN OF A GENIUS

Enriched Rats

Some of the most exciting work on enriching brains is being conducted in Berkeley by a dynamic and creative neuroanatomist named Marian Diamond. For years she has studied the brains of laboratory rats because they are a good, if greatly simplified, version of the human model. She has repeatedly demonstrated that environments enriched with toys and social interaction cause growing rat brains to develop more dendrites, more glial cells, and stronger synapses. She has found that it is important to keep adding new challenges in order to keep neural connections exercised—and growing. The very areas which develop most heavily as a result of this environmental stimulation are the ones in a human brain which make the most creative connections.

Stimulation enhances creative potential, up to a point. When does "good" become "too much"? Concerned that reports about her research might be causing parents to overload children, she is now investigating her suspicion that an excess of stimulation may cause the brain to shut down. An interesting and challenging environment is quite different from one which bombards the brain with too much of a good thing. It would be unfortunate if these rat studies, important as they are, caused parents to forget common sense in efforts to produce children with active and creative minds!

Even aging rat brains profit from vigorous mental activity, and new dendrite branches and supporting glial cells can develop into the last years of life. In fact, when young and old rats shared a cage, the older adults monopolized the toys and their brains grew more than did those of their offspring! Here's good evidence for creative "play" —*with* your child. It appears that meeting new challenges throughout life keeps cortical neurons firing vigorously and effectively!

The Brain of a Genius

One of Dr. Diamond's recent studies departed intriguingly from rat brains. "If you could study any brain in history, whose would it be?" she asks. "Einstein's!"

Einstein's brain had been perfectly preserved after his death, but no one had yet studied it when Dr. Diamond requested four special tissue samples. She was particularly interested in comparing two sections from each hemisphere with the same areas in more average male brains. By the intricate technique of staining cells and counting them under a microscope, she discovered that the brain of this genius was indeed different.

In these small but critical areas of frontal and parietal lobes, Einstein's brain contained significantly more glial cells per neuron. Dr. Diamond believes this ratio is associated with more vigorous use of these particular areas for higher thinking and reasoning. Remember, while the number of neurons does not increase after birth, the support systems grow in response to cognitive demands. The late-developing part of the parietal lobe where all senses are associated for meaning seemed to be unusually active—especially in the left hemisphere!

We could speculate endlessly about what happened to that developing brain while Einstein played with his favorite toy, a compass, and listened to music, his other preferred hobby. I decided to ask Dr. Diamond what implications she could draw for parents interested in raising bright and creative children. Musing for only a moment, this scientist-mother who has looked into the black box of thousands of growing brains and into the brain of a genius replied, "I'd tell them to give children the broadest picture."

THE BROADEST PICTURE

Creative parents give children the broad picture of an interesting and loving environment with freedom to explore. Children get their own focus—in an old toolshed, a corner of a city apartment, or a suburban garden. I treasure my wobbly heart in its old bottle cap as a reminder that the truly creative mind is forged, not only from stimulation, but also from time—time to experiment, to discover, to understand, and to get acquainted with the very special muse of childhood.

The child's brain has an instinctive knowledge of its timetable, but the creative mind is more than a schedule of neural connections. I hope you will accept the suggestions in this book, and your role in your child's development, as part of a greater process, never perfect, never finished. Learning is something that children do, not something that is done to them. You have the wisdom to guide the process but not the power to control it. Listen, watch, have patience, enjoy the journey—and the product will take care of itself.

Selected Bibliography

GENERAL REFERENCES

Bee, H., & Mitchell, S. *The Developing Person: A Life-Span Approach.* San Francisco: Harper & Row, 1980.

Cohen, D. *The Learning Child.* New York: Vintage Books, 1973.

The Diagram Group. *The Brain: A User's Manual.* New York: Berkley, 1982.

Fitzgerald, H., Strommen, E., & McKinney, J. *Developmental Psychology: The Infant and Young Child.* Homewood, Ill.: Dorsey, 1982.

Gardner, H. *Developmental Psychology.* Boston: Little, Brown, 1978.

Gholson, B., & Rosenthal, T. *Applications of Cognitive-Developmental Theory.* New York: Academic, 1984.

Hart, L. *Human Brain and Human Learning.* New York: Longman, 1983.

Hynd, G., & Obrzut, J. *Neuropsychological Assessment and the School-Age Child.* New York: Grune & Stratton, 1981.

Kandel. E., & Schwartz, J. *Principles of Neural Science.* New York: Elsevier North-Holland, 1981.

Kirk, U. (Ed.). *Neuropsychology of Language, Reading, and Spelling.* New York: Academic, 1983.

Luria, A. *The Working Brain.* New York: Basic Books, 1973.

Mussen, P., Conger, J., & Kagan, J. *Child Development and Personality (5th ed.).* New York: Harper & Row, 1979.

Restak, R. *The Brain: The Last Frontier.* New York: Warner Books, 1979.

———. *The Brain.* Toronto: Bantam, 1984.

Rosner, J. *Helping Children Overcome Learning Difficulties (2d ed.)*. New York: Walker, 1979.

Rourke, B. *Neuropsychology of Learning Disabilities: Essentials of Subtype Analysis*. New York: Guilford, 1985.

————, et al. *Child Neuropsychology*. New York: Guilford, 1983.

Rutter, M. (Ed.). *Developmental Neuropsychology*. New York: Guilford, 1983.

Spreen, O., et al. *Human Developmental Neuropsychology*. New York: Oxford University Press, 1984.

Strommen, E., McKinney, J., & Fitzgerald, H. *Developmental Psychology: The School-Aged Child*. Homewood, Ill.: Dorsey, 1983.

Yakolev, P., & Lecours, A. The myelogenetic cycles or regional development of the brain. In A. Minkowski (Ed.), *Regional Development of the Brain in Early Life*. Oxford: Blackwell, 1967.

CHAPTER 1

Bloom, F. Fetal alcohol syndrome. Paper presented at symposium: "The Ever-Changing Brain," San Rafael, Calif., 1985.

Eskenazi, B. Behavioral teratology: The effects of toxic chemicals on the developing brain. Paper presented at symposium: "The Ever-Changing Brain," San Rafael, Calif., 1985.

CHAPTER 2

Boddy, J. *Brain Systems and Psychological Concepts*. New York: Wiley, 1978.

Bradley, R., & Caldwell, B. The relation of infants' home environments to achievement test performance in first grade: A follow-up study. *Child Development*, 55, 803–809, 1984.

Colombo, J. The critical period concept: Research, methodology, and theoretical issues. *Psychological Bulletin*, 91, 2, 260–275, 1982.

Friedrich, O. What do babies know? *Time*, August 15, 1983.

Held, R. Plasticity in sensory motor systems. *Scientific American*, 213, 85, 1965.

Huttenlocher, P. Synapse elimination and plasticity in developing human cerebral cortex. *American Journal of Mental Deficiency*, 88, 5, 488–496, 1984.

Luddington-Hoe, S., and Golant, S. K. *How to Have a Smarter Baby:* The Infant Stimulation Program Explained in Full. New York: Rawson Associates, 1985.

MacLean, P. A mind of three minds: Educating the triune brain. In J. Chall & A. Mirsky, *Education and the Brain,* 77th Yearbook of the National Society for the Study of Education. University of Chicago Press, 1978.

Mehler, J., & Fox, R. *Neonate Cognition: Beyond the Blooming Buzzing Confusion.* Hillsdale, N.J.: Erlbaum, 1985.

Phillips, C., Zeki, S., & Barlow, H. Localization of function in the cerebral cortex. *Brain, 107,* 1, 327–362, 1984.

Shaheen, S. Neuromaturational and behavioral development: The case of childhood lead poisoning. *Developmental Psychology, 20,* 4, 542–550, 1984.

Siegel, L. Reproductive, perinatal and environmental factors as predictors of the cognitive and language development of preterm and full-term infants. *Child Development, 53,* 963–973, 1982.

Streissguth, A., et al. Intrauterine alcohol and nicotine exposure: Attention and reaction time in 4-year-old children. *Developmental Psychology: 20,* 4, 533–541, 1984.

CHAPTER 3

Belsky, J., et al. Assessing performance, competence, and executive capacity in infant play: Relations to home environment and security of attachment. *Developmental Psychology, 20,* 3, 406–417, 1984.

Case, R. *Intellectual Development: Birth to Adulthood.* New York: Academic, 1985.

Donaldson, M. *Children's Minds.* New York: Norton, 1978.

Flavell, J. *Cognitive Development.* Englewood Cliffs, N.J.: Prentice-Hall, 1977.

Gottfried, A. *Home Environment and Early Cognitive Development.* New York: Academic, 1984.

Greenspan, S., & Porges, S. Psychopathology in infancy and early childhood: Clinical perspectives on the organization of sensory and affective-thematic experience. *Child Development, 55,* 1, 49–70, 1984.

Liss, M. *Social and Cognitive Skills: Sex Roles and Children's Play.* New York: Academic, 1983.

Parkinson, C., et al. Rating the home environment of school-age children: A comparison with general cognitive index and school progress. *Journal of Child Psychology and Psychiatry and Allied Disciplines, 23,* 3, 329–333, 1982.

Pepler, D., & Rubin, K. (Eds.). *The Play of Children: Current Theory and Research.* New York: Karger, 1982.

Phillips, J. *Piaget's Theory: A Primer.* San Francisco: Freeman, 1981.

Rubin, K. Fantasy play: Its role in the development of social skills and social cognition. *New Directions for Child Development,* 9, 69–86, 1980.

CHAPTER 4

Ames, L. *Is Your Child in the Wrong Grade?* Flemington, N.J.: Programs for Education, Inc.

Ansara, A. Maturational readiness for school tasks. The Orton Society Reprint Series. Baltimore: The Orton Dyslexia Society.

Connors, K. *Hyperkenesis in Childhood: A Neuropsychological Approach.* Beverly Hills, Calif.: Sage, 1985.

Epstein, H. Phrenoblysis: Special brain and mind growth periods. *Developmental Psychology, 7,* 207–224, 1974.

————. Correlated brain and intelligence development in humans. In M. Hahn (Ed.), *Development and Evolution of Brain Size: Behavioral Implications.* New York: Academic, 1979.

Jansky, J. The marginally ready child. *Bulletin of the Orton Society, XXV,* 1975.

Levenson, D. Where do they belong? *Teacher,* March 1977.

CHAPTER 5

Conger, J., & Peterson, A. *Adolescence and Youth (3d ed.).* New York: Harper & Row, 1984.

Elkind, D. *A Sympathetic Understanding of the Child: Birth to Sixteen.* Boston: Allyn and Bacon, 1974.

Epstein, H. Growth spurts during brains development: Implications for educational policy. In J. Chall & A. Mirsky (Eds.), *1978 Yearbook of the National Society for the Study of Education.* University of Chicago Press, 1978.

Hasher, L., & Zacks, R. Automatic processing of fundamental information. *American Psychologist, 39,* 12, 1372–1388, 1984.

Hawley, R. *The Purposes of Pleasure.* Wellesley Hills, Mass.: Independent School Press, 1983.

Heath, R. *Marijuana and the Brain.* New Orleans: Department of Psychiatry and Neurology, Tulane University School of Medicine, 1981.

Levine, M. Beyond L.D. Address presented at A.C.L.D. Annual Conference, New Orleans, La., 1984.

Levine, M., Brooks, R., & Shonkoff, J. *A Pediatric Approach to Learning Disorders.* New York: Wiley, 1980.

Miller, L. Cannabis: Effects on memory and the cholinergic limbic system. *Psychological Bulletin, 94,* 3, 441–456, 1983.

Newcomb, M., et al. Mothers' influence on the drug use of their children: Confirmatory tests of direct modeling and mediational theories. *Developmental Psychology, 19,* 5, 714–726, 1983.

Stuss, D., & Benson, D. Neuropsychological studies of the frontal lobes. *Psychological Bulletin, 95,* 1, 3–28, 1984.

Tierno, M. The impact of cognitive change on personality development in middle schoolers. Paper presented at the Annual Meeting of Independent Schools of the Central States, Chicago, November 1984.

CHAPTER 6

Buzan, T. *Use Both Sides of Your Brain.* New York: Dutton, 1974.

Dennis, M., & Whitaker, H. Language acquisition following hemidecortication: Linguistic superiority of the left over the right hemisphere. *Brain and Language, 3,* 404–433, 1976.

Durden-Smith, J., & deSimone, D. *Sex and the Brain.* New York: Warner Books, 1983.

Frankel, M., & Rollins, H. Does mother know best? Mothers and fathers interacting with preschool sons and daughters. *Developmental Psychology, 19,* 5, 694–702, 1983.

Galaburda, A. Developmental dyslexia: Current anatomical research. *Annals of Dyslexia, 33,* 41–53, 1983.

Levy, J. The integrated mind of the asymmetric brain. Paper presented at National Association of Independent Schools Annual Meeting, New York, 1984.

Maccoby, E., Snow, M., & Jacklin, C. Children's dispositions and mother-child interaction at 18 months: A short-term longitudinal study. *Developmental Psychology, 20,* 3, 459–472, 1984.

McCarthy, B. *The 4Mat System: Teaching to Learning Styles with Right/Left Mode Techniques* (2d ed.). Oak Brook, Ill.: Excel, 1981.

Meece, J., et al. Sex differences in math achievement: Toward a model of academic choice. *Developmental Psychology, 91,* 2, 329–346, 1982.

Springer, S., & Deutsch, G. *Left Brain, Right Brain (rev. ed.).* New York: Freeman, 1985.

CHAPTER 7

deHirsch, K. *Language and the Developing Child.* Baltimore: The Orton Dyslexia Society, 1984.

deVilliers, P., & deVilliers, J. *Early Language.* Cambridge, Mass.: Harvard, 1979.

Garvey, C. *Children's Talk.* Cambridge, Mass.: Harvard, 1984.

Gleitman, L., et al. The current status of the motherese hypothesis. *Journal of Child Language, 11,* 1, 43–79, 1984.

McCartney, K. Effect of quality of day care environment on children's language development. *Developmental Psychology, 20,* 2, 244–260, 1984.

McLaughlin, B., et al. Mothers' and fathers' speech to their young children: Similar or different? *Journal of Child Language, 10,* 1, 245–252, 1983.

Prutting, C. Process: The action of moving forward progressively from one point to another on the way to completion. *Journal of Speech and Hearing Disorders, 44,* 3–30, 1979.

Tinsley, V., & Waters, H. The development of verbal control over motor behavior: A replication and extension of Luria's findings. *Child Development, 53,* 746–753, 1982.

CHAPTER 8

Brown, F. *Principles of Educational and Psychological Testing.* New York: Holt, 1983.

Feuerstein, R., et al. *Instrumental Enrichment.* Baltimore: University Park, 1980.

Friedman, M. (Ed.). *Intelligence and Learning.* New York: Plenum, 1981.

Gardner, H. *Frames of Mind: The Theory of Multiple Intelligences.* New York: Basic Books, 1983.

Lewis, M. *Origins of Intelligence.* New York: Plenum, 1983.

Lodico, M., et al. The effects of strategy-monitoring training on children's selection of effective memory strategies. *Journal of Experimental Child Psychology, 35,* 2, 263–277, 1983.

O'Connor, M., Cohen, S., & Parmalee, A. Infant auditory discrimination in preterm and full-term infants as a predictor of 5-year intelligence. *Developmental Psychology, 20,* 1, 159–165, 1984.

Ornstein, P. *Memory Development in Children.* Hillsdale, N.J.: Erlbaum, 1978.

Ramey, C., Yeats, K., & Short, E. The plasticity of intellectual development: Insights from preventive intervention. *Child Development, 55,* 1913–1925, 1984.

Ratner, H. Memory demands and the development of young children's memory. *Child Development, 55,* 2173–2191, 1984.

Scarr, S., & Weinberg, R. The Minnesota Adoption Studies: Genetic differences and malleability. *Child Development, 54,* 2, 260–267, 1983.

Wilson, R. The Louisville Twin Study: Developmental synchronies in behavior. *Child Development, 54,* 2, 298–316, 1983.

CHAPTER 9

Bryant, N. Getting meaning from words: The role of the angular gyrus. Paper presented at the Conference on Neuropsychology in the School and in the Clinic, Teachers College, Columbia University, New York, 1983.

Child Study Children's Book Committee. *Books to Read Aloud with Children Through Age 8.* New York: Bank Street College, 1984.

Durkin, D. *Children Who Read Early,* New York: Teachers College Press, 1966.

————. *Teaching Young Children to Read* (3d ed.). Boston: Allyn and Bacon, 1980.

Ellis, A. *Reading, Writing, and Dyslexia: A Cognitive Analysis.* London: Erlbaum, 1984.

Feitelson, D., et al. How effective is early instruction in reading? Experimental evidence. *Merrill-Palmer Quarterly, 28,* 4, 485–494, 1982.

Healy, J. The enigma of hyperlexia. *Reading Research Quarterly, 17,* 3, 319–338, 1982.

————, et al. A study of hyperlexia. *Brain and Language, 17,* 1–23, 1982.

Pirozzolo, F., & Wittrock, M. (Eds.). *Neuropsychological and Cognitive Processes in Reading.* New York: Academic, 1981.

Simpson, E. *Reversals: A Personal Account of Victory over Dyslexia.* New York: Pocket Books, 1979.

CHAPTER 10

Frith, U. (Ed.). *Cognitive Processes in Spelling.* New York: Academic, 1980.

Graves, D. *Writing: Teachers and Children at Work.* Exeter, N.H.: Heinemann, 1983.

Hodges, R. *Learning to Spell.* Urbana, Ill.: National Council of Teachers of English, 1981.

King, M., & Rentel, V. *How Children Learn to Write: A Longitudinal Study.* Final report. Washington, D.C.: National Institute of Education, 1981.

Rico, G. *Writing the Natural Way.* Boston: Houghton Mifflin, 1983.

Tkach, J. Educational software and typing skills. *G.C.T.,* March/April, 31–32, 1984.

Vail, P. *Clear and Lively Writing.* New York: Walker, 1981.

Walshe, R. *Every Child Can Write!* Rozelle, N.S.W.: Primary English Teaching Association, 1982.

Welty, E. *One Writer's Beginnings.* Cambridge, Mass.: Harvard, 1983.

CHAPTER 11

Briars, D., & Siegler, R. A featural analysis of preschoolers' counting knowledge. *Developmental Psychology, 20,* 4, 607–618, 1984.

Copeland, R. *How Children Learn Mathematics* (3d ed.). New York: Macmillan, 1979.

Hazen, A. Spatial exploration and spatial knowledge: Individual differences in very young children. *Child Development, 53,* 826–837, 1982.

Hildebrandt, S., & Tromba, A. *Mathematics and Optimal Form.* New York: Scientific-American Library, 1985.

CHAPTER 12

Clark, R. *Einstein: The Life and Times.* New York: World Publishing, 1971.

Diamond, M. Cortical plasticity. Address given at symposium: "The Ever-Changing Brain," San Rafael, Calif., August 1985.

————, et al. On the brain of a scientist: Albert Einstein. *Experimental Neurology, 88,* 198–204, 1985.

Gardner, H. *Art, Mind, and Brain: A Cognitive Approach to Creativity.* New York: Basic Books, 1982.

G.C.T. Box 66654, Mobile, Ala. 36660

Gifted Children Newsletter. 213 Honeywell Drive, Sewell, N.J. 08080

Hunt, M. *The Universe Within.* New York: Simon & Schuster, 1982.

Ostrander, S., & Schroeder, L. *Super-Learning.* New York: Laurel Books, 1979.

Silberstein-Storfer, M. *Doing Art Together.* New York: Simon & Schuster, 1982.

Tait, M., & Haack, P. *Principles and Processes of Music Education.* New York: Teachers College Press, 1984.

Torrance, E. *Guiding Creative Talent.* Englewood Cliffs, N.J.: Prentice-Hall, 1962.

Vail, P. *The World of the Gifted Child.* New York: Penguin, 1980.

Webb, J., et al. *Guiding the Gifted Child.* Columbus: Ohio Psychology Publishing Co., 1982.

Index